THE
NEWBERY
AWARD
READER

THE NEWBERY AWARD READER

edited by
CHARLES G. WAUGH
and
MARTIN H. GREENBERG

introduction by Virginia Hamilton

HARCOURT BRACE JOVANOVICH, PUBLISHERS
San Diego · New York · London

Copyright © 1984 by Charles G. Waugh and Martin H. Greenberg
Introduction copyright © 1984 by Harcourt Brace Jovanovich, Inc.

All rights reserved. No part of this publication may be reproduced or transmitted in any form or by any means, electronic or mechanical, including photocopy, recording, or any information storage and retrieval system, without permission in writing from the publisher.

Requests for permission to make copies of any part of the work should be mailed to: Permissions, Harcourt Brace Jovanovich, Publishers, Orlando, Florida 32887

"The Smith, the Weaver, and the Harper" from *The Foundling* by Lloyd Alexander. Copyright © 1973 by Lloyd Alexander. Reprinted by permission of Holt, Rinehart and Winston, Publishers.

"Emma Went, Too" from *Magical Melons, More Stories About Caddie Woodlawn* by Carol Ryrie Brink. Copyright © 1939, 1940, 1944 by Macmillan Publishing Company, renewed 1967, 1968, 1972 by Carol Ryrie Brink. Reprinted with permission of Macmillan.

"The Race in the Wilderness" from *Indian Encounters* by Elizabeth Coatsworth. Copyright © 1932 by Macmillan Publishing Company, renewed 1960 by Katherine C. Kelly. Reprinted with permission of Macmillan.

"Moses" by Walter D. Edmonds. Copyright © 1938 by Walter D. Edmonds. Copyright © renewed 1965 by Walter D. Edmonds. Reprinted by permission of Harold Ober Associates Incorporated.

"Rufus M." from *Rufus M.,* copyright © 1943, 1971 by Eleanor Estes. Reprinted by permission of Harcourt Brace Jovanovich, Inc.

"Na-Ha the Fighter" from *Tales From Silver Lands,* © 1924 by Charles J. Finger. Reprinted by permission of Mrs. Robert A. Leflar.

"The Wounded Wolf" by Jean Craighead George. Text copyright © 1978 by Jean Craighead George. Reprinted by permission of the author.

"M. C. Higgins, the Great" by Virginia Hamilton. Adapted with permission of Macmillan Publishing Company from *M. C. Higgins, the Great* by Virginia Hamilton. Copyright © 1974 by Virginia Hamilton.

E. L. Konigsburg, "The Catchee," in *Throwing Shadows.* Copyright © 1979 by E. L. Konigsburg. Reprinted with the permission of Atheneum Publishers.

"Poor Little Saturday" by Madeleine L'Engle. Copyright © 1956 by King-Size Publications, reprinted by permission of Lescher & Lescher, Ltd.

"The Christmas Fake: A Backwoods Christmas" (text only, pp. 115-125) from *Lois Lenski's Christmas Stories* by Lois Lenski (J. B. Lippincott). Copyright © 1968 by Lois Lenski. Reprinted by permission of Harper & Row Publishers, Inc.

"The Sampler" from *Young Americans* by Cornelia Meigs, © Copyright 1936, by Ginn and Company (Xerox Corporation). Used with permission.

"Garden of Broken Glass" exerpted from the book *Garden of Broken Glass* by Emily Cheney Neville. Copyright © 1975 by Emily Cheney Neville. Reprinted by permission of Delacorte Press.

Robert C. O'Brien, "Through the Valley," from *Z for Zachariah*. Copyright © 1975 by Robert C. O'Brien. Reprinted with the permission of Atheneum Publishers.

"Star of Night" (text, pp. 64-80) from *Angels and Other Strangers: Family Christmas Stories* by Katherine Paterson (Thomas Y. Crowell). Copyright © 1979 by Katherine Paterson. Reprinted by permission of Harper & Row Publishers, Inc.

"Ghost of the Lagoon" by Armstrong Sperry. Reprinted by permission of the author's Estate and the agents for the Estate, Scott Meredith Literary Agency, Inc., 845 Third Avenue, New York, New York 10022.

"The Highest Hit" by Nancy Willard. From *The Highest Hit,* copyright © 1978 by Nancy Willard. Reprinted by permission of Harcourt Brace Jovanovich, Inc.

"The Haste-Me-Well Quilt" from *Under the Little Fir* by Elizabeth Yates. Copyright © 1942 by Coward-McCann, Inc. Reprinted by permission of the author.

Library of Congress Cataloging in Publication Data
Main entry under title:
The Newbery Award reader.
Summary: A collection of short fictional works by eighteen winners of the Newbery Award, an award presented each year to an outstanding work of fiction for young people.
1. Children's stories, American. [1. Short stories]
I. Waugh, Charles G. II. Greenberg, Martin H.
PZ5.N38 1984   [Fic]   83-22592
ISBN 0-15-257034-9

Designed by Dalia Hartman

Printed in the United States of America

First edition

A   B   C   D   E

To our children, with love

Eric-Jon Waugh
Jenny-Lynn Waugh
Kari Greenberg
Kate Greenberg

CONTENTS

Introduction by Virginia Hamilton xi
Lloyd Alexander "The Smith, the Weaver, and the Harper" 1
Carol Ryrie Brink "Emma Went, Too" 11
Elizabeth Coatsworth "The Race in the Wilderness" 25
Walter D. Edmonds "Moses" 43
Eleanor Estes "Rufus M." 65
Charles J. Finger "Na-Ha the Fighter" 79
Jean Craighead George "The Wounded Wolf" 85
Virginia Hamilton "M.C. Higgins, the Great" 91
E. L. Konigsburg "The Catchee" 99
Madeleine L'Engle "Poor Little Saturday" 113
Lois Lenski "The Christmas Fake" 133
Cornelia Meigs "The Sampler" 147
Emily Neville "Garden of Broken Glass" 161
Robert C. O'Brien "Through the Valley" 179
Katherine Paterson "Star of Night" 245
Armstrong Sperry "Ghost of the Lagoon" 261
Nancy Willard "The Highest Hit" 271
Elizabeth Yates "The Haste-Me-Well Quilt" 295

INTRODUCTION

T HE WORLD IS FILLED with stories. In every country and with every people, the need to "tell" about what has happened to someone, with something, and to "talk" about fears, desires, and plain "imaginings" to one another has proved to be an ancient need. Storytelling has for ages been one of the most natural ways we have of communicating. Our literature for children and young adults reaches back into these long-ago times. Historically, children's literature began in the ancient storytelling period before the novel. Legends out of the long past, myths and fairy tales, are still very much alive today, and they influence modern story-writing considerably.

Contemporary literature draws upon the series of fictitious events known as narrative or story. Many writers in this book return again and again to established narrative themes, as in Lloyd Alexander's story, "The Smith, The Weaver, and The Harper," which embodies the maxim *To thine own self be true*. They use timeless prose forms such as the gentle *fantasy* of "Moses," a story from the 1930's by Walter D. Edmonds, and the stark *realism* of Katherine Paterson's "Star of Night," written in the 1970's.

Authors of young adult literature insist on writing what they want to write—and not what might be considered "good" for young people. Many of us write for our own satisfaction, in memory of the child within ourselves. We do remember the children we were. And we often pull upon the stuff of those dreams and longings from our younger lives in creating our fictions.

Whether adults or children, most of us read for pleasure. We read to enjoy ourselves, and there is nothing wrong with that. But one of the marks of an exceptional story is the feeling that there is much more to it than the obvious pleasure of reading it. One learns something one has not known before from the story. The reader is startled by what is there to be learned. The situations presented are astonishing in that they reveal characters, ideas, that had never been dreamed of by the reader before.

A story entertains by offering solace, encouragement, excitement, relaxation, or escape. The stories here run the gamut of subject matter and style. They represent over half a century of story-writing, of putting words together in ways that are unique and individual. Each story represents a miracle of words in making language meaningful in terms of human communication.

It is the writer's pleasure to transform vague images and

INTRODUCTION

desires into convincing fictions. A writer discovers the best way to write a particular story only by writing it. The making of it is often first and foremost a self-view, a looking inward that is translated into an outward force for life. The story-making is greater than the sum of fact, memory, and imagination. The finished narrative stands independently from the writer and is more magical than anything the author may have experienced.

As a John Newbery Award medalist, I receive letters from young people who in their schools and libraries belong to Newbery clubs or have discovered the pleasure of fine writing and storytelling on their own. They read a remarkable number of books written by the Award-winning authors.

It is truly a pleasure to introduce short works of fiction by eighteen of those authors who have been honored by the John Newbery Medal. This highest medal of achievement is given for "the most distinguished contribution to American literature for children" in any given year. The beauty of these stories lies in their variety, their superb execution, and the authors' individuality of expression. In the strength of language, the magic in words lives its artistry and meaning for us all.

Virginia Hamilton

Virginia Hamilton
Yellow Springs, Ohio

THE
NEWBERY
AWARD
READER

LLOYD ALEXANDER

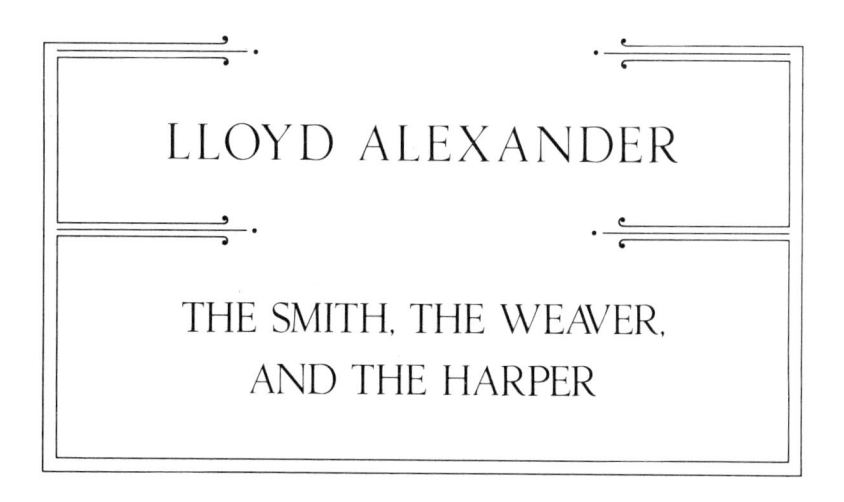

THE SMITH, THE WEAVER, AND THE HARPER

A powerful fantasy about death and greed . . .

There was a time in Prydain when craftsmen were so skillful their very tools held the secrets of their crafts. Of these, the hammer of Iscovan the smith could work any metal into whatever shape its owner wished. The shuttle of Follin the weaver could weave quicker than the eye could see, with never a knot or a tangle. The harp of Menwy the bard sounded airs of such beauty it lifted the hearts of all who heard it.

But Arawn, Lord of Death, coveted these things and set out

to gain them for himself, to lock them deep in his treasure house, so no man might ever have use of them.

And so it was that one day, working at his anvil, Iscovan saw a tall man standing in his doorway. The stranger was arrayed as a war-leader, sword at side, shield over shoulder; he wore a coat of mail whose links were so cleverly wrought and burnished it seemed smooth as satin and glittering as gold.

"Blacksmith," said the tall man, "the rowel of my spur is broken. Can you mend it?"

"There's no metal in all this world I can't mend, or shape, or temper," Iscovan answered. "A broken spur? A trifle! Here, put it on my anvil. With this hammer of mine I'll have it done in three strokes."

"You have a fair hammer," the warrior said, "but I doubt it can work metal such as this."

"Think you so?" cried Iscovan, stung by these words. "Well, now, see for yourself."

So saying, he laid the spur on his anvil, picked up his hammer, and began pounding away with all the strength of his burly arms.

At last, out of breath, his brow smudged and streaming, he stopped and frowned at the spur. It showed not the least mark from his battering.

Iscovan pumped the bellows of his forge, picked up the spur with his tongs, and thrust it into his furnace. There, heating it white hot, once again he set it on his anvil and hammered as hard as he was able, to no avail.

"Trouble yourself no more," the stranger told the puzzled blacksmith. "In my country, armorers shape metal harder than any you know. If you would do likewise, you must use a hammer like theirs."

With that, he reached into a leather sack hanging from his belt and took out a little golden hammer, which he handed to the smith.

"That toy?" Iscovan burst out. "Make sport of me and you'll have more than a broken spur to mend!"

"Try it, nevertheless," replied the stranger.

Laughing scornfully, the smith gripped the hammer and struck with all his force, sure the implement would break in his hand. Instead, sparks shot up, there came a roar of thunder, and his anvil split nearly in two. However, after that single blow, the spur was good as new.

Iscovan's jaw dropped, and he stared at the tall man, who said:

"My thanks to you, blacksmith. Now let me take my hammer and go my way."

"Wait," said Iscovan, clutching the tool. "Tell me, first, how I might get a hammer like yours."

"In my realm, these are treasured highly," replied the stranger. "You have only seen the smallest part of its worth. With such a hammer, a smith can forge weapons that lose neither point nor edge, shields that never split, coats of mail no sword can pierce. Thus arrayed, even a handful of warriors could master a kingdom."

"Tell me nothing of arms and armor," Iscovan replied. "I'm no swordsmith. My skill is with plow irons, rakes, and hoes. But, one way or another, I must have that hammer."

Now, Iscovan had always been a peaceful man; but even as he spoke these words, his head began spinning with secret thoughts. The stranger's voice seemed to fan embers in his mind until they glowed hotter than his forge. And Iscovan said to himself, "If this man speaks the truth, and no sword or spear can harm them, indeed a handful of warriors could master a kingdom, for who could stand against them? But the smith who had the secret—he would be master of all! And why not I instead of another?"

The stranger, who meantime had been watching Iscovan narrowly, said, "Blacksmith, you have done me a favor and by rights I owe a favor to you. So I shall give you this hammer. But for the sake of a fair bargain, give me yours in its place."

Iscovan hesitated, picking up his old hammer and looking fondly at it. The handle was worn smooth by long use, the iron head was nicked and dented; yet this hammer knew its craft as deeply as Iscovan himself, for it had taken to itself the skill of all smiths. It had well served Iscovan and brought him the honor of his workmanship. Nevertheless, considering what new power lay within his grasp, Iscovan nodded and said, "Done. So be it."

The stranger took Iscovan's iron hammer, leaving the gold one in the hands of the smith, and, without another word, strode from the forge.

No sooner had the stranger gone than Iscovan, with a triumphant cry, raised the hammer and gave his anvil a ringing blow. But even as he did, the hammer crumbled in his hand. The bright gold had turned to lead.

Bewildered, Iscovan stared at the useless tool, then ran from the forge, shouting for his own hammer back again. Of the stranger, however, there was no trace.

And from that time on, Iscovan drudged at his forge, never to find a hammer the equal of the one he had bartered away.

On another day, Follin the weaver was busy at his loom when a short, thickset man, ruddy-cheeked and quick-eyed, came into his weaving shed. Follin stopped plying his shuttle, which had been darting back and forth among the threads like a fish in water.

"Good greeting to you," said the stranger, clad in garments finer than any the weaver had ever seen before. His heavy cloak was of cloth of gold, embroidered in curious patterns. "My cloak is worn and shabby. Will you weave another for me?"

"I don't know where you're from," returned Follin, dazzled at the traveler's apparel, "but surely it's a rich realm if you call that handsome cloak shabby."

"It serves well enough to wear on a journey, to be stained and spattered," returned the traveler. "But in my country this is no better than a castoff. Even a beggar would scorn it."

Follin, meanwhile, had climbed down from his bench at the loom. He could not take his eyes from the stranger's cloak, and when he ventured to rub the hem between his thumb and fingers, he grew still more amazed. The cloth, although purest gold, was lighter than thistledown and softer than lamb's wool.

"I can weave nothing like this," Follin stammered. "I have no thread to match it, and the work is beyond even my skill."

"It would be a simple matter," said the traveler, "if you had the means." He reached into a leather sack he carried at his belt. "Here, try this shuttle instead of yours."

Doubtfully, Follin took the shuttle, which looked as if it had never been used, while his own was worn and polished and comfortable to his hand. Nevertheless, at the stranger's bidding, Follin threw the shuttle across the threads already on his loom.

That same instant, the shuttle began flying back and forth even faster than his old one. In moments, before the weaver's eyes, shimmering cloth of gold appeared and grew so quickly the loom soon held enough for a cloak.

"Weaver, my thanks to you," said the stranger, gesturing for Follin to take the new cloth off the loom. "What reward shall you ask?"

Follin was too dumbfounded to do more than wag his head and gape at the work of the wondrous shuttle. And so the traveler continued, "You have done me a favor. Now I shall do one for you. Keep the shuttle. Use it as it may best profit you."

"What?" cried Follin, scarcely believing his ears. "You mean to give me such a treasure?"

"Treasure it may be to you," replied the stranger, "not to me. In my country, such implements are commonplace. Nevertheless," he went on, "for the sake of a fair bargain, give me your shuttle in trade, and you shall have this one."

Now, Follin had never been a greedy man. But the traveler's words were like thin fingers plucking at the warp and weft of his thoughts. He had used his old shuttle all his life and knew it to be filled with the wisdom and pride of his workmanship. Even so, he told himself, no man in his wits could turn down such an exchange. Instead of cloth, he could weave all the gold he wanted. And so he said, "Done. So be it."

He handed his old shuttle to the traveler, who popped it into the leather sack and, without another word, left the weaving shed.

No sooner had the stranger gone out the door than Follin, trembling in excitement, leaped onto his bench and set about weaving as fast as he could. He laughed with glee, and his eyes glittered at the treasure that would be his.

"I'll weave myself a fortune!" he cried. "And when I've spent that, I'll weave myself another! And another! I'll be the richest man in all the land. I'll dine from gold plates, I'll drink from gold cups!"

Suddenly the flying shuttle stopped, split asunder, and fell in pieces to the ground. On the loom the gleaming threads turned, in that instant, to cobwebs and tore apart in shreds before Follin's eyes.

Distraught at the cheat, bewailing the loss of his shuttle, Follin ran from the weaving shed. But the traveler had gone.

And from that time on, Follin drudged at his loom, never to find a shuttle the equal of the one he had bartered away.

On another day, Menwy the bard was sitting under a tree, tuning his harp, when a lean-faced man, cloaked in gray and mounted on a pale horse, reined up and called to him, "Harper, my instrument lacks a string. Can you spare me one of yours?"

THE SMITH, THE WEAVER, AND THE HARPER

Menwy noticed the rider carried at his saddle bow a golden harp, the fairest he had ever seen. He got to his feet and strode up to the horseman to admire the instrument more closely.

"Alas, friend," said Menwy, "I have no strings to match yours. Mine are of the common kind, but yours are spun of gold and silver. If it plays as nobly as it looks, you should be proud of it."

"In my country," said the rider, "this would be deemed the meanest of instruments. But since it seems to please you, so you shall have it. For the sake of a fair bargain, though, give me yours in exchange."

"Now, what a marvelous place the world is!" Menwy answered lightly. "Here's a fellow who rides out of nowhere and asks nothing better than to do me a favor. And would I be so ungrateful as to turn it down? Come, friend, before there's any talk of trading this and that, let's hear a tune from that handsome harp of yours."

At this, the rider stiffened and raised a hand as if the bard had threatened him; but, recovering himself, he replied, "Prove the instrument for yourself, harper. Take it in your hands, listen to its voice."

Menwy shook his head. "No need, friend. For I can tell you now, even though yours sang like a nightingale, I'd rather keep my own. I know its ways, and it knows mine."

The rider's eyes flickered for an instant. Then he replied, "Harper, your fame has spread even as far as my realm. Scorn my gift as you will. But come with me and I swear you shall serve a king more powerful than any in Prydain. His bard you shall be, and you shall have a seat of honor by his throne."

"How could that be?" asked Menwy, smiling. "Already I serve a ruler greater than yours, for I serve my music."

Now, Menwy was a poet and used to seeing around the edge of things. All this while, he had been watching the gray-cloaked horseman; and now as he looked closer, the rider and the golden harp seemed to change before his eyes. The frame of the instrument, which had appeared so fair, he saw to be wrought of dry bones, and the strings were serpents poised to strike.

Though Menwy was as brave as any man, the sight of the rider's true face behind its mask of flesh froze the harper's blood. Nevertheless, he did not turn away, nor did his glance waver as he replied, "I see you for what you are, Lord of Death. And I fear you as all men do. For all that, you are a weak and pitiful king. You can destroy but never build. You are less than the humblest creature, the frailest blade of grass. For these live, and every moment of their lives is a triumph over you. Your kingdom is dust; only the silent ending of things, never the beginnings."

At that, Menwy took his harp and began to play a joyful melody. Hearing it, the horseman's face tightened in rage; he drew his sword from its sheath and with all his might he struck at the bard.

But the blow missed its mark and instead struck the harp, shattering it to bits. Menwy, however, flung aside the pieces, threw back his head, and laughed in defiance, calling out, "You fail, Death-Lord! You destroy the instrument, but not its music. With all your power, you have gained only a broken shell."

In that moment, when the harp had been silenced, arose the songs of birds, the chiming of brooks, the humming of wind through grass and leaves; and all these voices took up the strands of melody, more beautiful than before.

And the Lord of Death fled in terror of life.

LLOYD ALEXANDER (1924-   ) won the Newbery Medal in 1969 for *The High King,* one of his "Prydain" series of books. In addition, he won the National Book Award in 1971 for *The Marvelous Misadventures of Sebastian.* Among his many other outstanding books are *The Wizard in the Tree* (1975), *The Town Cats and Other Tales* (1977), *The First Two Lives of Lukas-Kasha* (1978), *Black Cauldron* (a Newbery Honor Book in 1966), and *Westmark* (1982).

CAROL RYRIE BRINK

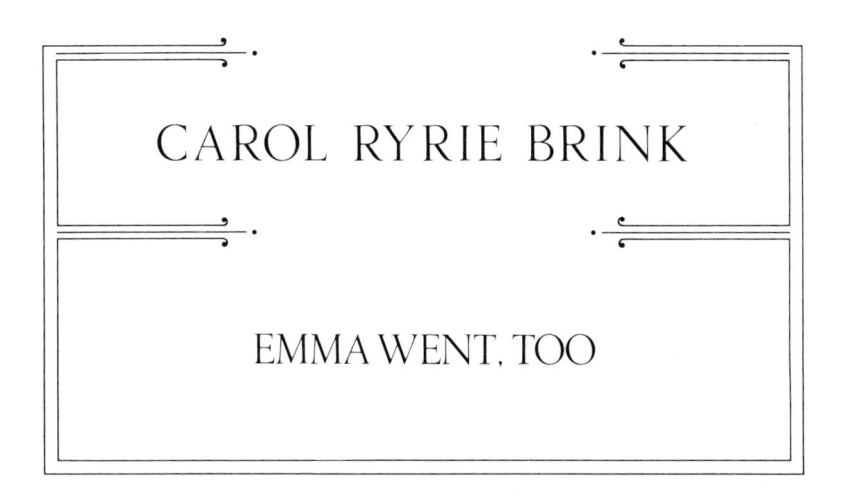

EMMA WENT, TOO

*Sometimes the journey is more
important than the destination....*

CADDIE, LIDA SILBERNAGLE, and Emma McCantry all started early to walk into Eau Galle to see the Medicine Show. They were going to have supper at Lida's grandma's, and Mr. Woodlawn was going to drive them home after the show was over. Caddie's brothers had gone to Eau Galle with Father in the morning.

Caddie had on her good blue dress and Lida a new bonnet with artificial cherries on it. Emma didn't have anything new to wear, but she felt lucky enough to be getting to go at all. There were always so many things to do at home that Mrs. McCantry didn't like to do because they spoiled her hands. But neither Emma nor Mrs. McCantry cared how Emma's hands looked, so it was often hard to get away. Of course, Emma had the eggs to deliver to the crossroads store on the way, and the candle mold to return to Grandma Butler at the second farm before the crossroads, and the Star of Bethlehem quilt pattern to borrow from the blacksmith's wife; but she did *not* have to take a baby along to mind, and that was something. Emma sighed. It wasn't that she minded looking after the younger children or running her mother's errands; but it was so nice to have a day to herself once in a while, and time to go somewhere with the other girls.

"They say it's a dandy show," said Caddie. "Robert Ireton saw it in Durand last week. The man who runs it is called Dr. Hearty, and he sings and plays the banjo and does sleight-of-hand tricks. He has an old spotted horse and he carries his show along with him in his wagon."

"Does he have a trick dog, too?" asked Lida.

"Oh, yes. That's about the best part. They say his medicine cures everything that you could have, but I guess Dr. Nightingale doesn't think much of it. Most people go to see the show, not to buy the medicine."

"I'm sure I don't want any medicine," said Lida, "but it will be fun to hear banjo singing and see magic. Did a medicine show ever come out here before?"

"Not that I ever heard of."

Emma jogged along beside them with the basket of eggs on one arm and the candle mold under the other, and she didn't say a word but she kept smiling. She thought to herself that she had never seen a show at all and this was going to be quite wonderful. When they cut across the pasture a bobolink whistled at them, and Emma whistled back at it—a true bobolink call.

EMMA WENT, TOO

"I wish I could do that," said Caddie, puckering up her lips to try.

"Emma can make lots of birds' whistles, can't you, Emma?" asked Lida.

Emma smiled and pursed up her lips, and out came the sound the robins make just before rain.

They turned in at Grandma Butler's place. Caddie and Lida sat down in the hammock under the pines to wait while Emma took the candle mold around to the back door.

"Oh, Emma," said Grandma Butler. "I'm so glad you've come by. I was just wondering what in the world I'd do. Johnny forgot to take the cow to pasture this morning before he left, and she's been bawling her head off ever since. I'd have taken her long ago, but my legs are full of rheumatics today. If you'll just drive her down for me, Johnny will see that she gets home tonight."

Emma thought of telling Grandma Butler that she was on her way to Eau Galle to see Dr. Hearty's wonderful Medicine Show, but she didn't like to disappoint people and she could hear the cow bawling mournfully in the barn. It wouldn't take long, and if she hurried she could catch the girls before they got to the crossroads. She ran around the house and told them to walk kind of slow and she would catch them up as soon as she could. Then, with the basket of eggs on one arm and a stick in the other hand, Emma drove the old cow down to the pasture.

The cow took her time about getting there and kept stopping every few steps to eat by the way, but finally she was safe behind pasture bars and Emma could hurry once more. She crawled under the pasture fence and skirted the swampy place behind Butler's farm. A redwing blackbird, swaying on a reed, gave a flutelike call and Emma whistled back at him. She was used to swampland and the birds that lived there. She took a shortcut across fields, and she could see Caddie and Lida on the road ahead of her.

13

When she came to the crossroads, they were still ahead of her. They waved and called, "Hurry up, Emma!"

"You go on. I'll catch up with you," called Emma.

But she was beginning to wonder if she would, for she would have to take the other branch of the crossroad for nearly a quarter of a mile to go by the blacksmith's house. Of course there was a lane there that made a shortcut back to the main road to Eau Galle, and if she hurried she might catch them before they came into town.

She ran into the crossroads store with her basket of eggs. Both Mr. Hooper and his brother were busy attending to customers and Emma had to wait. She tapped her toe impatiently on the floor. The three little Hooper boys were playing tag around the cracker and gingersnap barrels, but they stopped and came to stand and stare at Emma.

"You goin' to the Medicine Show to Eau Galle?"

"I aim to," said Emma, smiling. "Are you?"

"Pa won't let us," they said dismally. "We ain't never seen a show like that with torchlight and magic and banjo singin'."

"I never have, either," said Emma. "I'm real pleased to get away to go."

Mr. Hooper took her basket now and began counting the eggs with great deliberation.

"Mis' McCantry want any groceries?"

"No. You're to credit the eggs to her account, please."

"Which way you going?"

"I'm going by the blacksmith's house to borrow a quilt pattern and then by the lane into Eau Galle."

"Fine!" said Mr. Hooper. "You're just the person I'm looking for. There's a letter here come for Mr. Tatum, and you can drop it by for the old man without going fifty steps out of your way. I'd send the little boys, but the last time they took a letter to him they dropped it in the mud and he couldn't half read it. Now he won't have them on the place. But I know you're always careful, Emma."

"Yes, sir," said Emma.

She wasn't surprised because, ever since the family had come back and settled on the corner of the Woodlawn and Nightingale places, people had trusted her with their errands. Somehow they never trusted her mother or Pearly, but they always trusted Emma. It was not very convenient if one were in a hurry. She stuck the letter in her pocket and hurried faster than ever.

It was considerably more than fifty steps out of her way to Mr. Tatum's door, but perhaps Mr. Hooper had forgotten. The old man was a long time answering her knock and, when he came, he looked as if he had been sleeping.

"Letter, eh?" he said, peering at it shortsightedly. "You'll have to come in and read it to me, my dear. I've broken my spectacles."

Emma sighed. This was beginning to assume the proportions of a bad dream—one of those dreams in which you try so hard to get somewhere on time, and everything conspires to stop you. She stepped inside the door and broke the seal of the letter. How untidy Mr. Tatum's kitchen was! There were dirty pans and dishes in the sink, and the floor couldn't have been swept for days. If only she hadn't been in such a hurry—

"It's from your daughter, Hazel," said Emma. "She says she'll be up by the steamer on Thursday afternoon."

"Thursday?" said the old man. "Ain't that today?"

Emma thought. Yes, the girls had said, "Ask your mother to let you off *Thursday* afternoon, because there's going to be a medicine show in Eau Galle."

"That's right," said Emma. "It's today. The steamer ought to get in any time now."

"My land!" said Mr. Tatum. "Look at this house, and Hazel neat as a pin! But I've had lumbago in my back for nearly a week."

"You tell me what to do," said Emma. "I'm a mighty hand at tidying."

She flew around the way she had to do at home on a Saturday morning. While the kettle boiled she swept the floor, and when the water was hot she clattered through the dishes and pans. Mr. Tatum straightened up the beds and picked up the old newspapers that he had left lying on the front-room floor. The house began to look better.

"What you got to eat?" asked Emma.

"Ham an' potatoes," said Mr. Tatum doubtfully.

"Anything in the garden?"

"Rhubarb. But I ain't pulled it for a long time on account of my back."

"Rhubarb sauce an' hot biscuits," said Emma to herself.

She ran out into the garden and found the rhubarb. It was rather old now, but it would do. The sun was getting low in the sky; almost any moment Mr. Tatum's daughter might come walking up the path. She washed the rhubarb and cut it up and put it on in a saucepan with a little water. Mr. Tatum peeled the potatoes and sliced the ham while she mixed up the biscuits. When the rhubarb began to bubble and turn soft and pink, she added the sugar to it and took it off to cool.

"Now you put the biscuits in the oven as soon as you start the ham, and you'll have a real nice supper for her."

"Won't you stay an' eat, Emma?"

"No, I'm in kind of a hurry," said Emma. "Thanks just the same."

She ran down the road to the blacksmith's house. The sun was going lower. Cowbells tinkled across the fields. A catbird called and, without stopping to think, Emma answered it.

"Mis' Peavy, Mama wants to know please can she borrow your Star of Bethlehem quilt pattern?"

"Why, yes, Emma, if she'll think to return it."

"*I'll* remember," Emma said.

"It may take me a minute to hunt it up. Will you hold the baby for me while I look?"

"Yes, ma'am," said Emma.

She sat in the big rocker and held the baby. It was the first time she had sat down since morning, and it made her realize that she was tired. The blacksmith's wife was taking a long time to find the quilt pattern, but it didn't matter now. Emma knew that she was too late. Supper would be over at Lida's grandma's before she could get to Eau Galle. She might still be in time to see the Medicine Show; but it would soon be getting dark, and if she should miss the girls in the crowd she would have no way of getting home again that night. She tried to think back over the afternoon and wonder if she could have hurried a little more here or there. But it didn't seem as if she would have done anything differently, even if she could. An unexpected tear rolled down the side of Emma's nose, but she brushed it hastily away. The Peavy baby was warm and soft to hold, and he was going to sleep in her arms.

When she left the Peavys' farm with the quilt pattern in her pocket, the sun had just slipped below the horizon and the sky was all clear and softly green like glass. There were two tiny pink clouds overhead, and the first star was just beginning to wink experimentally.

Down the road ahead of her Emma saw something that had not been there when she came by before. It was an odd-looking red wagon—almost like a little house on wheels, and something seemed to have gone wrong with it. One of the wheels was sunk in a muddy rut of the road, and a man in a stovepipe hat was out examining the extent of the damage.

Emma came up alongside and looked on.

"I guess you broke your axle, mister."

"Snakes an' fishes!" said the man. "I guess I did!"

A little spotted dog jumped out of the wagon and came to bark at Emma. A fat spotted horse craned its neck around and rolled its eyes to see why the wagon wouldn't budge. There were gold filigree designs around the top of the red caravan, and iron sockets that looked as if they might be made for holding torches. The man wore a long frock coat and a marvelous flowered waistcoat. It was all very strange. Emma's heart began to beat more quickly.

"Trouble, trouble all day long!" said the man. "I never see the like. First the mare throws a shoe and I have to wait to get her reshod. Then the sheriff wants to see my license and I've got to go five miles out of my way—and now this! I'll never get to Eau Galle in time for the show."

"Why, that's just the way it's been with me!" said Emma in surprise. "I started out real early this afternoon; but somebody stopped me every way I turned, and I'll never get to Eau Galle in time for the show."

"Then we're in the same boat, sister," said the big man, smiling. His troubles really seemed to sit upon him very lightly. "Do you know where there's a blacksmith?"

"Yes, I just come from his house. His shop's down to the crossroads—not far."

He opened the back of the red van, and Emma saw that it was lined with racks full of bottles. Suddenly her heart stood still, and then it began to pound at double its usual rate. She went around to the side of the wagon to make sure. Yes, it was there in red and gold letters.

DR. HEARTY'S MARVELOUS CURE-ALL

"But . . . but . . ." said Emma breathlessly. "You *are* the show."

"At your service, ma'am," said Dr. Hearty cheerfully. He had taken a long pole out of the wagon and now he began to rig up a crude sort of lever for hoisting the wheel out of the rut. "You take the horse's bridle—will you, sister?—and get him to move along right smart when I give you the word."

"Yes, sir," said Emma, trotting to the horse's head.

Her thoughts were in a turmoil. Why, there wouldn't be any show in Eau Galle tonight! Dr. Hearty was here—in the road— no farther along than Emma McCantry.

Emma and Dr. Hearty coaxed and lifted and prodded and groaned for nearly half an hour before they got the horse and the disabled caravan as far as the crossroads and the blacksmith's shop. But they were both cheerful about it.

Dr. Hearty seemed to accept everything that came along as pleasantness, and to Emma this was real adventure. A barn swallow flew over and Emma couldn't help imitating its eerie cry.

"Can you do more of those?" asked Dr. Hearty curiously.

"About ten, I guess," said Emma carelessly.

There were usually quite a few people around the crossroads on a fine evening, but most of them had gone into Eau Galle tonight to see the Medicine Show. Those who remained were people who wished they might go but were prevented from doing so, such as the little Hooper boys and old man Toomey, with the wooden leg, and the men who had to tend shop or forge. These remaining few came out and stood about the caravan in open-mouthed amazement.

The sight of even so small a crowd made Dr. Hearty's eyes sparkle. While the blacksmith went to work on the broken axle, Dr. Hearty began to make a speech.

"La-*dees* and *Gent*lemen," he said, "if you cannot go to Dr.

Hearty's highly educating and entertaining display of music, art, and magic, Dr. Hearty will come to you."

He took out a worn old banjo and began such a lively tune that the little Hooper boys could not resist jigging and doing handsprings all over the grass. When the jig was finished, Dr. Hearty struck more plaintive chords and raised his rich bass voice in a sad ballad, "Dying at the Door."

> *"Through the dark streets I am wand'ring alone,*
> *Bowed down and weary with hope overthrown;*
> *Seeking from torturing memory rest,*
> *Trying to stifle the pain at my breast.*
> *Stained tho' I am, yet on this cruel night*
> *I'm seeking again my old home's firelight.*
> *Oh, you who once loved me, forgive, I implore;*
> *Oh, pity me tonight, for I'm dying at your door.*
> *Have pity tonight for I'm dying at your door.*
>
> *"Weary, sighing, hopeless, dying,*
> *What a change from days of yore.*
> *Father, mother, husband, children,*
> *I am dying at your door."*

Emma couldn't help wiping her eyes on the corner of her apron. The mouths of the little Hooper boys had gone down at the corners. In fact, Dr. Hearty's audience was almost in tears over the sad fate of the heroine of the ballad, when he stopped singing as suddenly as he had begun.

"Pardon me, miss, but you've a half-dollar sticking out of your ear."

Emma was perfectly amazed to have Dr. Hearty reach out and pluck a half-dollar quite painlessly out of her ear. It was a very nimble half-dollar indeed; for after it had disappeared under a silk handkerchief, it suddenly popped up again in old man Toomey's beard, was once more lost in Dr. Hearty's stovepipe hat, and finally came to light in the youngest Hooper boy's pocket.

"And now," said Dr. Hearty, "a little local talent, my friends. My able assistant, Miss Emma, will now favor us with her birdcall imitations."

Emma was as much astonished as when Dr. Hearty found a half-dollar in her ear, but she wasn't frightened.

"This is the robin's early-morning song," she said, pursing up her lips. "This is the bobolink. . . . This is the redwing. . . ."

When she had finished they all applauded. Even the blacksmith stopped working on the axle to clap his hands, and Emma found herself making a curtsy just like a regular actor.

"And now, again, my friends," said Dr. Hearty, "to demonstrate to you the salubrious properties of my Marvelous Cure-All, I should like you to witness its remarkable effect on a poor old man."

In a moment the spotted dog, dressed in a small pair of trousers, with spectacles on his nose, came walking around the caravan on his hind legs. He appeared to be in great distress and presently lay down as if at death's door. Dr. Hearty felt his pulse and asked him various questions concerning his health, to which the little dog replied with barks and dismal whines. When all seemed lost, a sip of Dr. Hearty's Cure-All miraculously restored him to health and vivacity—to the extreme delight of Emma and the little boys.

"I'd like a bottle of that myself," said Mr. Hooper. "Have you et, Dr. Hearty?"

"No," said Dr. Hearty, "but I'd admire to do so. Will you trade me some supper for a bottle of Cure-All?"

"Step right over to the store, doctor, an' we'll do business."

"My able assistant is also unfed," said the doctor.

"That's all right," said Mr. Hooper. "Come right in, Emma. I'll feed ye both."

The store was mellow with lamplight. Emma sat on a cracker barrel and Dr. Hearty leaned on a counter beside her. Crackers and cheese had never tasted finer. It was a rare meal and spiced with magic, for Dr. Hearty seemed as clever at extracting crackers from people's ears as he had been with half-dollars. Crackers came out of the lamp chimney and disappeared mysteriously into flour sacks, and gingersnaps materialized out of thin air.

It was a lovely evening, full of adventure. But at last the axle was mended, and Emma knew that she must be on her way home.

"Come into Eau Galle tomorrow, Emma," said Dr. Hearty, "and I'll let you do your bird imitations for all the people."

Emma smiled and shook her head.

"My mother couldn't spare me off another day, I guess."

"Well, anyway, here's a parting gift," said the doctor, "and thank you kindly for helping me get out of the mud hole."

He held out a shiny new bottle of Dr. Hearty's Marvelous Cure-All.

Emma took it with reverence and awe.

"I don't seem to need much medicine," she said, "but I'll always keep it just like this to remember you by."

It was cool and fresh walking home in the starlight with so many things to think about and the wonderful bottle clutched under her arm.

When she was almost at the little lane that turned down between the Woodlawns' and the Nightingales' places, she heard Mr. Woodlawn's wagon come rattling along behind her.

"Oh, Emma, whatever happened to you?" cried the girls. "But it's just as well you didn't come. What do you think? There wasn't any show at all!"

"Do tell!" said Emma, turning in at the lane. "I'm real sorry that you didn't get to see the show!"

Behind the barn a whippoorwill gave out its wistful cry, and Emma answered it.

CAROL RYRIE BRINK *(1895–1981)* won the Newbery Medal in 1936 for *Caddie Woodlawn.* Her numerous other excellent books for children include *Magical Melons: More Stories About Caddie Woodlawn* (1944), *Two Are Better Than One* (1968), *The Bad Times of Irma Baumlein* (1972), and *Mademoiselle Misfortune* (1936).

ELIZABETH COATSWORTH

THE RACE IN THE WILDERNESS

A fact-based story of colonial adventure and disguise . . .

OH, TAMAR WAS TIRED of the airs of her half brother, Roger! He was so proud because his mother had been English while hers had been Indian! It mattered little to Roger that Tamar's mother had been a princess. It was early in the eighteenth century and to be a boy and heir to a Virginian estate were great things, indeed. Tamar was only a girl and a half-Indian girl at that. And now he was to ride with his father and Govenor Spotswood to discover the lands beyond the mountains while Tamar was to remain at home where she belonged.

But Tamar had her own pride, and besides, in a fit of anger, she had wagered her Indian grandmother's crown that she, too, would go on the governor's gay expedition. But that was more easily said than done.

Tamar ate her solitary supper. Then, with a pounding heart, she wrote a letter and addressed it to Mrs. Macdonald, the housekeeper, sanding the ink with a careful hand in spite of her excitement. Next she put on her oldest dress and tiptoed down the stairs. She heard Scipio, the black butler, moving in the dining room and waited until his back was turned before she passed the wide door on noiseless feet. Keeping in the shadow of the trees, she started toward the river down which the moon was making a silver road, but a few yards from the great house she hesitated and turned back. Running swiftly, she rounded the wing and, moving on tiptoe outside kitchens and bake rooms, came to the weaver's house, where a candle was burning.

"John Dummer," she said in a low voice from the door. "Are you there, John Dummer?"

He stirred and answered her.

"Take care of the cosset lamb while I am gone, John Dummer," she said and was off before he could speak again.

The Indians were breaking up their encampment, stowing their few belongings into the bows of two forty-foot canoes, putting out their fires, rolling up the woven mats of their lodges. All was silent commotion when one of the squaws, glancing up, saw someone staring at her from the shadow.

"How," she said.

The girl spoke and moved nearer.

"Opechancanough," she said. "I would see Opechancanough."

The woman pointed him out where he stood by himself,

staring toward river and moon as though unconscious of any of the preparations for departure going on about him.

Tamar had a sudden knowledge. *I must be quiet as a stone or he will not do as I wish.*

She slipped down to the river and bathed her hot hands in the cool water, laying her damp fingers across her eyes. Then she slowly approached her mother's brother, and when she spoke her voice was remote from all feeling.

"Greetings, my uncle," she said. "I have a favor I would ask of you."

He looked at her without change of expression.

"Greetings," he said. "What is the wish of my sister's daughter?"

"My father and brother are going beyond the mountains with the governor, and I wish to go with them, with my cousin and the other guides."

"This is a foolish wish," said Opechancanough. "You are a girl and half a paleface. If your father had wished you to go, you should have gone on horseback with the others. That is all."

Tamar waited. She counted all the stars she could see between the moon and the river. In a voice as cool as lapping water she spoke again.

"The part of me that is white has been brought up all these years in the great house. I do not even speak the language of my mother's people. But in me sometimes the blood calls for the forest, for the dwellings by the spring under the trees, for the small fires that burn without smoke. For once, let me taste the life that my mother lived. I am strong. I can walk many miles without tiring. If I were dressed as an Indian boy, no one would notice me. My brother despises me because I am not all English. I have wagered with him the Weyanoke crown itself that I would go on this expedition."

"A foolish wager," said Opechancanough, staring away into the night. "See, a fish leaped!" He was silent, then added with the shadow of a smile, "I, too, have made foolish wagers in my youth." He seemed to think of the past, then roused.

"Your father makes too much of you," he said sternly, and Tamar's heart sank. "But"—she waited watching his impassive face touched with moonlight—"the Weyanoke crown must not be lost to a headstrong boy."

The squaws who took Tamar in hand laughed and joked as they dressed her, and one held a pine knot while the others boiled bark and deepened the brown of her face and chest and then painted them with red clay. When at last the squaws were through, it was an Indian boy who stood before them in leggings and deerskin shirt, dark eyes dancing with excitement.

Opechancanough grunted approval.

"Walk with straight feet," he said. "Place one foot before the other. Obey your cousin, Scarred Wolf, in everything. Keep a silent mouth. We will see how good an Indian you can make."

Tamar sat in the prow of one of the canoes, watching the dark, low banks slip past them. Sometimes they went by plantations, and she smelled earth and the rank odor of tobacco plants as they passed the wharves and the far-off lights of a great house; but mostly the country was still scarcely touched by the presence of man and they skirted only forests.

The trees near her were brightened by moonlight. She saw the glisten on holly leaves and ivy, and when an owl swooped past them, every feather lay in its place, pale and soft. The fish that leaped about them made widening rings of narrow brightness so that sometimes the canoes seemed to be passing through networks and spangles of silver; the path of the moon followed them up the river and marked the wake that stretched behind them like the broad flanges of an arrow of which they formed the point.

On the far side of the river the trees were dark on a pallid sky and when, as sometimes happened, the other canoe came abreast the one in which Tamar sat lulled by the soft gurgle of water at the bow, the figures seemed to her to loom grave and dark against the light, more like spirits than human beings. Occasionally an Indian said a few words whose meaning she did not know; it did not trouble her. This was like her dreams, and she felt as though her heart had become a spring from which a dark, quiet happiness was flowing into the night.

Nevertheless, after a time she fell asleep, to be wakened by a touch and a voice saying, "Come, Raccoon."

The chill of the false dawn was in the air as Tamar followed the four young Indians up the slope of lawn toward Lilac Banks. She saw their lean, sinewy figures outlined before her on a pale, strawberry-stained sky. She might almost have been walking with four panthers—four panthers that were friendly to her and allowed her to share their hunting.

It was with alien eyes that she watched the great house awake and saw the servants lead out the horses and the mules. The governor rode over to speak to the guides, and she saluted him.

"I have brought my young brother, the Raccoon, with me," said Scarred Wolf. "It is time he learned to follow trail."

The governor tossed the boy a silver coin; the Raccoon caught it nimbly and slipped it into his belt, continuing to stare as Colonel Antony went by and meeting for a calm second the glance of Roger. As young Caesar passed, however, the Indian boy was bending over the fire. But young Caesar had many things to think of more important than Indians and Indian boys. Kitty Fisher had a saddle sore from a saddle blanket's having slipped; it had gone unnoticed by Mr. Reid, the schoolmaster, whose head was in the clouds, in heaven over the adventure. He came to the Indian camp fire, drawn as a bee to clover by the presence of the savage and disinherited heirs of the land he loved. He even put his hand on the Raccoon's shoulder, his blue eyes peering into a face that to him was filled with romantic interest.

"My brother is shy and speaks no English," said Scarred Wolf. "Now we must make ready for the trail."

Mr. Reid patted the Raccoon's shoulder and returned toward Lilac Banks thinking how much like Tamar the boy looked. *I suppose they may even be cousins,* he thought. *Perhaps Indian children look alike. But his glance is prouder and colder than Tamar's.*

When the expedition set out, the guides led the way, on foot, in a swift stride, keeping ahead of the horses. The Raccoon carried on his back a light burden laced with thongs. In the cool of the morning, the walking was an adventure. But they were still in low tidewater country and, as the sun grew hot and hotter and the dense trees cut off the breeze, the Raccoon dragged a little behind the others. At the resting place by a stream where the servants lit fires and prepared a luncheon on cloths spread with fruits and meats and biscuits and wine, the Indian boy flung himself on his back to rest.

Scarred Wolf taunted him.

"Is this the strength of which you boasted?" he asked. "You are a branch easily broken. Go fetch water."

When the boy came back to the guides, he was given a handful of parched corn.

"They ride on horses and can afford to fill their bellies," said Scarred Wolf, "but we are on our feet. This is enough."

Once more the cavalcade was on its way, and now the boy was limping, so that the governor noticed it and sent one of the servants forward with a horse. But the Raccoon shook his head.

"He was only dancing," remarked Scarred Wolf, and after that by a great effort the Raccoon forced himself once more into the stride of the others. As the hours lengthened, the walking became easier and the agony in his feet seemed less.

That evening he fetched the water for the others without being told and found the sticks for their fire, laying them in a circle with their ends together, requiring little wood, as he had noticed Opechancanough's fire was made. Every muscle in his body ached, and he could scarcely swallow the venison that he was given.

I was mad to dream I could do this, thought Tamar; but the other half of her that was the Raccoon gritted his teeth and thought, *I will*—and fell asleep watching the play of firelight on the undersides of beech leaves through which a few stars shone.

Scarred Wolf woke him in the morning with harsh words; but as the boy went about his tasks he noticed that someone during the night had sewn soles of heavier hide in his moccasins. He looked at his cousin, who did not return his glance. Somewhere the horn sounded to horse, and he heard the governor's merry voice cry, "Gentlemen, we are one day nearer the mountains!"

And, slinging his load on his back, the Raccoon broke into the swift Indian stride of the four guides who led the cavalcade.

The days went by, and the summer adventurers drew nearer and nearer to the mountains. The weather was hot and fine, and the air of merriment with which the expedition had begun only deepened with the passing hours. The governor was a man who could do serious business gaily. They would find out what sort of land lay beyond the mountains that the French were beginning to claim, but they would make a frolic of the adventure if they could. The long line of horses and mules moved leisurely enough. The gentlemen stopped to hunt deer and elk; they sang as they ate and drank beneath the trees. Sometimes they slept at the houses of planters, sometimes in their own tents. Roger grew into the beginnings of manhood, sharing the days with his father and the other men, and Mr. Reid rode with flapping elbows and knees, scarcely noticing his horse, so intent was he on the birds that rose about them, the cornfields standing in full tassel, the snake fences, the hawks wheeling in the blue sky, and the forests of beech and oak, pine, walnut, and sassafras, hung with curtains and festoons of vines and intersected by narrow game trails.

With every day the character of the country was changing, growing more rolling. Here, Mr. Reid noted, the forest was master, and the truce between the woodland and the field was here not yet begun. Instead of mansions, he saw cabins of logs stripped of their bark built in clearings where the stumps still stood ragged in the midst of the corn or served the thin cattle as barbaric fences, their roots interlacing into a crude barrier. Here man was on sufferance. It was the wilderness that laid down the terms under which he might be allowed to live, a small, mean creature, at its fringes. The courage of the men and women whom he saw in the clearings gave Mr. Reid a new admiration for the spirit of mankind; but it was of the wilderness he dreamed—the wilderness that stretched over hill and valley as far as his thought could pierce, still savage and untamed.

The Raccoon now could walk all day and swing into camp untired. He slept on the bare ground and drank water from his hands and ate sparingly of what he was given. Now he could speak in the Indian language, though with a haltingness that the whites never suspected.

Crouched over the fire, with the darkness like a blanket about his shoulders as he had always dreamed, he talked with his companions, who—now that he had proved himself—were no longer harsh.

"Scarred Wolf, tell me the story of the first Opechancanough, our ancestor," he begged.

Scarred Wolf enjoyed talking to new ears.

"He was a great fighter," he said, "bold as an elk in the fall and cunning as a weasel. He was Powhatan's brother and hated the English. In those days he led twenty-four hundred warriors. It was he who was the hand and mind behind the massacre of the whites that took place many, many moons ago, when he hoped to sweep the last of the palefaces into the sea from which they came. His dream failed, though he grew to be an old man, so old that he could no longer follow the war trail; but even then he had himself carried on a litter by young braves and still led the fighting."

The Raccoon stared off into the faintly stirring shadows. His blood was warrior's blood on both sides, and the first Opechancanough on his litter seemed as real and near as Admiral Stafford, his father's ancestor, who had fought the Spanish.

In these days the Raccoon was learning to live very close to the earth. He heard sounds that he had never heard before. Everything he saw and smelled meant something to him. By the behavior of the birds and squirrels, by the turn of the leaves, by the smallest breaking of a twig, he learned to read what was taking place unseen about him; though even then Scarred Wolf laughed at his ignorance.

"You have been wasting your life indoors studying out of books made from paper," said the Indian. "That is dead wisdom. Are not the sky, and these trees, better teachers than Mr. Reid? It was from this red earth you were born, and your dust someday will blow on these winds. There is a spirit here that moves in the shadows, and cries out with the voice of the swans, and walks among the trees, and strikes with the arrows of lightning. Empty your heart of pride, and watch, for not a grass blade moves without a reason and that reason is important for you to learn."

At last there came a day when Scarred Wolf pointed silently from a hilltop and the Raccoon had his first sight of the blue ridge of the mountains cutting the skyline. To someone raised in the flat tidewater country, it appeared very wonderful to see the land tilted thus against the clouds. The rivers had reached their falls now and narrowed to freshwater streams in which the tides no longer ran; the road had narrowed, too, to a trail; and instead of coaches with outriders they now met occasional peddlers with their lines of packhorses, trafficking on the wilderness trail, taking in cloth, sugar, rum, tools, and medicines to the scattered cabins and bringing out the precious beaver skins—tall, morose-looking men in coonskin caps, with guns slung at their saddlebows and eyes almost as learned in forest lore as Scarred Wolf's own. Governor Spotswood was as courteous to a woodsman as to a great landowner, and more than once he stopped the pack-trains and invited the peddlers to dine with him, giving them such food and drink as they had never tasted before, spread on damask cloths and served on fine china.

It was during one of these trail-side repasts that the rivalry between Rambler and Grenadier was brought to a head. The governor had been questioning Sam Hutton, a well-known wilderness man, about what he knew of the country beyond the mountains, and after luncheon he had examined some of the fine beaver pelts with which the packhorses were loaded and in turn showed Sam Hutton the horses of his own expedition.

The peddler ran an experienced eye over the animals.

"Nice young horse, that strawberry," he remarked, jerking a thumb toward Rambler. The governor smiled.

"He belongs to young Stafford," he answered. "I should imagine that he is the best horse we have."

"Then you would be mistaken, sir," said his secretary quickly. "He's a good enough horse for one Virginia-bred, I admit, but my Grenadier would show him his place at any distance."

"It's possible, sir," said the governor, displeased by the interruption, "but I myself have not such a preference for all things English."

Sam Hutton brought his big hands together in a clap.

"A race, gentlemen!" he exclaimed. "What better chance for a race? I'll bet on the Virginia colt, beaver skins against tobacco at Mr. Byrd's trading house at the falls."

"I'll take you," said Mr. Bridge with an ugly smile.

"If there's to be a race, it must be tomorrow when the horses are rested," said the governor. "And remember, Mr. Hutton, the laws about betting. We'll pitch camp here, and, Mr. Hutton, you and your men must be our guests. Are you willing, Colonel Antony, that your son should race the colt?"

"Roger must answer for himself, sir," said Colonel Antony. "But I know he has long been an admirer of Mr. Bridge's Grenadier, so I believe he will be glad to show him some sport."

Roger bowed eagerly.

In a few minutes it was known throughout the camp that there was to be a race next day, and a hundred wagers were laid, openly among the gentlemen, and secretly among the rangers and servants. Even the Indians were interested, and the Raccoon was greatly excited by the news. A quarter mile through a natural clearing was staked out in preparation, and everyone was airing his knowledge of horseflesh.

After supper the Raccoon felt a strong impulse to look at the two horses, but he was anxious that neither Roger nor young Caesar should see him, so he stood in the shadow of the trees watching the animals in the dusk. Suddenly his attention was caught by voices.

A man's voice, which he recognized as Mr. Bridge's, was saying in low, urgent tones, "You will do as I tell you, George, or you'll have cause to regret it. There's no danger to you. Early in the morning, before the grooms are up, take two or three strong horsehairs . . ."

Then the figures moved away, and the Raccoon could see the

English secretary leaning toward his groom urging and explaining something; but what that something was, the Indian boy could not hear, though he followed quietly among the trees trying to come again within earshot.

When the others were all asleep, the Raccoon lay long pondering. Had the secretary only been talking of some charm to help his horse, some harmless superstition? But if so, why did George hang back? No, the Raccoon thought, there must be danger to Rambler. He could not discuss it with Scarred Wolf, who knew much about deer but little about horses. And at last he fell into a deep sleep, still uncertain what Mr. Bridge had meant by his curious words.

It was broad daylight when the Raccoon woke. The Indians had gone so silently that no crackling twig had wakened him. He heard a hunting horn blow and the sound of cheering and knew that it was a signal for the beginning of the race. There was something wrong, he remembered, but he had not been able to guess it; and then, as he sprang up from the ground, the explanation came to him as clearly as though a voice had spoken, and he ran off toward the crowd in the clearing, running with all the swiftness he had learned in these last days.

The crowd was gathered—gentlemen, peddlers, rangers, servants—looking small against the background of savage and indifferent trees behind them. The horses were already in place but the governor was talking with the riders. As the Raccoon ran, he saw Grenadier advance to another position a little farther along the course and knew that the black was being given a handicap because he carried the heavier rider. Raccoon's breath was coming in gasps. He saw Joseph Bentley raise a pistol toward the sky, and at that moment he burst panting through the crowd and threw himself on his knees, on the ground, his quick brown fingers searching above Rambler's nearest hoof, while a volley of surprised exclamations sounded over his head.

"What's this? What's this?" cried Mr. Bentley in a sputter, lowering his pistol uncertainly.

"Give the lad a moment," said the governor. "Let's see what he is doing."

Rambler, usually impatient of strangers, stood still as the Indian boy crouched beside him.

"What's the trouble?" asked Roger, leaning down from the saddle.

Mr. Bridge rode back scowling.

"Is this delay necessary, sir?" he asked the governor. "Let someone give that boy a hiding for interrupting his betters."

"Let him alone," said the governor, who was watching the Indian boy with great interest.

Just as the Raccoon thought that he must be mistaken, his fingers, steady in spite of his nervousness, felt something infinitely narrow and strong fastened tightly about Rambler's left hind fetlock. Drawing his knife, he severed it, and he rose to his feet holding three or four horsehairs that had been knotted above the hoof.

"Ha!" said the governor. "I have heard of that trick for barely laming a horse. Boy, what do you know of this?"

The Raccoon shook his head and tried to escape through the crowd. His one desire now was to get away from the eyes that were looking at him—Roger's and Colonel Antony's, Mr. Reid's and young Caesar's.

But as he turned, the lash of a riding crop came stinging across his face and another blow fell on his shoulder. Mr. Bridge had ridden up to him and, shouting angrily, "You put it there, yourself, you Indian pup!" was raining blows upon him. It was

Mr. Reid who sprang from the crowd and caught the secretary's wrist in his big, clumsy hand.

"For shame, sir!" he cried in passion. "The boy speaks no English. He cannot defend himself."

Roger had jumped from Rambler and was running forward, white with anger, when the governor's cool tones cut through the storm.

"Gentlemen, gentlemen!" he said smoothly. "Stop where you are. Mr. Reid, release Mr. Bridge's wrist. He will not strike the boy again. Sir, I am accustomed to being obeyed when I speak.

"Now, gentlemen, we have witnessed the detection of a foul act such as no man of honor would be guilty of. We know that heavy bets were made on this race and must suppose this to be the work of some unknown person who was deeply interested. We all owe this Indian boy a debt of gratitude, but none more than Mr. Bridge, who has been spared the embarrassment of being winner in an unfair race. Mr. Bridge and Roger Stafford, I desire you to shake one another's hands and the race will then be run."

Roger's face flushed and he hesitated as Mr. Bridge held out his hand, his teeth showing between pale lips.

"Gentlemen!" said the governor again, and one felt the force that usually lay hidden under his friendliness and merriment.

Unwillingly, Roger put his hand in the other man's, bowed to the governor, and swung into the saddle in silence. He had not glanced at his father for advice.

Egad, thought the colonel, well pleased, *my son is growing into a man, it seems.*

Roger sat in his saddle looking straight ahead of him as Mr. Bridge rode past him to the starting point. The pistol spoke, and the two horses leaped forward almost with one bound. For a hundred yards Grenadier held the lead, but Rambler was running furiously.

"Faith!" said the colonel out loud, "it's as though he were as angry as Roger."

The boy's spirit seemed to have passed into the horse—his stride was almost an onslaught, and as he tore by Grenadier he reached sideways toward the other horse with open mouth, and only Roger's quick jerk at the rein swept him past his rival and on to the finish line. There was great applause among all the gathering.

"Virginia forever!" exclaimed the governor, smiling.

But Roger listened to the congratulations all about him with an absentminded look. His eyes glanced here and there but did not find what they were seeking.

"Excuse me, sir," he said to the governor. "I have an errand I must do."

"I guess what the young man's errand is," said Sam Hutton. "A pretty race, Governor Spotswood, and we wilderness men are mightily obliged to you for letting us see the English horse beaten. Not that fine things don't come out of England, like yourself, sir, and none finer, if you'll excuse the liberty, sir."

The governor smiled and turned to Mr. Bridge, who had ridden up. His eyes hardened at seeing Grenadier's sides bloodied by the spurs. The secretary was still riding with a heavy hand on the curb.

"Do not blame your horse, Mr. Bridge," said the governor, still politely. "He is not accustomed yet to the land. If you will come to my tent, sir, at noon, I have important dispatches I will ask you to carry for me to the burgesses. And as we are nearing the end of our expedition, it will be wiser if you will await our return at the capital."

"I shall be only too glad, sir," said Mr. Bridge. "It will be a stride nearer London. And I am expecting word of a legacy that will make it necessary for me to return to my estates. To tell you the truth, sir, I shall not be sorry to leave this wilderness"—he made a gesture with his hands—"and—" he paused, smiled insolently, and added, "its varied inhabitants."

"Leave 'em as fast as you like," said Sam Hutton cheerfully, turning his back full on the secretary, and through a contemptuous silence Mr. Bridge rode away from the summer adventure.

But meantime, Roger had thrown his reins to young Caesar and, after a word or two of instructions as to the care of the horse and a pat on Rambler's sweat-darkened neck, he was off toward the edge of the clearing.

He found the Raccoon sitting quietly, stitching sinew through a newly cut pair of moccasins, a red welt across his cheek. The other Indians were there also. Roger put his hand on the younger boy's shoulder.

"He doesn't speak my tongue," he said to Scarred Wolf, "but tell him my heart is grateful to him. I wish that I might have taken the blows that he received. Tell him I hope that someday I may be his friend when he needs one, as he this day has been mine."

Roger hesitated. He had a purse with a jingle of gold coins in it; but, looking into the eyes of the Indian boy, he had another impulse. At his belt hung a fine knife in a silver sheath, newly come from London on the *Merryweather*—a thing of which he was very fond and whose loss he would feel. He unbuckled it and put it in the Raccoon's hands.

"Tell him I give him my knife and hope that good fortune goes with it," he said. "Let it remind him of this day and of the debt I owe him."

The Indian boy still stared into his face. For a moment Roger thought he saw tears, but in an instant they were gone, if they had ever been there. The other boy said something in his own tongue, in a low voice.

"He says that he thanks you and is glad of your friendship," translated Scarred Wolf, and, eased in heart, Roger turned back toward the tent he shared with his father. For some reason he thought of Tamar. Oh, better that she should be kin to the Raccoon than to some gentleman he could name! He was ashamed to think that he had been ashamed of her blood.

Meantime, there was silence among the Indians. The Raccoon had thrust the knife into his belt and gone on with his work on the moccasin.

After a while, Scarred Wolf laughed. "These white men are blind," he said. "His hand was on your shoulder, yet he never knew."

The boy said nothing, and there was another silence.

"Blind as a snake shedding its skin," said Scarred Wolf again. "But he will be a man yet, this brother of yours, whose friendship will be well worth having."

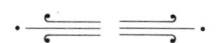

ELIZABETH COATSWORTH *(1893–   )* won the Newbery Medal in 1931 for *The Cat Who Went to Heaven*. The author of dozens and dozens of children's books, she shows her vivid imagination in books like *You Say You Saw a Camel?* (1958), *Lonely Maria* (1960), *Princess and the Lion* (1963), *Marra's World* (1975), *The Werefox* (1975), *Snow Parlor and Other Bedtime Stories* (1972), *They Walk in the Night* (1969), and *All-Of-A-Sudden Susan* (1974).

WALTER D. EDMONDS

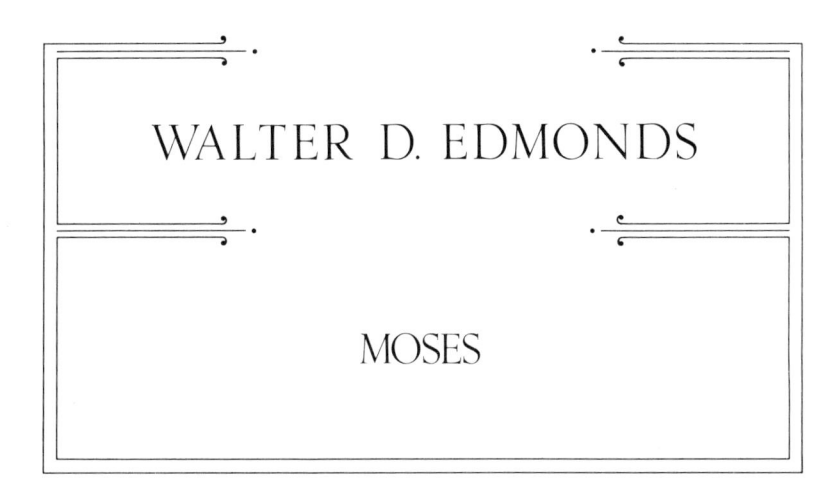

MOSES

A hilarious tale of a heavenly dog . . .

It was a long climb. The scent was cold, too; so faint that when he found it behind the barn he could hardly trust himself. He had just come back from Filmer's with a piece of meat, and he had sat down behind the barn and cracked it down; and a minute later he found that scent reaching off, faint as it was, right from the end of his nose as he lay.

He had had the devil of a time working it out at first, but up here it was simple enough except for the faintness of it. There didn't appear to be any way to stray off this path; there wasn't any brush, there wasn't any water. Only he had to make sure of it, when even for him it nearly faded out, with so many other, stronger tracks overlaying it. His tail drooped, and he stumbled a couple of times, driving his nose into the dust. He looked gaunt when he reached the spot where the man had lain down to sleep.

The scent lay heavier there. He shuffled round over it, sifting the dust with an audible clapping of his nostrils to work out the pattern the man had made. It was hard to do, for the dust didn't take scent decently. It wasn't like any dust he had ever come across, either, being glittery, like mica, and slivery in his nose. But he could tell after a minute how the man had lain, on his back, with his hands under his head, and probably his hat over his eyes to shield them from the glare, which was pretty dazzling bright up this high, with no trees handy.

His tail began to cut air. He felt better, and all of a sudden he lifted up his freckled nose and let out a couple of short yowps and then a good chest-swelled belling. Then he struck out up the steep going once more. His front legs may have elbowed a little, but his hind legs were full of spring, and his tail kept swinging.

That was how the old man by the town entrance saw him, way down below.

The old man had his chair in the shadow of the wall with a black and yellow parasol tied to the back of it as an extra insurance against the sun. He was reading the Arrivals in the newspaper, the only column that ever interested him; but he looked up sharply when he heard the two yowps and the deep chest-notes that, from where he sat, had a mysterious, floating quality. It was a little disturbing; but when he saw a dog was the cause he reached out with his foot and shoved the gate hard, so that it swung shut and latched with a sound like a gong. Only one dog had ever come here, and that sound had been enough to discourage him; he had hung round for a while, though, just on the edge, and made the old man nervous. He said to himself that he wasn't going to watch this one, anyway, and folded the paper in halves the way the subway commuter had showed him and went on with the Arrivals.

After a while, though, he heard the dog's panting coming close and the muffled padding of his feet on the marble gate-stone. He shook the paper a little, licked his thumb, and turned over half a sheet and read on through the Arrivals into the report of the Committee on Admissions. But then, because he was a curious old man, and kindhearted, noticing that the panting had stopped—and because he had never been quite up to keeping his resolves, except once—he looked out of the gate again.

The dog was sitting on the edge of the gate-stone, upright, with his front feet close under him. He was a rusty-muzzled, blue-tick foxhound, with brown ears, and eyes outlined in black like an Egyptian's. He had his nose inside the bars and was working it at the old man.

"Go away," said the old man. "Go home."

At the sound of his voice the hound wrinkled his nose soberly and his tail whipped a couple of times on the gate-stone, raising a little star dust.

"Go home," repeated the old man, remembering the dog that had hung around before.

He rattled the paper at him, but it didn't do any good. The dog just looked solemnly pleased at the attention, and a little hopeful, and allowed himself to pant a bit.

This one's going to be worse than the other, the old man thought, groaning to himself as he got up. He didn't know much about dogs, anyway. Back in Galilee there hadn't been dogs that looked like this one—just pariahs and shepherds and the occasional Persian greyhound of a rich man's son.

He slapped his paper along the bars; it made the dog suck in his tongue and move back obligingly. Peter unhooked his shepherd's staff from the middle crossbar, to use in case the dog tried to slip in past him, and let himself out. He could tell by the feeling of his bare ankles that there was a wind making up in the outer heavens, and he wanted to get rid of the poor creature before it began really blowing round the walls. The dog backed off from him and sat down almost on the edge, still friendly, but wary of the shepherd's staff.

Why can't the poor dumb animal read? thought Peter, turning to look at the sign he had hung on the gatepost.

The sign read:

TAKE NOTICE

NO

DOGS

SORCERERS

WHOREMONGERS

MURDERERS

IDOLATERS

LIARS

WILL

BE

ADMITTED

When he put it up, he had thought it might save him a lot of trouble; but it certainly wasn't going to help in the case of this dog. He expected he would have to ask the Committee on Admissions to take the matter up; and he started to feel annoyed with them for not having got this animal on the list themselves. It was going to mean a lot of correspondence and probably the Committee would send a memorandum to the Central Office suggesting his retirement again, and Peter liked his place at the gate. It was quiet there, and it was pleasant for an old man to look through the bars and down the path, to reassure the frightened people, and, when there was nothing else to do, to hear the winds of outer heaven blowing by.

"Go away. Go home. Depart," he said, waving his staff; but the dog only backed down onto the path and lay on his wishbone with his nose between his paws.

II

Peter went inside and sat down and tried to figure the business out. There were two things he could do. He could notify the Committee of the dog's arrival, or he could give the information to the editor. The Committee would sit up and take notice for once if they found the editor had got ahead of them. It would please the editor, for there were few scoops in Heaven. And then, as luck would have it, the editor himself came down to the gate.

The editor wasn't Horace Greeley or anybody like that, with a reputation in the newspaper world. He had been editor of a little country weekly that nobody in New York, or London, or Paris had ever heard of. But he was good and bursting with ideas all the time. He was now.

"Say, Saint Peter," he said, "I've just had a swell idea about the Arrivals column. Instead of printing all the 'arrivals' on one side and then the 'expected guests' on the other, why not just have one column and put the names of the successful candidates in uppercase type? See?" He shoved a wet impression under Peter's nose and rubbed the back of his head nervously with his ink-stained hand. "Simple, neat, dignified."

Peter looked at the galley and saw how simple it would be for him, too. He wouldn't have to read the names in lowercase at all. It would make him feel a lot better not to know. Just check the uppercase names as they came to the gate.

He looked up at the flushed face of the editor, and his white beard parted over his smile. He liked young, enthusiastic men, remembering how hard, once, they had been to find.

"It looks fine to me, Don," he said. "But the Committee won't like losing all that space in the paper, will they?"

"Probably not," the editor said ruefully. "But I thought you could pull a few wires with the Central Office for me."

Peter sighed.

"I'll try," he said. "But people don't pay attention to an old man, much, Don. Especially one who's been in service."

The editor flushed and muttered something about bums.

Peter said gently, "It doesn't bother me, Don. I'm not ashamed of the service I was in." He looked down to his sandals. He wondered whether there was any of the dust of that Roman road left on them after so long a time. Every man has his one great moment. He'd had two. He was glad he hadn't let the second one go. "I'll see what I can do, Don."

It was a still corner, by the gate; and, with both of them silently staring off up the avenue under the green trees to where the butterflies were fluttering in the shrubbery of the public gardens, the dog decided to take a chance and sneak up again.

He moved one foot at a time, the way he had learned to do behind the counter in the Hawkinsville store, when he went prospecting toward the candy counter. These men didn't hear him any more than the checker players in the store did, and he had time to sniff over the gatepost thoroughly. It puzzled him; and as the men didn't take any notice, he gumshoed over to the other post and went over that, too.

It was queer. He couldn't smell dog on either of them and they were the best-looking posts he had ever come across. It worried him some. His tail drooped and he came back to the gate-stone and the very faint scent on it, leading beyond the gate, that he had been following so long. He sat down again and put his nose through the bars, and after a minute he whined.

It was a small sound, but Peter heard it.

"That dog," he said.

The editor whirled round, saying, "What dog?" and saw him.

"I was going to let you know about him, only I forgot," said Peter. "He came up a while ago, and I can't get rid of him. I don't know how he got here. The Committee didn't give me any warning and there's nothing about him in the paper."

"He wasn't on the bulletin," said the editor. "Must have been a slipup somewhere."

"I don't think so," said Peter. "Dogs don't often come here. Only one other since I've been here, as a matter of fact. What kind of a dog is he, anyway? I never saw anything like him." He sounded troubled and put out, and the editor grinned, knowing he didn't mean it.

"I never was much of a dog man," he said. "But that's a likely-looking foxhound. He must have followed somebody's scent up here. Hi, boy!" he said. "What's your name? Bob? Spot? Duke?"

The hound lowered his head a little, wrinkled his nose, and wagged his tail across the stone.

"Say," said the editor. "Why don't I put an ad in the Lost and Found? I've never had anything to put there before. But you better bring him in and keep him here till the owner claims him."

"I can't do that," said Peter. "It's against the Law."

"No dogs. Say, I always thought it was funny there were no dogs here. What happens to them?"

"They get removed," said Peter. "They just go."

"That don't seem right," the young editor said. He ruffled his back hair with his hand. "Say, Saint," he asked, "who made this law anyway?"

"It's in Revelations. John wasn't a dog man, as you call it. Back in Galilee we didn't think much of dogs, you see. They were mostly pariahs."

"I see," said the editor. His blue eyes sparkled. "But, say! Why can't I put it in the news? And write an editorial? By golly, I haven't had anything to raise a cause on since I got here."

Peter shook his head dubiously. "It's risky," he said.

"It's a free country," exclaimed the editor. "At least nobody's told me different. Now probably there's nothing would mean so much to the owner of that dog as finding him up here. You get a genuine dog man and this business of passing the love of women is just hooey to him."

"Hooey?" Peter asked quietly.

"It just means he likes dogs better than anything. And this is a good dog, I tell you. He's cold-tracked this fellow, whoever he is, Lord knows how. Besides, he's only one dog, and look at the way the rabbits have been getting into the manna in the public garden. I'm not a dog man, as I said before, but believe me, Saint, it's a pretty thing on a frosty morning to hear a good hound hightailing a fox across the hills."

"We don't have frost here, Don."

"Well," said the editor, "frost or no frost, I'm going to do it. I'll have to work quick to get it in before the forms close. See you later."

"Wait," said Peter. "What's the weather report say?"

The editor gave a short laugh.

"What do you think? Fair, moderate winds, little change in temperature. Those twerps up in the bureau don't even bother to read the barometer anymore. They just play pinochle all day, and the boy runs that report off on the mimeograph machine."

"I think there's a wind making up in the outer heavens," Peter said. "When we get a real one, it just about blows the gate-stone away. That poor animal wouldn't last a minute."

The editor whistled. "We'll have to work fast." Then suddenly his eyes blazed. "All my life I wanted to get out an extra. I never had a chance, running a weekly. Now, by holy, I will."

He went off up the avenue on the dead run. Even Peter, watching him go, felt excited.

"Nice dog," he said to the hound; and the hound, at the deep, gentle voice, gulped in his tongue and twitched his haunches. The whipping of his tail on the gate-stone made a companionable sound for the old man. His beard folded on his chest and he nodded a little.

III

He was dozing quietly when the hound barked.

It was a deep, vibrant note that anyone who knew dogs would have expected the minute he saw the spring of those ribs; it was mellow, like honey in the throat. Peter woke up tingling with the sound of it and turned to see the hound swaying the whole hind half of himself with his tail.

Then a high, loud voice shouted, "Mose, by Jeepers! What the hell you doing here, you poor dumb fool?"

Peter turned to see a stocky, short-legged man who stuck out more than was ordinary, both in front and behind. He had on a gray flannel shirt, and blue denim pants, and a pair of lumberman's rubber packs on his feet, with the tops laced only to the ankle. There was a hole in the front of his felt hat where the block had worn through. He wasn't, on the whole, what you might expect to see walking on that Avenue. But Peter had seen queer people come to Heaven and he said mildly, "Do you know this dog?"

"Sure," said the stout man. "I hunted with him round Hawkinsville for the last seven years. It's old Mose. Real smart dog. He'd hunt for anybody."

"Mose?" said Peter. "For Moses, I suppose."

"Maybe. He could track anything through hell and high water."

"Moses went through some pretty high water," said Peter. "What's your name?"

"Freem Brock. What's yours?"

Peter did not trouble to answer, for he was looking at the hound; and he was thinking he had seen some people come to Heaven's gate and look pleased, and some come and look shy, and some frightened, and some a little shamefaced, and some satisfied, and some sad (maybe with memories they couldn't leave on earth), and some jubilant, and a whole quartet still singing "Adeline" just the way they were when the hotel fell on their necks in the earthquake. But in all his career at the gate he had never seen anyone express such pure, unstifled joy as this rawboned hound.

"Was he your dog?" he asked Freeman Brock.

"Naw," said Freem. "He belonged to Pat Haskell." He leaned his shoulder against the gatepost and crossed one foot over the other. "Stop that yawping," he said to Mose, and Mose lay down, wagging. "Maybe you ain't never been in Hawkinsville," he said to Peter. "It's a real pretty village right over the Black River. Pat kept store there and he let anybody take Mose that wanted to. Pretty often I did. He liked coming with me because I let him run foxes. I'm kind of a fox hunter," he said, blowing out his breath. "Oh, I like rabbit-hunting all right, but there's no money in it. . . . Say," he broke off, "you didn't tell me what your name was."

"Peter," said the old man.

"Well, Pete, two years ago was Mose's best season. Seventy-seven fox was shot ahead of him. I shot thirty-seven of them myself. Five crosses and two blacks in the lot. Yes, sir. I heard those black foxes had got away from the fur farm and I took Mose right over there. I made three hundred and fifty dollars out of them hides."

"He was a good dog, then?" asked Peter.

"Best foxhound in seven counties," said Freem Brock. He kicked the gate with his heel in front of Mose's nose and Mose let his ears droop. "He was a fool to hunt. I don't see no fox signs up here. Plenty rabbits in the Park. But there ain't nobody with a gun. I wish I'd brought my old Ithaca along."

"You can't kill things here," said Peter.

"That's funny. Why not?"

"They're already dead."

"Well, I know that. But it beats me how I got here. I never did nothing to get sent to this sort of place. Hell, I killed them farm foxes and I poached up the railroad in the *pre*-serve. But I never done anything bad."

"No," said St. Peter. "We know that."

"I got drunk, maybe. But there's other people done the same before me."

"Yes, Freem."

"Well, what the devil did I get sent here for, Pete?"

"Do you remember when the little girl was sick and the town doctor wouldn't come out at night on a town case, and you went over to town and made him come?"

"Said I'd knock his teeth out," said Freem, brightening.

"Yes. He came. And the girl was taken care of," said Peter.

"Aw," Freem said, "I didn't know what I was doing. I was just mad. Well, maybe I'd had a drink, but it was a cold night, see? I didn't knock his teeth out. He left them in the glass." He looked at the old man. "Jeepers," he said. "And they sent me here for that?"

Peter looked puzzled. "Wasn't it a good reason?" he asked. "It's not such a bad place."

"Not so bad as I thought it was going to be. But people don't want to talk to me. I tried to talk to an old timber-beast named Boone down the road. But he asked me if I ever shot an Indian, and when I said no he went along. You're the only feller I've seen that was willing to talk to me," he said, turning to the old man. "I don't seem to miss likker up here, but there's nowhere I can get to buy some tobacco."

Peter said, "You don't have to buy things in Heaven."

"Heaven?" said Freeman Brock. "Say, is that what this is?" He looked frightened all at once. "That's what the matter is. I don't belong here. I ain't the kind to come here. There must have been a mistake somewhere." He took hold of Peter's arm. "Listen," he said urgently. "Do you know how to work that gate?"

"I do," said Peter. "But I can't let you out."

"I got to get out."

Peter's voice grew gentler. "You'll like it here after a while, Freem."

"You let me out."

"You couldn't go anywhere outside," Peter said.

Freem looked through the bars at the outer heavens and watched a couple of stars like water lilies floating by below. He said slowly, "We'd go someplace."

Peter said, "You mean you'd go out there with that dog?"

Freem flushed. "I and Mose have had some good times," he said.

At the sound of his name, Mose's nose lifted.

Peter looked down at the ground. With the end of his shepherd's staff he thoughtfully made a cross and then another overlapping it and put an X in the upper left-hand corner. Freem looked down to see what he was doing.

"You couldn't let Mose in, could you, Pete?"

Peter sighed and rubbed out the pattern with his sandal. "I'm sorry," he said. "The Committee don't allow dogs."

"What'll happen to the poor brute, Pete?"

Peter shook his head.

"If you ask me," Freem said loudly, "I think this is a hell of a place."

"What's that you said?"

Peter glanced up. "Hello, Don," he said. "Meet Freem Brock. This is the editor of the paper," he said to Freem. "His name's Don."

"Hello," said Freem.

"What was that you said about Heaven being a hell of a place?" asked the editor.

Freem drew a long breath. He took a look at old Mose lying outside the gate with his big nose resting squashed up and sideways against the bottom crossbar; he looked at the outer heavens, and he looked at the editor.

"Listen," he said. "That hound followed me up here. Pete says he can't let him in. He says I can't go out to where Mose is. I only been in jail twice," he said, "but I liked it better than this."

The editor said, "You'd go out there?"

"Give me the chance."

"What a story!" said the editor. "I've got my extra on the Avenue now. The cherubs will be coming this way soon. It's all about the hound, but this stuff is the genuine goods. 'Guest prefers to leave Heaven. Affection for old hunting dog prime factor in his decision.' It's human interest. I tell you it'll shake the Committee. By holy, I'll have an editorial in my next edition calling for a celestial referendum."

"Wait," said Peter. "What's the weather report?"

"What do you think? 'Fair, moderate winds, little change in

temperature.' But the Central Office is making up a hurricane for the South Pacific and it's due to go by pretty soon. We got to hurry, Saint."

He pounded away up the Avenue, leaving a little trail of star dust in his wake.

Freem Brock turned on Saint Peter. "He called you something," he said.

Peter nodded. "Saint."

"I remember about you now. Say, you're a big shot here. Why can't you let Mose in?"

Peter shook his head. "I'm no big shot, Freem. If I was, maybe —"

His voice was drowned out by a shrieking up the Avenue.

"Extry! Extry! Special Edition. Read all about it. Dog outside Heaven's Gate. Dog outside . . ."

A couple of cherubs were coming down the thoroughfare, using their wings to make time. When he saw them, Freem Brock started. His shoulders began to itch self-consciously and he put a hand inside his shirt.

"My gracious," he said.

Peter, watching him, nodded. "Everybody gets them. You'll get used to them after a while. They're handy, too, on a hot day."

"For the love of Pete," said Freem.

"Read all about it! Dog outside Heaven's Gate. Lost dog waiting outside . . ."

"He ain't lost!" cried Freem. "He never got lost in his life."

" 'Committee at fault,' " read Peter. "Thomas Aquinas isn't going to like that," he said.

"It don't prove nothing," said Freem.

"Mister, please," said a feminine voice. "The editor sent me down. Would you answer some questions?"

"Naw," said Freem, turning to look at a young woman with

red hair and a gold pencil in her hand. "Well, what do you want to know, lady?"

The young woman had melting brown eyes. She looked at the hound. "Isn't he cute?" she asked. "What's his name?"

"Mose," said Freem. "He's a cute hound all right."

"Best in seven counties," said Peter.

"May I quote you on that, Saint?"

"Yes," said Peter. "You can say I think the dog ought to be let in." His face was pink over his white beard. "You can say a hurricane is going to pass, and that before I see that animal blown off by it I'll go out there myself—I and my friend Freem. Some say I'm a has-been, but I've got some standing with the public yet."

The girl with red hair was writing furiously with a little gold glitter of her pencil. "Oh," she said.

"Say I'm going out, too," said Freem. "I and Pete."

"Oh," she said. "What's your name?"

"Freeman Brock, Route 5, Boonville, New York, U. S. A."

"Thanks," she said breathlessly.

"How much longer before we got that hurricane coming?" asked Freem.

"I don't know," said the old man anxiously. "I hope Don can work fast."

"Extry! Owner found. Saint Peter goes outside with hound, Moses. Committee bluff called. Read all about it."

"How does Don manage it so fast?" said Peter. "It's like a miracle."

"It's science," said Freem. "Hey!" he yelled at a cherub.

They took the wet sheet, unheeding of the gold ink that stuck to their fingers.

"They've got your picture here, Pete."

"Have they?" Peter asked. He sounded pleased. "Let's see."

It showed Peter standing at the gate.

"It ain't bad," said Freem. He was impressed. "You really mean it?" he asked. Peter nodded.

"By cripus," Freem said slowly, "you're a pal."

Saint Peter was silent for a moment. In all the time he had minded Heaven's Gate, no man had ever called him a pal before.

IV

Outside the gate, old Mose got up on his haunches. He was a weather-wise dog, and now he turned his nose outward. The first puff of wind came like a slap in the face, pulling his ears back, and then it passed. He glanced over his shoulder and saw Freem and the old man staring at each other. Neither of them had noticed him at all. He pressed himself against the bars and lifted his nose and howled.

At his howl both men turned.

There was a clear gray point way off along the reach of the wall, and the whine in the sky took up where Mose's howl had ended.

Peter drew in his breath.

"Come on, Freem," he said, and he opened the gate.

Freeman Brock hesitated. He was scared now. He could see that a real wind was coming, and the landing outside looked almighty small to him. But he was still mad, and he couldn't let an old man like Peter call his bluff.

"All right," he said. "Here goes."

He stepped out, and Mose jumped up on him and licked his face.

"Get down, darn you," he said. "I never could break him of that trick," he explained shamefacedly to Peter. Peter smiled, closing the gate behind him with a firm hand. Its gonglike note echoed through Heaven just as the third edition burst upon the Avenue.

Freeman Brock was frightened. He glanced back through the bars, and Heaven looked good to him. Up the Avenue a crowd was gathering. A couple of lanky, brown-faced men were in front. They started toward the gate.

Then the wind took hold of him and he grasped the bars and looked outward. He could see the hurricane coming like an express train running through infinity. It had a noise like an express train. He understood suddenly just how the victim of a crossing accident must feel.

He glanced at Peter.

The old saint was standing composedly, leaning on his staff with one hand, while with the other he drew Mose close between his legs. His white robe fluttered tight against his shanks and his beard bent sidewise like the hound's ears. He had faced lack of faith, in others; what was worse, he had faced it in himself; and a hurricane, after all, was not so much. He turned to smile at Freem. "Don't be afraid," he said.

"Okay," said Freem, but he couldn't let go the gate.

Old Mose, shivering almost hard enough to rattle, reached up and licked Peter's hand.

One of the brown-faced men said, "That's a likely-looking hound. He the one I read about in the paper?"

"Yep," said Freem. He had to holler now.

Daniel Boone said, "Let us timber-beasts come out with you, Saint, will you?"

Peter smiled. He opened the gate with a wave of his hand, and ten or a dozen timber-beasts—Carson, Bridger, Nat Foster —all crowded through and started shaking hands with him and Freeman Brock. With them was a thin, mild-eyed man.

"My name's Francis," he said to Freem when his turn came. "From Assisi."

"He's all right," Daniel Boone explained. "He wasn't much of a shot, but he knows critters. We better get holt of each other, boys."

It seemed queer to Freem. Here he was going to get blown to eternity and he didn't even know where it was, but all of a sudden he felt better than he ever had in his life. Then he felt a squirming round his legs and there was Mose, sitting on his feet, the way he would on his snowshoes in cold weather when they stopped for a sandwich on earth. He reached down and took hold of Mose's ears.

Let her blow to blazes, he thought.

She blew.

The hurricane was on them. The nose of it went by, sweeping the wall silver. There was no more time for talk. No voices could live outside Heaven's gate. If a man had said a word, the next man to hear it would have been some poor heathen aborigine on an island in the Pacific Ocean, and he wouldn't have known what it meant.

The men on the gate-stone were crammed against the bars. The wind dragged them bodily to the left, and for a minute it looked as if Jim Bridger were going, but they caught him back. There were a lot of the stoutest hands that ever swung an axe in that bunch holding onto Heaven's gate, and they weren't letting go for any hurricane—not yet.

But Freem Brock could see it couldn't last that way. He didn't care, though. He was in good company, and that was what counted the most. He wasn't a praying man, but he felt his heart swell with gratitude, and he took hold hard of the collar of Mose and felt the license riveted on. A queer thing to think of, a New York State dog license up there. He managed to look down at it, and he saw that it had turned to gold, with the collar gold under it. The wind tore at him as he saw it. The heart of the hurricane was on him now like a million devils' fingers.

Well, Mose, he thought.

And then in the blur of his thoughts a dazzling bright light came down and he felt the gate at his back opening and he and Peter and Francis and Daniel and the boys were all drawn back into the peace of Heaven, and a quiet voice belonging to a quiet man said, "Let the dog come in."

"Jesus," said Freem Brock, fighting for breath, and the quiet man smiled, shook hands with him, and then went over and placed his arm around Peter's shoulders.

V

They were sitting together, Freem and Peter, by the gate, reading the paper in the morning warmth, and Peter was having an easy time with the editor's new type arrangement. "Gridley," he was reading the uppercase names, "Griscome, Godolphin, Habblestick, Hafey, Hanlon, Hartwell, Haskell . . ."

"Haskell," said Freem. "Not Pat?"

"Yes," said Peter. "Late of Hawkinsville."

"Not in big type?"

"Yes."

"Well, I'll be . . . Well, that twerp. Think of that. Old Pat." Peter smiled.

"By holy," said Freem. "Ain't he going to be amazed when he finds Mose up here?"

"How's Mose doing?"

"He's all right now," said Freem. "He's been chasing the rabbits. I guess he's up there now. The dew's good."

"He didn't look so well, I thought," Peter said.

"Well, that was at first," said Freem. "You see, the rabbits just kept going up in the trees and he couldn't get a real run on any of them. There, he's got one started now."

Peter glanced up from the paper.

Old Mose was doing a slow bark, kind of low, working out the scent from the start. He picked up pace for a while, and then he seemed to strike a regular knot. His barks were deep and patient.

And then, all of a sudden, his voice broke out—that deep, ringing, honey-throated baying that Freem used to listen to in the late afternoon on the sand hills over the Black River. It went away through the public gardens and out beyond the city, the notes running together and fading and swelling and fading out.

"He's pushing him pretty fast," said Freem. "He's going to get pretty good on these rabbits."

The baying swelled again; it came back, ringing like bells. People in the gardens stopped to look up and smile. The sound of it gave Peter a warm, tingling feeling.

Freem yawned.

"Might as well wait here till Pat Haskell comes in," he said.

It was pleasant by the gate, under the black and yellow parasol. It made a shade like a flower on the hot star dust. They didn't have to talk, beyond just, now and then, dropping a word between them as they sat.

After a while they heard a dog panting and saw old Mose tracking down the street. He came over to their corner and lay down at their feet, lolling a long tongue. He looked good—a little fat, but lazy and contented. After a minute, though, he got up to shift himself around, and paused as he sat down, and raised a hind leg, and scratched himself behind his wings.

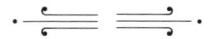

WALTER D. EDMONDS (1903–) won the Newbery Medal in 1942 for *The Matchlock Gun*. He is also a distinguished recipient of the National Book Award (for *Bert Breen's Barn,* 1975) and the Christopher Award. Other notable books include *Seven American Stories* (1970), *Wolf Hunt* (1970), *The Story of Richard Storm* (1974), and *The Night Raider and Other Stories* (1980).

ELEANOR ESTES

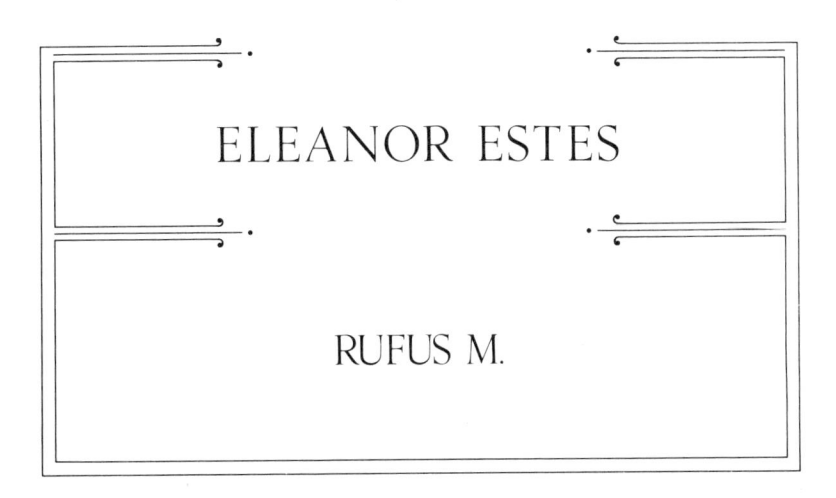

RUFUS M.

Rufus will do anything to get a library card, in this tale of small-town life from a child's point of view. . . .

R*UFUS M. THAT'S THE WAY* Rufus wrote his name on his heavy arithmetic paper and on his blue-lined spelling paper. *Rufus M.* went on one side of the paper. His age, *seven,* went on the other. Rufus had not learned to write his name in school, though that is one place for learning to write. He had not learned to write his name at home, either, though that is another place for learning to write. The place where he had learned to write his name was the library, long ago, before he ever went to school at all. This is the way it happened.

One day when Rufus had been riding his scooter up and down the street, being the motorman, the conductor, the passengers, the steam, and the whistle of a locomotive, he came home and found Joey, Jane, and Sylvie, all reading in the front yard. Joey and Jane were sitting on the steps of the porch and Sylvie was sprawled in the hammock, a book in one hand, a chocolate-covered peppermint in the other.

Rufus stood with one bare foot on his scooter and one on the grass and watched them. Sylvie read the fastest. This was natural since she was the oldest. But Joey turned the pages almost as fast, and Jane went lickety-cut on the good parts. They were all reading books and he couldn't even read yet. These books they were reading were library books. The library must be open today. It wasn't open every day, just a few days a week.

"I want to go to the library," said Rufus. "And get a book," he added.

"We all just came home from there," said Jane, while Joey and Sylvie merely went on reading as though Rufus had said nothing. "Besides," she added, "why do you want a book, anyway? You can't even read yet."

This was true, and it made Rufus mad. He liked to do everything that they did. He even liked to sew if they were sewing. He never thought whether sewing was for girls only or not. When he saw Jane sewing, he asked Mama to let him sew, too. So Mama tied a thread to the head of a pin and Rufus poked that in and out of a piece of goods. That's the way he sewed. It looked like what Jane was doing, and Rufus was convinced that he was sewing, too, though he could not see much sense in it.

Now here were the other Moffats, all with books from the library. And there were three more books stacked up on the porch that looked like big people's books without pictures. They were for Mama, no doubt. This meant that he was the only one here who did not have a book.

"I want a book from the library," said Rufus. A flick of the page as Sylvie turned it over was all the answer he got. It seemed to Rufus as though even Catherine-the-cat gave him a scornful glance because he could not read yet and did not have a book.

Rufus turned his scooter around and went out of the yard. Just wait! Read? Why, soon he'd read as fast as they did, if not faster. Reading looked easy. It was just flipping pages. Who couldn't do that?

Rufus thought that it was not hard to get a book out of the library. All you did was go in, look for a book that you liked, give it to the lady to punch, and come home with it. He knew where the library was, for he had often gone there with Jane and some of the others. While Jane went off to the shelves to find a book, he and Joey played the game of Find the Duke in the Palmer Cox Brownie books. This was a game that the two boys had made up. They would turn the pages of one of the Brownie books, any of them, and try to be the first to spot the Duke, the Brownie in the tall hat. The library lady thought that this was a noisy game and said she wished they would not play it there. Rufus hoped to bring a Brownie book home now.

"Toot-toot!" he sang to clear the way. Straight down Elm Street was the way to the library; the same way that led to Sunday school, and Rufus knew it well. He liked sidewalks that were white the best, for he could go the fastest on these.

"Toot-toot!" Rufus hurried down the street. When he arrived at the library, he hid his scooter in the pine trees that grew under the windows beside the steps. Christmas trees, Rufus called them. The ground was covered with brown pine needles, and they were soft to walk upon. Rufus always went into the library the same way. He climbed the stairs, encircled the light on the granite arm of the steps, and marched into the library.

Rufus stepped carefully on the strips of rubber matting that led to the desk. This matting looked like dirty licorice. But it wasn't licorice. He knew because once when Sylvie had brought him here when he was scarcely more than three he had tasted a torn corner of it. It was not good to eat.

The library lady was sitting at the desk playing with some cards. Rufus stepped off the matting. The cool, shiny floor felt good to his bare feet. He went over to the shelves and luckily did find one of the big Palmer Cox Brownie books there. It would be fun to play the game of Find the Duke at home. Until now he had played it only in the library. Maybe Jane or Joe would play it with him right now. He laughed out loud at the thought.

"Sh-sh-sh, quiet," said the lady at the desk.

Rufus clapped his chubby fist over his mouth. Goodness! He had forgotten where he was. *Do not laugh or talk out loud in the library.* He knew these rules. Well, he didn't want to stay here any longer today, anyway. He wanted to read at home with the others. He took the book to the lady to punch.

She didn't punch it, though. She took it and she put it on the table behind her and then she started to play cards again.

"That's my book," said Rufus.

"Do you have a card?" the lady asked.

Rufus felt in his pockets. Sometimes he carried around an old playing card or two. Today he didn't have one.

"No," he said.

"You'll have to have a card to get a book."

"I'll go and get one," said Rufus.

The lady put down her cards. "I mean a library card," she explained kindly. "It looks to me as though you are too little to have a library card. Do you have one?"

"No," said Rufus. "I'd like to, though."

"I'm afraid you're too little," said the lady. "You have to write your name to get one. Can you do that?"

Rufus nodded his head confidently. Writing. Lines up and

down. He'd seen that done. And the letters that Mama had tied in bundles in the closet under the stairs were covered with writing. Of course he could write.

"Well, let's see your hands," said the lady.

Rufus obligingly showed this lady his hands, but she did not like the look of them. She cringed and clasped her head as though the sight hurt her.

"Oh," she gasped. "You'll just have to go home and wash them before we can even think about joining the library and borrowing books."

This was a complication upon which Rufus had not reckoned. However, all it meant was a slight delay. He'd wash his hands and then he'd get the book. He turned and went out of the library, found his scooter safe among the Christmas trees, and pushed it home. He surprised Mama by asking to have his hands washed. When this was done, he mounted his scooter again and returned all the long way to the library. It was not just a little trip to the library. It was a long one. A long one and a hot one on a day like this. But he didn't notice that. All he was bent on was getting his book and taking it home and reading with the others on the front porch. They were all still there, brushing flies away and reading.

Again Rufus hid his scooter in the pine trees, encircled the light, and went in.

"Hello," he said.

"Well," said the lady. "How are they now?"

Rufus had forgotten he had had to wash his hands. He thought she was referring to the other Moffats. "Fine," he said.

"Let me see them," she said, and she held up her hands.

Oh! His hands! Well, they were all right, thought Rufus, for Mama had just washed them. He showed them to the lady. There was a silence while she studied them. Then she shook her head. She still did not like them.

"*Ts, ts, ts!*" she said. "They'll have to be cleaner than that."

Rufus looked at his hands. Supposing he went all the way home and washed them again, she still might not like them. However, if that is what she wanted, he would have to do that before he could get the Brownie book . . . and he started for the door.

"Well, now, let's see what we can do," said the lady. "I know what," she said. "It's against the rules, but perhaps we can wash them in here." And she led Rufus into a little room that smelled of paste where lots of new books and old books were stacked up. In one corner was a little round sink, and Rufus washed his hands again. Then they returned to the desk. The lady got a chair and put a newspaper on it. She made Rufus stand on this because he was not big enough to write at the desk otherwise.

Then the lady put a piece of paper covered with a lot of printing in front of Rufus, dipped a pen in the inkwell, and gave it to him.

"All right," she said. "Here's your application. Write your name here."

All the writing Rufus had ever done before had been on big pieces of brown wrapping paper with lots of room on them. Rufus had often covered those great sheets of paper with his own kind of writing at home. Lines up and down.

But on this paper there wasn't much space. It was already covered with writing. However, there was a tiny little empty space and that was where Rufus must write his name, the lady said. So, little space or not, Rufus confidently grasped the pen with his left hand and dug it into the paper. He was not accustomed to pens, having always worked with pencils until now, and he made a great many holes and blots and scratches.

"Gracious," said the lady. "Don't bear down so hard! And why don't you hold it in your right hand?" she asked, moving the pen back into his right hand.

Rufus started again scraping his lines up and down and all over the page, this time using his right hand. Wherever there was an empty space he wrote. He even wrote over some of the print for good measure. Then he waited for the lady, who had gone off to get a book for some man, to come back and look.

"Oh," she said as she settled herself in her swivel chair, "is that the way you write? Well . . . it's nice, but what does it say?"

"Says Rufus Moffat. My name."

Apparently these lines up and down did not spell Rufus Moffat to this lady. She shook her head.

"It's nice," she repeated. "Very nice. But nobody but you knows what it says. You have to learn to write your name better than that before you can join the library."

Rufus was silent. He had come to the library all by himself, gone back home to wash his hands, and come back because he wanted to take books home and read them the way the others did. He had worked hard. He did not like to think he might have to go home without a book.

The library lady looked at him a moment and then she said quickly, before he could get himself all the way off the big chair, "Maybe you can *print* your name."

Rufus looked at her hopefully. He thought he could write better than he could print, for his writing certainly looked to him exactly like all grown people's writing. Still, he'd try to print if that was what she wanted.

The lady printed some letters on the top of a piece of paper. "There," she said. "That's your name. Copy it ten times and then we'll try it on another application."

Rufus worked hard. He worked so hard the knuckles showed white on his brown fist. He worked for a long, long time, now with his right hand and now with his left. Sometimes a boy or a girl came in, looked over his shoulder, and watched, but he paid no attention. From time to time the lady studied his work, and she said, "That's fine. That's fine." At last she said, "Well, maybe now we can try." And she gave him another application.

All Rufus could get, with his large, generous letters, in that tiny little space where he was supposed to print his name, was *R-u-f.* The other letters he scattered here and there on the card. The lady did not like this, either. She gave him still another blank. Rufus tried to print smaller and this time he got *Rufus* in the space, and also he crowded in an *M* at the end. Since he was doing so well now, the lady herself printed the *offat* part of Moffat on the next line.

"This will have to do," she said. "Now take this home and ask your mother to sign it on the other side. Bring it back on Thursday and you'll get your card."

Rufus's face was shiny and streaked with dirt where he had rubbed it. He never knew there was all this work to getting a book. The other Moffats just came in and got books. Well, maybe they had had to do this once, too.

Rufus held his hard-earned application in one hand and steered his scooter with the other. When he reached home, Joey, Jane, and Sylvie were not around any longer. Mama signed his card for him, saying, "My! So you've learned how to write!"

"Print," corrected Rufus.

Mama kissed Rufus and he went back out. The lady had said to come back on Thursday, but he wanted a book today. When the other Moffats came home, he'd be sitting on the top step of the porch, reading. That would surprise them. He smiled to himself as he made his way to the library for the third time.

Once his application blew away. Fortunately it landed in a thistle bush and did not get very torn. The rest of the way Rufus clutched it carefully. He climbed the granite steps to the library again, only to find that the big, round, dark-brown doors were closed. Rufus tried to open them, but he couldn't. He knocked at the door, even kicked it with his foot, but there was no answer. He pounded on the door, but nobody came.

A big boy strode past with his newspapers. "Hey, kid," he said to Rufus. "Library's closed!" And off he went, whistling.

Rufus looked after him. The fellow had said the library was closed. How could it have closed so fast? He had been here such a little while ago. The lady must still be here. He did want his Brownie book. If only he could see in, he might see the lady and get his book. The windows were high up, but they had very wide sills. Rufus was a wonderful climber. He could shinny up trees and poles faster than anybody else on the block. Faster than Joey. Now, helping himself up by means of one of the pine trees that grew close to the building, and by sticking his toes in the ivy and rough places in the bricks, he scrambled up the wall. He hoisted himself up on one of the sills and sat there. He peered in. It was dark inside, for the shades had been drawn almost all the way down.

"Library lady!" he called, and he knocked on the windowpane. There was no answer. He put his hands on each side of his face to shield his eyes, and he looked in for a long, long time. He could not believe that she had left. Rufus was resolved to get a book. He had lost track of the number of times he had been back and forth from home to the library, and the library home. Maybe the lady was in the cellar. He climbed down, stubbing his big toe on the bricks as he did so. He stooped down beside one of the low, dirt-spattered cellar windows. He couldn't see in. He lay flat on the ground, wiped one spot clean on the window, picked up a few pieces of coal from the sill, and put them in his pocket for Mama.

"Hey, lady," he called.

He gave the cellar window a little push. It wasn't locked, so he opened it a little and looked in. All he could see was a high pile of coal reaching up to this window. Of course he didn't put any of *that* coal in his pocket, for that would be stealing.

"Hey, lady," he yelled again. His voice echoed in the cellar, but the library lady did not answer. He called out, "Hey, lady," every few seconds, but all that answered him was an echo. He pushed the window open a little wider. All of a sudden it swung wide open and Rufus slid in, right on top of the coal pile, and *crash, clatter, bang!* He slid to the bottom, making a great racket.

A little light shone through the dusty windows, but on the whole it was very dark and spooky down here, and Rufus really wished that he was back on the outside looking in. However, since he was in the library, why not go upstairs quick, get the Brownie book, and go home? The window had banged shut, but he thought he could climb up the coal pile, pull the window up, and get out. He certainly hoped he could, anyway. Supposing he couldn't and he had to stay in this cellar! Well, that he would not think about. He looked around in the dusky light and saw a staircase across the cellar. Luckily his application was still good. It was torn and dirty, but it still had his name on it, *Rufus M,* and that was the important part. He'd leave this on the desk in exchange for the Brownie book.

Rufus cautiously made his way over to the steps, but he stopped halfway across the cellar. Somebody had opened the door at the top of the stairs. He couldn't see who it was, but he did see the light reflected and that's how he knew that somebody had opened the door. It must be the lady. He was just going to say, "Hey, lady," when he thought, *Gee, maybe it isn't the lady. Maybe it's a spooky thing.*

Then the light went away, the door was closed, and Rufus was left in the dark again. He didn't like it down here. He started to go back to the coal pile to get out of this place. Then he felt of his application. What a lot of work he had done to get a book, and now that he was this near to getting one, should he give up? No. Anyway, if it was the lady up there, he knew her and she knew him and neither one of them was scared of the other. And Mama always said there's no such thing as a spooky thing.

So Rufus bravely made his way again to the stairs. He tiptoed up them. The door at the head was not closed tightly. He pushed it open and found himself right in the library. But goodness! There in the little sink room right opposite him was the library lady!

Rufus stared at her in silence. The library lady was eating. Rufus had never seen her do anything before but play cards, punch books, and carry great piles of books around. Now she was eating. Mama said not to stare at anybody while they were eating. Still, Rufus didn't know the library lady ate, so it was hard for him not to look at her.

She had a little gas stove in there. She could cook there. She was reading a book at the same time that she was eating. Sylvie could do that, too. This lady did not see him.

"Hey, lady," said Rufus.

The librarian jumped up out of her seat. "Was that you in the cellar? I thought I heard somebody. Goodness, young man! I thought you had gone home long ago."

Rufus didn't say anything. He just stood there. He had gone home and he had come back lots of times. He had the whole thing in his mind; the coming and going, and going and coming, and sliding down the coal pile, but he did not know where to begin, how to tell it.

"Didn't you know the library is closed now?" she demanded, coming across the floor with firm steps.

Rufus remained silent. No, he hadn't known it. The fellow had told him, but he hadn't believed him. Now he could see for himself that the library was closed so the library lady could eat.

If the lady would let him take his book, he'd go home and stay there. He'd play the game of Find the Duke with Jane. He hopefully held out his card with his name on it.

"Here this is," he said.

But the lady acted as though she didn't even see it. She led Rufus over to the door.

"All right now," she said. "Out with you!" But just as she opened the door the sound of water boiling over on the stove struck their ears, and back she raced to her little room.

"Gracious!" she exclaimed. "What a day!"

Before the door could close on him, Rufus followed her in and sat down on the edge of a chair. The lady thought he had gone and started to sip her tea. Rufus watched her quietly, waiting for her to finish.

After a while the lady brushed the crumbs off her lap. And then she washed her hands and the dishes in the little sink where Rufus had washed his hands. In a library a lady could eat and could wash. Maybe she slept here, too. Maybe she lived here.

"Do you live here?" Rufus asked her.

"Mercy on us!" exclaimed the lady. "Where'd you come from? Didn't I send you home? No, I don't live here, and neither do you. Come now, out with you, young man. I mean it." The lady called all boys "young man" and all girls "Susie." She came out of the little room and she opened the big brown door again. "There," she said. "Come back on Thursday."

Rufus's eyes filled up with tears.

"Here's this," he said again, holding up his application in a last desperate attempt. But the lady shook her head. Rufus went slowly down the steps, felt around in the bushes for his scooter, and with drooping spirits mounted it. Then for the second time that day, the library lady changed her mind.

"Oh, well," she said, "come back here, young man. I'm not

supposed to do business when the library's closed, but I see we'll have to make an exception."

So Rufus rubbed his sooty hands over his face, hid his scooter in the bushes again, climbed the granite steps, and, without circling the light, went back in and gave the lady his application.

The lady took it gingerly. "My, it's dirty," she said. "You really ought to sign another one."

"And go home with it?" asked Rufus. He really didn't believe this was possible. He wiped his hot face on his sleeve and looked up at the lady in exhaustion. What he was thinking was: All right. If he had to sign another one, all right. But would she just please stay open until he got back?

However, this was not necessary. The lady said, "Well, now, I'll try to clean this old one up. But remember, young man, always have everything clean—your hands, your book, everything, when you come to the library."

Rufus nodded solemnly. "My feet, too," he assured her.

Then the lady made Rufus wash his hands again. They really were very bad this time, for he had been in a coal pile, and now at last she gave Rufus the book he wanted—one of the Palmer Cox Brownie books. This one was *The Brownies in the Philippines*.

And Rufus went home.

When he reached home, he showed Mama his book. She smiled at him and gave his cheek a pat. She thought it was fine that he had gone to the library and joined all by himself and taken out a book. And she thought it was fine when Rufus sat down at the kitchen table, was busy and quiet for a long, long time, and then showed her what he had done.

He had printed *Rufus M.* That was what he had done. And that's the way he learned to sign his name. And that's the way he always did sign his name for a long, long time.

But, of course, that was before he ever went to school at all, when the Moffats still lived in the old house, the yellow house on New Dollar Street; before this country had gone into the war; and before Mr. Abbot, the curate, started leaving his overshoes on the Moffats' front porch.

ELEANOR ESTES (1906–) won the Newbery Medal in 1952 for *Ginger Pye*. She is particularly noted for her authentic accounts of childhood experiences, which can be found in such marvelous books as *The Moffats* (1941), *The Hundred Dresses* (a Newbery Honor Book in 1945), *The Middle Moffat* (a Newbery Honor Book in 1943), *Rufus M.* (a Newbery Honor Book in 1944), and *The Moffat Museum* (1983).

CHARLES J. FINGER

NA-HA THE FIGHTER

A South American folktale of a doomed hero and his epic struggle . . .

I N THE FAR SOUTH near Cape Horn there is a place of many islands, and it is a corner of the world where winds are piercing cold and great black clouds scurry across a lead-gray sky. From snow-clad mountains slide rivers of ice from which break off mighty pieces to fall into the sea with thunder-sounds. It is a land wrinkled into narrow valleys that are always gloomy and cold and wet. Cold, ice-cold, is the gray-green sea, and the wild cries of a million seabirds fill the air. Sometimes great albatrosses sweep up the channels between the high, jagged mountains or drop low to sail over penguin-crowded rocks, and sometimes the mountain echoes are deep-toned with the booming of walrus and the barking of seals. But people are few. There are Indians there, poor, gentle folk who fish in the sea and who know nothing but a life of cold, and they paddle or sit crouching in their canoes, taking no heed of the biting wind and the snow that falls on their naked bodies.

Long years ago, the people of that land were sadly at the mercy of the wild, hairy folk who lived under the sea. To be sure, there were long periods when they were left in peace to do their fishing, though from their canoes they could look down into the waters and see the undersea people walking on the sands at the bottom, very shadowy and vague, though, in the greenish light. Still, it was clear enough, for those who watched, to see their hair-covered bodies, their long and serpentlike arms, and their noseless faces.

But again, there were times when the undersea men marched in great numbers out of the water and caught the land men, dragging them down to their deaths. In such numbers they came that there was no resisting them. Nor was there escape, for the undersea people could walk on the water, going faster than the wind itself. With earsplitting booming they would form themselves into a wide circle about the canoes, then draw nearer in wild rushes or strange slidings and drag the frightened men into the green-gray water. Sometimes a few only were taken, and those that were left, looking down, might see the undersea folk dragging their fellows to great rocks to which they bound them with ropes of leathery kelp.

One day the undersea people caught Na-Ha, a youth strong as a wild wind, whose muscles were knotted like oak branches, one who smiled when danger came. Five of the noseless people attacked him, and of the five, Na-Ha sent three to the bottom of the sea with broken necks, for though he smote them with his clenched fist alone, they staggered back and swiftly sank, and the blood that gushed from their mouths made a spreading pink cloud in the water. But soon the sea was alive with wild, raging faces, and the roaring of them was like the southeast wind in the forest trees, yet Na-Ha stood in his little canoe, cold and calm, and the smile did not leave his lips. Stealthily they crept toward him, none at first daring to attack, until with a fierce noise and clamor all rushed together, leaping upon him in his canoe and bearing it down by sheer press and weight, Na-Ha in the midst of the tangled mass of hair-covered creatures. Some who saw that fight said that the sudden silence when the waters closed over them hurt the ears like a thunderclap, but the true-hearted Na-Ha was the last to disappear, and while he smote the black-haired ones furiously, the smile of scorn was still on his face.

Like a picture in a dream, some saw the fight among the rocks at the bottom of the sea, saw the noseless ones crowding about the lad, saw others leaping over the heads of those who did not dare to near him, saw others again creeping in the sea sand, trailing kelp ropes to bind him. Many fell in that battle under the sea, and the low waves that lapped the shore were red with blood that day. How it ended none knew, for with the dying light and the sand clouds that hung in the water, all became gray at last and then swiftly faded.

That night the land people wept for Na-Ha the untamed, Na-Ha whose spear was like lightning, Na-Ha whose canoe rode the waves like the brown storm-birds. Tales were whispered of how he never bent beneath a load, of how in the blackest night he drove his boat before the storm, of how once he swept out to sea after a great whale and slew it, so that his people were saved from the hunger-death.

But with the screaming of the morning sea gulls Na-Ha came

to them again, walking up out of the sea, and his face was set and stern. Nor did he say a word until he had eaten and thought awhile.

The tale he told was of the underseas and of his wandering after the battle in which he left so many dead in bloody sand. He had been sore-pressed, he said, but had broken away and come to a door in a cave, which he entered. It was a vast cavern in which he found himself, so vast that he could not at first see the end, and the roof of it he never saw, it being lost in a strange, cool green light. The floor of the place was of gold dust and silver sand, and out of it grew networks of white rocks about which swam fish of many gay colors, while everywhere seaweeds swayed in gently moving water.

Soon he came to a place where, on a seat of white, sat a woman with bent head, and she was fair of skin and her golden hair floated in the water like a cloud. Being bidden, Na-Ha told her the tale of the fight and how the earth people were woe-ridden because of the evil work of the undersea folk.

Patiently she listened, her cheek on her hand, and her eyes large with grief, and when Na-Ha had done she told him that there was but one way to free his people and that was the way of the white death. Much more she told him and then gave him a great seashell and made him know that when he blew it, the great cold that lies under the seven stars would be freed and the undersea people driven for all time to their own place. Then she stepped from her seat and, taking Na-Ha by the hand, gazed at him long.

"Many there are, Na-Ha, who live not to know of the good that they do. He who looses the white death must himself be stilled. This I tell you, Na-Ha, lest your heart fail you," she said.

That was all, for he did not tell the tale of how he came again to the land, but he showed them the great shell and said that his mind was made up to free his own people, though he himself slept the sleep. At that the people set up a great shout and there were not lacking those who offered to sound the blast, saying that it were better for Na-Ha to lead the people. But that Na-Ha refused and added that the undersea woman had told him that before the blast was blown all the land people should take themselves and their belongings to a far land under the sun, for staying where they were, it would do but small good to drive the undersea people to their own place forever, seeing that they themselves must also be ice-stiffened.

Then arose a confusion of talk, many being unwilling to leave the land where their fathers and the fathers of their fathers had lived, but Na-Ha prevailed and overruled them, and soon the day came when there was a great movement and canoes were loaded and the land people set off for the country under the sun. So Na-Ha was left alone.

Over the length and the breadth of the land Na-Ha walked, to see if by mischance some had been left, but there were none. And when the sea hen and the albatross and the gull and the brown storm birds saw the hair-covered, noseless people come out of the sea, when with the black loneliness of night the snow came and the land waters were prisoned under glassy ice, when the morning sun looked on a world of rime and crystal frost, then Na-Ha put the great shell to his lips and blew a blast that woke the echoes.

So the world soon grew faint and sleepy, and all living creatures except the noseless ones fled or flew after the land people, and there was strange stillness everywhere. Trees that had been green grew horned and black and then ghost white. And the black wind came raging and furious, and grinding, groaning ice-mountains swam in the sea and locked the land, and hills were cased in beryl walls.

Seeing all that, for a time the undersea folk were full of delight, believing themselves to be masters of the land, but soon they feared the glistening white of the world, the black scurrying clouds, and the fast-thickening ice. So they sought the sea, but no sea was there, only thick-ribbed ice across which swept snow-laden, stinging winds, and instead of the quiet of the underwater there was the calm of the white death. Under the eaves of the rocks they crouched, but it was small help, for with the biting cold they shriveled and shrank. Close they hugged themselves, their elbows thrust into their hairy sides, their legs bent, making themselves small. And thus they stayed, nevermore to be as they were. For in that great cold the underwater people became seals, and seals they remained.

Well and bravely stood Na-Ha while all this came to pass, scornful of the death that clawed at him. Nor did he lie down to die until the great cold had passed away and his people returned to find the underwater folk forevermore bound to their own place, powerless to harm, looking always with wide, wondering eyes, lest the mighty Na-Ha again steal upon them and bring the great white death.

CHARLES J. FINGER (1869–1941) won the Newbery Medal in 1925 for *Tales From Silver Lands*. He was the author of over sixty books of adventure and biography, including *Adventure Under Sapphire Skies* (1931), *Golden Tales of Faraway* (1940), *Tales Worth Telling* (1927), and *Travels of Marco Polo* (1924).

JEAN CRAIGHEAD GEORGE

THE WOUNDED WOLF

A gripping account of a wolf pack's loyalty to a wounded member . . .

A WOUNDED WOLF CLIMBS Toklat Ridge, a massive spine of rock and ice. As he limps, dawn strikes the ridge and lights it up with sparks and stars. Roko, the wounded wolf, blinks in the ice fire, then stops to rest and watch his pack run the thawing Arctic valley.

They plunge and turn. They fight the mighty caribou that struck young Roko with his hoof and wounded him. He jumped between the beast and Kiglo, leader of the Toklat pack. Young Roko spun and fell. Hooves, paws, and teeth roared over him. And then his pack and the beast were gone.

Gravely injured, Roko pulls himself toward the shelter rock. Weakness overcomes him. He stops. He and his pack are thin and hungry. This is the season of starvation. The winter's harvest has been taken. The produce of spring has not begun.

Young Roko glances down the valley. He droops his head and stiffens his tail to signal to his pack that he is badly hurt. Winds wail. A frigid blast picks up long shawls of snow and drapes them between young Roko and his pack. And so his message is not read.

A raven scouting Toklat Ridge sees Roko's signal. "Kong, kong, kong," he bells—death is coming to the ridge; there will be flesh and bone for all. His voice rolls out across the valley. It penetrates the rocky cracks where the Toklat ravens rest. One by one they hear and spread their wings. They beat their way to Toklat Ridge. They alight upon the snow and walk behind the wounded wolf.

"Kong," they toll with keen excitement, for the raven clan is hungry, too. "Kong, kong"—there will be flesh and bone for all.

Roko snarls and hurries toward the shelter rock. A cloud of snow envelopes him. He limps in blinding whiteness now.

A ghostly presence flits around. "Hahahahahahaha," the white fox states—death is coming to the Ridge. Roko smells the fox tagging at his heels.

The cloud whirls off. Two golden eyes look up at Roko. The snowy owl has heard the ravens and joined the deathwatch.

Roko limps along. The ravens walk. The white fox leaps. The snowy owl flies and hops along the rim of Toklat Ridge. Roko stops. Below the ledge out on the flats the musk-ox herd is circling. They form a ring and all face out, a fort of heads and horns and fur that sweeps down to their hooves. Their circle means to Roko that an enemy is present. He squints and smells the wind. It carries scents of thawing ice, broken grass—and earth. The grizzly bear is up! He has awakened from his winter's sleep. A craving need for flesh will drive him.

Roko sees the shelter rock. He strains to reach it. He stumbles. The ravens move in closer. The white fox boldly walks beside him. "Hahaha," he yaps. The snowy owl flies ahead, alights, and waits.

The grizzly hears the eager fox and rises on his flat hind feet. He twists his powerful neck and head. His great paws dangle at his chest. He sees the animal procession and hears the ravens' knell of death. Dropping to all fours, he joins the march up Toklat Ridge.

Roko stops; his breath comes hard. A raven alights upon his back and picks the open wound. Roko snaps. The raven flies and circles back. The white fox nips at Roko's toes. The snowy owl inches closer. The grizzly bear, still dulled by sleep, stumbles onto Toklat Ridge.

Only yards from the shelter rock, Roko falls.

Instantly the ravens mob him. They scream and peck and stab at his eyes. The white fox leaps upon his wound. The snowy owl sits and waits.

Young Roko struggles to his feet. He bites the ravens. Snaps the fox. And lunges at the stoic owl. He turns and warns the grizzly bear. Then he bursts into a run and falls against the shelter rock. The wounded wolf wedges down between the rock and barren ground. Now protected on three sides, he turns and faces all his foes.

The ravens step a few feet closer. The fox slides toward him on his belly. The snowy owl blinks and waits, and on the ridge rim roars the hungry grizzly bear.

Roko growls.

The sun comes up. Far across the Toklat Valley, Roko hears his pack's "hunt's end" song. The music wails and sobs, wilder than the bleating wind. The hunt song ends. Next comes the roll call.

Each member of the Toklat pack barks to say that he is home and well.

"Kiglo here," Roko hears his leader bark. There is a pause. It is young Roko's turn. He cannot lift his head to answer. The pack is silent. The leader starts the count once more. "Kiglo here." —A pause. Roko cannot answer.

The wounded wolf whimpers softly. A mindful raven hears. "Kong, kong, kong," he tolls—this is the end. His booming sounds across the valley. The wolf pack hears the raven's message that something is dying. They know it is Roko, who has not answered roll call.

The hours pass. The wind slams snow on Toklat Ridge. Massive clouds blot out the sun. In their gloom Roko sees the deathwatch move in closer. Suddenly he hears the musk-oxen thundering into their circle. The ice cracks as the grizzly leaves. The ravens burst into the air. The white fox runs. The snowy owl flaps to the top of the shelter rock. And Kiglo rounds the knoll.

In his mouth he carries meat. He drops it close to Roko's head and wags his tail excitedly. Roko licks Kiglo's chin to honor him. Then Kiglo puts his mouth around Roko's nose. This gesture says "I am your leader." And by mouthing Roko, he binds him and all the wolves together.

The wounded wolf wags his tail. Kiglo trots away.

Already Roko's wound feels better. He gulps the food and feels his strength return. He shatters bone, flesh, and gristle and shakes the scraps out on the snow. The hungry ravens swoop upon them. The white fox snatches up a bone. The snowy owl gulps down flesh and fur. And Roko wags his tail and watches.

For days Kiglo brings young Roko food. He gnashes, gorges, and shatters bits upon the snow.

A purple sandpiper winging north sees ravens, owl, and fox. And he drops in upon the feast. The long-tailed jaeger gull flies down and joins the crowd on Toklat Ridge. Roko wags his tail.

One dawn he moves his wounded leg. He stretches it and pulls himself into the sunlight. He walks—he romps. He runs in circles. He leaps and plays with chunks of ice. Suddenly he stops. The "hunt's end" song rings out. Next comes the roll call.

"Kiglo here."

"Roko here," he barks out strongly.

The pack is silent.

"Kiglo here," the leader repeats.

"Roko here."

Across the distance comes the sound of whoops and yipes and barks and howls. They fill the dawn with celebration. And Roko prances down the Ridge.

JEAN CRAIGHEAD GEORGE (1919–) won the Newbery Medal in 1973 for *Julie of the Wolves*. Among her other honors are the Aurianne Award, conferred in 1958, and the George G. Stone Center for Children's Books award, received in 1969. Her books include *My Side of the Mountain* (a Newbery Honor Book in 1960), *The Wounded Wolf* (1978), *The Cry of the Crow* (1980), *Coyote in Manhattan* (1968), and *The Summer of the Falcon* (1979).

VIRGINIA HAMILTON

M. C. HIGGINS, THE GREAT

"For the want of a question, the tunnel would be a grave for both of them...."

The lake lay as serene and peaceful as when they had left it. Way down at the other end was the ridge. In between the ridge and the rocky end where now he and the girl crouched was the tent, like an intruder in the sun. All around them were pines, undergrowth, greens and browns closing in the magical shimmer of the lake.

He and the girl hung onto rocks just above the waterline. The children were clinging a foot above them.

"The tunnel's right down there," M.C. told her. "About

eight to ten feet down. Maybe twelve feet long and that's a couple of body lengths." He paused, looking out over the lake. "Now I lead," he told her. "I lead and we hold together like this." With his right hand, he took hold of her left arm, forcing her to balance herself with her back against the rocks. "Hold on to my arm just above the wrist."

"Like this?" She grabbed his arm with fingers stronger than he'd expected. So close to her, he felt shy but calm.

"We jump here, we get more power," he told her. "We get down faster, but it has to be done just right."

"How?" she said.

M.C. didn't know how. He was figuring it all out as he went along, working fast in his head the best way to jump and the quickest way to get through the tunnel.

"Best way is . . . if I jump backward and you jump frontward." He spoke carefully. "See, I hit and go in facing the tunnel. I have your left arm and you are pulled over. You follow in just in back of me. Now. In the tunnel, you have your right arm free and I have my left." They would use their free arms to push them through, and they could kick with their feet.

"Tunnel sides are moss," he said. "Push off from them when you bump them. It'll feel slimy, but it won't hurt."

"Okay," she said.

"Pay no mind to fishes," he went on. "Most times, they're but just a few. They don't do nothing but get out of your way."

She nodded. M.C. could feel her tension through her arm.

"You are ready?" Macie asked from above them.

M.C. looked at the girl. "I'm ready," she said.

"You have to hold out for most of a minute."

"I can do it," she said.

"If you lose air, just stay calm," M.C. said. "I can get us out."

"I said I can do it!"

Her anger cut through him again, making him ashamed, though he didn't know why.

They leaped out and plunged. They hit the water at the same time, but M.C. went under first because he was heavier. The girl turned, facing him before her head went under. That was good, but pulling her after him slowed M.C. It seemed to take forever to get down to the tunnel level. Water closed in on them. Sounds became muffled and then no sound at all. They were alone as never before. And there was nothing for M.C. to do but get it over with.

M.C. liked nothing better than being in the deep, with sunlight breaking into rays of green and gold. Water was a pressure of delicious weight as he passed through it, down and down. It was as if feeling no longer belonged to him. The water possessed it and touched along every inch of him.

He pulled out of his downward fall at the sight of the gaping tunnel opening. He no longer felt the girl next to him. He knew she was there with him by the impression she made on the deep. And he would remember her presence, her imprint, on this day for weeks.

Bending her wrist forward, he stretched her arm out straight as he kicked hard into the tunnel. Here the water was cooler, and it cast a gray shimmer that was ghostly. Pressure grew like a ball and chain hanging on his right shoulder. It was the girl like a deadweight.

Kick with your feet!

With a powerful scissoring of his legs, he tried to swim midway between the ceiling and the bottom of the tunnel.

Push off with your hand!

Her dead pressure dragged him down. His knees banged hard against the bottom. His back hit the tunnel side as he realized she was struggling to get away. Fractions of seconds were lost as he tried twisting her arm to pull her body into line. Fishes slid over his skin, tickling and sending shivers to his toes. They must have touched the girl, for he had no moment to brace himself as she shot up on her back toward the ceiling.

Won't make it.

Horror, outrage stunned him. He had taken for granted the one thing he should have asked her. For the want of a question, the tunnel would be a grave for both of them.

She kicked futilely against the tunnel side and rose above him, twisting his arm straight up.

Yank, like Macie will pull down on a balloon.

If he could get the girl turned over, they might have a chance. But his breath seemed to be gone.

Not a grave, it's a tunnel.

In his lungs, emptiness was pain. But the will not to fail was there in his burning chest, in his free arm pushing hard against the deep. His legs were still loose and working. Then a sudden surge of strength, like a second wind.

Be M.C. Higgins, the Great.

He yanked the balloon down—he mustn't break the string. At the same time he propelled himself forward, knowing she would follow as she turned over.

An awful pounding in his head snapped his brain open. M.C. shot out of the tunnel like a cork from a jug of cider. And arching his back, he swung mightily with his right arm.

Dark balloon to the light above.

He hadn't the strength to hurl her to the surface. But he was right behind her. Before she could struggle down again, he was there, pulling at her. She opened her mouth in a pitiful attempt to breathe. He pounded her back, hoping to dislodge water. And held her close a split second to calm her. She was rigid.

Girl, don't drown.

Swiftly he caught her ankles and tossed her up over his head. She broke the surface. He was there, feeling sweet air just when he would have had to open his mouth or have his lungs collapse.

M.C. fought against dizziness, aware that he had his hand on her neck in a bruising clasp to hold her up. He had to let go or break it.

The girl was gagging, trying to breathe. He heard his own breath in a harsh, raw heaving. He was daydreaming a distant cheering. Then he saw the children, feet jumping up and down on the grassy bank. A swirl of rocks before he realized the girl was sinking. He must have let her go. But he had the sense to catch her again around the waist.

Still M.C. Still the leader. He had taken her through the tunnel, and they were back in the world together. Still, all the blame was his. But he could fix it. Could keep the children from knowing about her.

Moaning cry, coughing, she clung to him.

"No." He knocked her hands away. With just the pressure of his arm and shoulder on her back, he forced her flat out. As though she were dog-paddling, he glided her into the land. The feet of the children jumping on the grassy bank fell back and were still.

Macie stood there on the bank, closest to M.C.'s head.

"She's weak," he said to Macie. "See if you can help pull her some . . . my wind is gone."

Macie clasped the girl's arms. M.C. had her by the waist. Halfway out of the water, she kicked M.C. away. She slithered and kneed her way over the bank. On the grass, she hunched into a ball and, struggling to breathe, closed her eyes.

Dark balloon.

M.C. climbed out and crawled a distance to collapse on his

back. He was away from the girl, with the children between them, but he kept his eye on her. They were close together in his mind, where a vision had started. Day after day, they swam the lake. Hour upon hour, they sunned themselves on shore.

M.C.'s chest wouldn't stop its heave and fall. His mouth watered with stomach bile as the pounding ache spread out across his forehead.

None of them moved. For a long while neither Harper nor Macie asked a question. Lennie Pool never did say much.

M.C. felt as if every muscle were trying to get out of his skin. He was sick with exhaustion. But light out of the sky bore into him, warming and relaxing him. It was a healing band on his eyelids. As the ache in his forehead moved off, tunnel and water filled his mind. His eyes shot open, blinding the awful memory.

Seeing that M.C. was awake, Macie came over to him. "You did it!" she said happily. "Were you scared?"

He knew he would vomit if he tried to talk. He swallowed.

"You sure took your time. Was it any trouble?" Macie asked.

"Just took it easy," he said finally.

The girl brought up pool water she had swallowed. A while later, she sat up shakily on her knees. In a slow, mechanical sweep, she brushed grass and twigs from her clothes.

M.C. raised his head. "You all right?" he asked her.

When she stood, the children stood with her. M.C. was on his feet as well, as though he moved only when she moved.

Slowly she seemed to change. He watched her grow stronger, throwing her head back, thrusting out her chin.

"I went all the way through that tunnel," she said, smiling vaguely. "I could have drowned—I can't even swim a lick."

The children gaped at her. Shocked, they turned to M.C.

"And you took her down?" Macie gasped. "You took her clear through . . . you didn't even know!"

The kids began to giggle, jostling one another, with the girl looking solemnly on.

M.C. felt the heat of shame rising in his neck. Only this one secret between them, but the girl wouldn't have it. She made him stand there with the kids laughing at him. He stared at his hands, at the jagged nails that he bit down to the skin.

"I can't stand a lying kid," the girl said.

He said evenly, "I'm not any kid. And I didn't lie."

"You told your sister we took it easy," she said, smirking.

"*I* took it easy," he said. "If I hadn't, you wouldn't be here."

The children stared at him. The girl looked uncertain.

"It's no joke not to tell somebody you can't swim," he said.

"Somebody didn't ask me," she said sullenly.

"Didn't need to ask—you should've told me!"

"I just wanted to see it. I didn't know it was going to be so long."

"So you want to see something and we almost drown?" He was shaking now with the memory of the tunnel. "Ever think of somebody but yourself?"

The girl shrank back. Uncomfortably, they watched her. M.C. hadn't meant to make her appear stupid. But she was quick to apologize.

"I'm sorry," she said simply. "You told me you were some M.C., the Great. . . ."

The look she gave him, as if she knew only he could have saved her, made him feel proud. He had to smile. "You have some good nerve. A lot of real good nerve," he said at last.

VIRGINIA HAMILTON (1936–   ) won the Newbery Medal in 1975 for *M. C. Higgins, the Great.* One of the most honored of contemporary children's writers, she has won the Edgar Allan Poe Award of the Mystery Writers of America (1974) and the National Book Award (1975). Her always entertaining books include *The Time-Ago Tales of Jahdu* (1969), *The Planet of Junior Brown* (a Newbery Honor Book in 1972), *Arilla Sun Down* (1976), *House of Dies Drear* (1968), *Zeely* (1967), and *Sweet Whispers, Brother Rush* (a Newbery Honor Book in 1983).

E. L. KONIGSBURG

THE CATCHEE

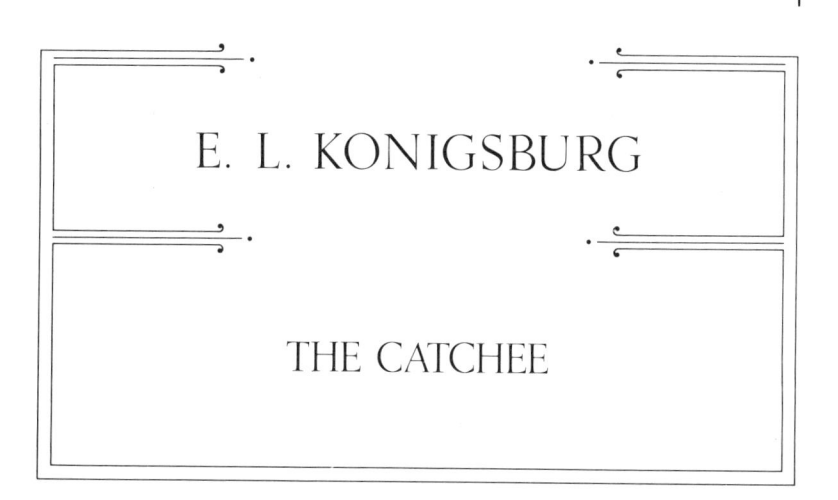

The world is made up of two kinds of people: the catchers and the catchees. And it doesn't take Avery long to find out which kind he is. . . .

When I was six years old, my brother Orville was twelve. Orville was a schoolboy patrol. He wore a Day-Glo red hat and a Day-Glo red strap that zagged across his chest and he carried a pole with a Day-Glo red flag at the end of it. There was probably nothing doing at school that Orville enjoyed more than schoolboy patrolling. He would stand at the corner and wait for the light to change, and when it did, he would walk out into the street and hold out the pole until everyone who should have crossed the street had. That was his duty. I would stand on the curb and wait for him. That was my duty. My mother had put Orville in charge of my transportation to and from school. Our transportation then was walking, and I wasn't allowed to cross the street without him.

Sometimes Orville stood on the corner long after everyone had emptied from the school building, and he'd walk home with me and with his pole with the Day-Glo red flag on the end of it. He'd walk over to the big industrial park that was growing up behind where we lived. Orville would pick a building and direct the people coming out.

There were no red lights in the industrial park. There were signs that had eight sides and some that had three. Orville would line up with one of the eight-siders, and he'd lower his pole with the Day-Glo red flag at the end of it and allow people to cross the street in front of him. They'd come out like popcorn: Nothing for a long time, then one and two at a time, and then they'd come out a whole hopperful at a time. Most of the people coming out of the office buildings were girls. A lot of them smiled at Orville, and next to schoolboy patrolling, Orville liked those smiles best. He was twelve; he had begun liking girls when he was eleven. I would stand on the curb and wait for Orville.

Orville had tried most of the buildings in the industrial park. The Remington became his favorite, and he always went back to it.

One day Orville was waiting outside the Remington. There was a little breeze that day, and that was another thing Orville liked a lot because the breezes would blow the girls' skirts up, and when I asked Orville why he enjoyed that so much, he answered that he could see Schenectady. I didn't understand what he meant then, when Orville was already twelve, and I was still six.

Orville was at the best part of his patrolling that day, the part where the girls came out in twoses and threeses, that being the part where he got the most smiles, when he told me that he had to go to the bathroom. I was surprised, because Orville didn't usually have to do ordinary things at inconvenient times. He told me to step off the curb and hold the pole with the Day-Glo red flag while he visited the bathroom in the Remington.

"You can't go in there," I said.

"Well, I sure can't go out here," he answered.

So Orville marched into the Remington, and for the first time I stood off the curb all by myself. I held the pole across the street, and the cars stopped, and the people crossed. I began to see why Orville enjoyed schoolboy patrolling so much. I was enjoying it pretty much myself, although it didn't matter to me whether it was boys crossing or girls.

I had raised the pole once and let it down again when I felt someone tap me on my shoulder. I thought Orville was finished and wanted me to give him back his pole. I wouldn't turn around. I felt the poke on my shoulder again. I lowered the pole and stiffened my shoulders. "Listen," I snarled, "I'll give it back to you after the next batch crosses."

A voice, a voice that wore a uniform, answered, "Don't you know that it's illegal to impersonate a traffic officer?"

I turned around and saw that not only the voice but also the man who owned it wore a uniform. He took the pole with the Day-Glo red flag from me and, with his arm over my shoulder, walked me and the pole to the exit of the industrial park. As he guided me out, he told me how lucky I was that none of the cars had chosen to ride right through my flag. I could have gotten run over, standing off the curb like that, he said. In between everything else he said was the message: Don't do it anymore. Ever. Again.

I waited for Orville on the sidewalk just outside the industrial park. Orville wasn't long in coming. He had gone to the bathroom just before the policeman came, and he finished just after the policeman took me with him.

While I waited, I figured out my life. I realized that the

world is made up of two kinds of people: the catchers and the catchees. I was a catchee.

The next time it happened was a week later or maybe a month. When you can't tell time, it's hard to measure it. I was still in the first grade, and I had not yet learned all the short vowel sounds. It was after school, and Orville had given me money for a limeade from the Minute Market on the corner on the same side of the street as the school. Orville was schoolboy patrolling and doing it and doing it. I finished the limeade and slurped all the ice from the bottom. I held onto the paper cup for three red lights' worth of crossings after that, and the cup began to get mushy. I walked back to the corner where the Minute Market was, and I put the empty limeade in a container. The next thing I knew, I was being dragged by the back of my collar to the principal's office. The sixth-grade teacher, Miss Elkins, was dragging me. She was also yelling at me, telling me that I had committed a federal offense. It wasn't until I got to the principal's office that I learned that I had mailed the limeade cup. What I had thought had said *litters* had said *letters*. I explained to the principal that I didn't think that it was a federal offense to be only halfway through the short vowel sounds. The principal agreed, and Miss Elkins, realizing that it wasn't my fault that I was only halfway, agreed, too. But she wasn't too happy about it. She said that her birthday card to someone special was probably blurred to where it couldn't be delivered. She looked sideways at the principal when she said "someone special."

Orville was waiting for me when I came out of the principal's office. That was the first time he had had to wait for me instead of vice versa.

"What kept you, Avery?" he asked.

"I put a limeade cup through the United States mail," I said. Then I explained to him what had happened.

THE CATCHEE

Miss Elkins was Orville's teacher then. He put his arm around my shoulder as we began to walk home and he said, "You know, Avery, if Miss Elkins were walking out of the Remington and a breeze blew her skirts way up past Schenectady, I wouldn't bother to look past New Rochelle."

There was only one spot where Orville's arm touched my shoulder that afternoon, and it was there for only three blocks, and that was many years ago, but to this day I could still point to exactly where it was.

By the time I got into Miss Elkin's sixth grade myself, the industrial park had bulldozed its way over our old neighborhood of small houses. With the money my folks got for selling our old house, they had bought a new one. Not exactly new. It was middle-aged. It was also middle-sized and the middle house on the block. We were now on the edge of rows of bigger houses. We knew there wouldn't be an industrial park moving up on us again because behind us was the old Talmadge estate that had been sold to developers. They were building houses on it. The new houses got bigger and bigger, row after row, the farther back from us you went. On the river row, they were as big as motels and had about that many bathrooms.

I was a schoolboy patrol in the sixth grade, but we were bused. We never took our flagpoles home. They still had Day-Glo red, but they were locked up every night. Schoolboy patrolling wasn't what it had been when Orville had been it. And now it was called *school patrol,* not *schoolboy patrol,* because girls did it, too.

Orville had moved on to high school. All the girls that he had discovered now discovered him. He divided his spare time between talking on the telephone and working as a bag boy at the A & P. He never put his arm around my shoulder, and he made jokes all the time, out of everything.

I had managed to live a pretty normal life for a catchee. I

had learned that the teacher would call on me for the *other* math problem, the one I had not done. In the fourth grade I was the only kid in my class who got lice, athlete's foot, and poison ivy. I was probably the only kid in history who got them all at the same time. The only parts of me that didn't itch were my fingernails and, every now and then, the roof of my mouth.

"Cooties, crud, and creeping eruption," Orville said. He did a little shuffle with his feet and snapped his fingers to give it rhythm. I didn't think Orville was funny.

By the sixth grade I had learned that when they let people through seven at a time, I would be eighth. And that in the supermarket I would get the one cart out of seventy-five that had a stuck left rear wheel. And in the sixth grade I resumed my career as a police catchee.

After we moved, I had a lot of odd jobs. Some of my steady lawn-mowing customers were hand-me-downs from Orville. He had to give them up to become a bag boy because there wasn't enough daylight when he got home. A lot of my piecework was for people who lived in the big houses along the river. I would feed and care for their parakeets when they went out of town. I would walk and brush their dogs; a lot of miniature poodles live in big houses. I was also hired to keep birdseed in the feeder and water in the birdbath. But the worst job I had was baby-sitting with some azaleas.

Mrs. Wilkie had hired me. Mrs. Wilkie was a very worried lady who was going to Europe for three weeks. She was worried that her infant azaleas would die. Her house was so new that all the wall space around the light switches was spotless and the air inside it smelled fresh-sawed. And it was so big that if you put up a sign that said EMERGENCY, it could be mistaken for a hospital.

There were so many new houses in the neighborhood that things that should automatically go on were going off. Even on our edge, where the houses weren't as big as hospitals, we had our convenience problems: water for one thing and electricity for another. When it got very hot outside, and the air conditioners were set to switch on, they didn't. The power was so low that there wasn't enough of it in the wires to throw the switches. Walk past any box of circuit breakers at supper time, and you could hear them moaning.

It sometimes took so long to fill the tub for a bath that you could turn the faucet on full force and go draw a map of the entire United States, marking the state capitals, Schenectady and New Rochelle, and five major rivers, and still have the tub only half full when you were finished. My mother was so pleased with her new-to-us middle-aged house that she never complained about its modern inconveniences or about having to wait until midnight to have enough water pressure to wash the dishes.

The first Saturday that Mrs. Wilkie was gone, I wandered over to her house to water. It was hot September. The electricity had been quaking in our house all day. When I got to the Wilkies', I saw that there was no garden hose outside. I walked around back and didn't find one there, either. It would be a hot walk back to our house to get ours. I saw her sliding glass doors leading to her bedroom, and with just a little extra tug—about what you'd give to a lawn mower going uphill—I could open them. I figured that I would go through the house to her garage and get the hose. I never thought of it as breaking in.

I was halfway across the living room when the alarm went off. If you've never been inside an empty house with a burglar alarm going off inside it, I can only tell you that your head feels like a giant sinus cavity with an air-raid alert inside.

I ran over to the entrance hall and threw every switch within sight, but the alarm wouldn't quit. Then I went into the hall closet and found the box of circuit breakers and threw every one there.

The house went quiet. Everything suddenly sounded so hushed that I felt it necessary to tiptoe into the garage.

While I was in the garage, trying to uncoil one hundred and fifty feet of green garden hose from one hundred and twenty-five feet of black garden hose, I heard a voice come over the loudspeaker: "All right, come on out." I paid no attention. I went on with my work. The voice came again. Closer and louder, and in uniform this time. "All right, come on out: We've got the house surrounded."

I realized they wanted me. So I came out. My hands were up from lifting the garage door, and the policemen told me to keep them exactly that way.

I walked down the driveway to the waiting police car. Mrs. Wilkie's neighbors saw me and said, "Why, it's Avery Basford." The cops asked if I would mind telling them what I was doing in there. I told them that I wouldn't mind telling them, and I didn't. But it took me thirty-five minutes to do it.

It seems that Mrs. Wilkie had been as worried about her house as she had been about her azaleas. She had asked her neighbors to listen for the alarm and to call the police if they heard it go off. Now, ordinarily, the minute that I pushed on the sliding glass door, the alarm would have gone off, and the neighbors would have found me outside, and ordinarily I could have explained to them. Ordinarily, I would never have been trapped inside. Ordinarily, Mrs. Wilkie's neighbors would not have reasoned that only a professional burglar would know how to enter a house and shut off an alarm. Ordinarily.

Ordinarily.

If everything had happened ordinarily, I would have found some other way to get trapped. For I was a catchee.

I became a police catchee again a little later that year, and it happened because of my Christmas spirit.

THE CATCHEE

My mother was not only pleased with our new house, she was also proud of it. She hardly believed me when I told her that our whole house would fit inside the Wilkies' living room and dining room. "Bigger," she said, "isn't necessarily prettier." To her, there was nothing prettier in this whole world than our middle-sized picture window with our big Christmas tree just behind it.

She invited the ladies from our old neighborhood over for a party. Everyone from our old neighborhood had scattered to different middle-sized houses. She called it a class reunion.

"What class?" I asked.

"Low-income class," she answered.

I arrived home from school just as the ladies were opening the gifts that they were exchanging with each other. Sister Arnetta gave my mother a pair of underpants. My mother wouldn't stop raving about them. She called them panties, not underpants, and she said they were precious. She said that the only thing that Sister Arnetta could have done nicer would have been to give her a pair in each color of the rainbow.

That solved my problem about what to get my mother for Christmas.

I went to her room that night and I took the underpants from the box they came in. The box was from Eaton's, so I supposed that the panties were, too. I put them in a plain brown paper bag from the grocery store, and I layered the bag between my math and social studies books. I decided that I would go to town straight from school and buy my mother those same precious panties in as many colors of the rainbow as I could afford.

I found Eaton's department of underwear with no trouble at all, but I had not counted on how pastel it would be. In my black skin, blue jeans, and maroon sweater, I felt like a walking exclamation point in a sea of whispers.

No one took my being there seriously. No one asked, "May I help you?" So I tried to help myself. I pulled a corner of the precious panties from the plain brown paper bag, and I tried to match them with the assortment that was on top of the counter. But I couldn't tell if they were the precious kind or some other. All the materials looked alike, and they were all basically the same shape. I needed to see the label for size and variety.

The label on women's underpants is on the inside. I figured that if I could get a hold on it, I could let it poke out of the bag. Then I would only have to match numbers. I reached into the bag to let my fingers do the walking and was gazing over the counter and up at the ceiling as I concentrated on the touch system inside the bag.

I felt a tap on my shoulder.

The tap wore a uniform. So did the voice. "Better come along with me, sonny."

I turned around and saw a store security guard.

"What's the matter?" I asked.

"Where did you get those panties?" he asked, looking at the bag.

"From my mother," I answered.

"Did she give them to you as an advance Christmas present?" His tone was sarcastic.

"These panties are not mine," I said.

"Oh, I believe that they're not yours. But it's your job to convince me that they're your mother's. Just show them to me, and if they've been worn, you won't have to say one more thing to me."

"They're brand-new."

The guard smiled. "That's what I thought. Can you show me a receipt?"

"No. They were a gift. People never put receipts in with gifts."

THE CATCHEE

"They never put them in with stolen goods, either. Suppose you come along with me, sonny."

I knew it would get down to that.

He took me to an office where some manager sat behind a desk. "I found this young fellow shoplifting in ladies' bloomers," he said.

"No, you didn't." I explained quietly. "You only caught me feeling them."

The two men exchanged looks.

"I brought these panties from home. *Bloomers,* if you want to call them that."

"To whom do you say they belong?" the manager asked.

"To my mother."

"Suppose we call her and check it out."

"Oh, please don't do that. She won't be at all surprised."

"You mean that you've been in trouble before?"

I could see that anything I said would be used against me. That was one of the problems of being a catchee. "Look," I said, "call my big brother, Orville. He works at the A & P." I looked at my watch. "He gets the car on Wednesdays because he brings the groceries home. If you get hold of him now, he'll stop here on his way home and straighten everything out."

I was left in the manager's outer office in my own custody until Orville came. We got it all straightened out. And the manager even walked us over to the department of underwear and introduced us to a saleslady who wore a badge saying MISS HINKEL. Miss Hinkel helped me find the underpants. I could afford one pink and one pale blue so I paid for them, and we left.

As we were driving home, I said to Orville, "You know, Orville, this never would have happened if I weren't a catchee. I've been a catchee all my life."

Orville understood what I meant by catchee because he had

noticed it about me. Orville said that he had thought about it, and he thought, too, that it was time to talk to me about it.

"Avery," he said, "being a catchee can make you two things. It can make you very honest."

"I believe that, brother. I can see that. I don't stand a chance being anything but honest."

"And," Orville added, taking a hand from the steering wheel to pat my knee, "it can make you very brave."

"How can it do that?" I asked.

"Well, Ave," he said, "it can make you brave this way. Most guys never know whether or not they're going to get caught. They just never know, and they live in fear of it. But you—you being a catchee—never have to worry about *whether*. You just don't know *when*. Don't you see, Ave? You are never afraid because you are always prepared for the worst. Like when the guy in the department store fingered you. You stayed calm. You didn't lose your temper. You didn't go crying to Mama and give your surprise away. You stayed cool. You are free of fear. And that, Avery, makes a guy very brave. Honest and brave. That's a great combination. I think you're going to be a leader of men, brother."

I liked what Orville said. A clarinet began playing inside me. I didn't even tell Orville thank you. I sat there holding that box of panties, pink and pale blue, Christmas-wrapped, and the white ones in the plain brown bag. I sat there and listened to that clarinet; it was playing "honest and brave" inside me.

We came to the intersection of Heavener and Forsythe, and Orville drove right through a yellow light, yellow making it to red before we were all the way across.

Orville looked over at me. We smiled at each other. Both of us were glad that it wasn't me driving.

E. L. KONIGSBURG (1930–   ) won the Newbery Medal in 1968 for *From the Mixed-up Files of Mrs. Basil E. Frankweiler.* Among her many excellent, imaginative novels for children are *Jennifer, Hecate, Macbeth, William McKinley, and Me, Elizabeth* (a Newbery Honor Book in 1968), *The Dragon in the Ghetto Caper* (1974), *Father's Arcane Daughter* (1976), and *Journey to an 800 Number* (1982).

MADELEINE L'ENGLE

POOR LITTLE SATURDAY

A story of witches and ghosts on a lonely Southern Georgia plantation . . .

THE WITCH WOMAN LIVED in a deserted, boarded-up plantation house, and nobody knew about her but me. Nobody in the nosy little town in south Georgia where I lived when I was a boy knew that if you walked down the dusty main street to where the post office ended it and then turned left and followed that road a piece until you got to the rusty iron gates of the drive to the plantation house, you could find goings-on would make your eyes pop out. It was just luck that I found out. Or maybe it wasn't luck at all. Maybe the witch woman wanted me to find out because of Alexandra. But now I wish I hadn't, because the witch woman and Alexandra are gone forever and it's much worse than if I'd never known them.

Nobody'd lived in the plantation house since the Civil War when Colonel Londermaine was killed and Alexandra Londermaine, his beautiful young wife, hung herself on the chandelier in the ballroom. A while before I was born some northerners bought it, but after a few years they stopped coming and people said it was because the house was haunted. Every few years a gang of boys or men would set out to explore the house but nobody ever found anything, and it was so well boarded up it was hard to force an entrance, so by and by the town lost interest in it. No one climbed the wall and wandered around the grounds except me.

I used to go there often during the summer because I had bad spells of malaria when sometimes I couldn't bear to lie on the iron bedstead in my room with the flies buzzing around my face, or out on the hammock on the porch with the screams and laughter of the other kids as they played, torturing my ears. My aching head made it impossible for me to read, and I would drag myself down the road, scuffling my bare, sunburned toes in the dust, wearing the tattered straw hat that was supposed to protect me from the heat of the sun, shivering and sweating by turns. Sometimes it would seem hours before I got to the iron gates near which the brick wall was lowest. Often I would have to lie panting on the tall, prickly grass for minutes until I gathered strength to scale the wall and drop down on the other side.

But once inside the grounds it seemed cooler. One funny thing about my chills was that I didn't seem to shiver nearly as much when I could keep cool as I did at home where even the walls and the floors, if you touched them, were hot. The grounds were filled with live oaks that had grown up unchecked everywhere and afforded an almost continuous green shade. The ground was covered with ferns that were soft and cool to lie on, and when I flung myself down on my back and looked up, the roof of leaves was so thick that sometimes I couldn't see the sky at all. The sun that managed to filter through lost its bright, pitiless glare and came in soft yellow shafts that didn't burn you when they touched you.

One afternoon, a scorcher early in September, which is usually our hottest month (and by then you're fagged out by the heat, anyhow), I set out for the plantation. The heat lay coiled and shimmering on the road. When you looked at anything through it, it was like looking through a defective pane of glass. The dirt road was so hot that it burned even through my calloused feet, and as I walked clouds of dust rose in front of me and mixed with the shimmying of the heat. I thought I'd never make the plantation. Sweat was running into my eyes, but it was cold sweat, and I was shivering so that my teeth chattered as I walked. When I managed finally to fling myself down on my soft green bed of ferns inside the grounds, I was seized with one of the worst chills I'd ever had in spite of the fact that my mother had given me an extra dose of quinine that morning and some 666 Malaria Medicine to boot. I shut my eyes tight and clutched the ferns with my hands and teeth to wait until the chill had passed, when I heard a soft voice call:

"Boy."

I thought at first I was delirious, because sometimes I got light-headed when my bad attacks came on; only then I remembered that when I was delirious I didn't know it; all the strange things I saw and heard seemed perfectly natural. So when the voice said, "Boy," again, as soft and clear as the mockingbird at sunrise, I opened my eyes.

Kneeling near me on the ferns was a girl. She must have been about a year younger than I. I was almost sixteen so I guess she was fourteen or fifteen. She was dressed in a blue and white gingham dress; her face was very pale, but the kind of paleness that's supposed to be, not the sickly pale kind that was like mine showing even under the tan. Her eyes were big and very blue. Her hair was dark brown and she wore it parted in the middle in two heavy braids that were swinging in front of her shoulders as she peered into my face.

"You don't feel well, do you?" she asked. There was no trace of concern or worry in her voice. Just scientific interest.

I shook my head. "No," I whispered, almost afraid that if I talked she would vanish, because I had never seen anyone here before, and I thought that maybe I was dying because I felt so awful, and I thought maybe that gave me the power to see the ghost. But the girl in blue and white checked gingham seemed as I watched her to be good flesh and blood.

"You'd better come with me," she said. "She'll make you all right."

"Who's she?"

"Oh—just Her," she said.

My chill had begun to recede by then, so when she got up off her knees, I scrambled up, too. When she stood up her dress showed a white ruffled petticoat underneath it, and bits of green moss had left patterns on her knees and I didn't think that would happen to the knees of a ghost, so I followed her as she led the way toward the house. She did not go up the sagging, half-rotted steps that led to the veranda, about whose white pillars wisteria vines climbed in wild profusion, but went around to the side of the house where there were slanting doors to a cellar. The sun and rain had long since blistered and washed off the paint, but the doors looked clean and were free of the bits of bark from the eucalyptus tree that leaned nearby and that had dropped its bits of dusty peel on either side; so I knew that these cellar stairs must frequently be used.

The girl opened the cellar doors. "You go down first," she said. I went down the cellar steps, which were stone and cool against my bare feet. As she followed me she closed the cellar doors after her and as I reached the bottom of the stairs we were in pitch darkness. I began to be very frightened until her soft voice came out of the black.

"Boy, where are you?"

"Right here."

"You'd better take my hand. You might stumble."

We reached out and found each other's hands in the darkness. Her fingers were long and cool and they closed firmly around mine. She moved with authority as though she knew her way with the familiarity born of custom.

"Poor Sat's all in the dark," she said, "but he likes it that way. He likes to sleep for weeks at a time. Sometimes he snores awfully. Sat, darling!" she called gently. A soft, bubbly, blowing sound came in answer, and she laughed happily. "Oh, Sat, you are sweet!" she said, and the bubbly sound came again. Then the girl pulled at my hand and we came out into a huge and dusty kitchen. Iron skillets, pots, and pans were still hanging on either side of the huge stove, and there was a rolling pin and a bowl of flour on the marble-topped table in the middle of the room. The girl took a lighted candle off the shelf.

"I'm going to make cookies," she said as she saw me looking at the flour and the rolling pin. She slipped her hand out of mine. "Come along." She began to walk more rapidly. We left the kitchen, crossed the hall, went through the dining room, its old mahogany table thick with dust, although sheets covered the pictures on the walls. Then we went into the ballroom. The mirrors lining the walls were spotted and discolored; against one wall was a single delicate gold chair, its seat cushioned with pale rose and silver woven silk; it seemed extraordinarily well preserved. From the ceiling hung the huge chandelier from which Alexandra Londermaine had hung herself, its prisms catching and breaking up into a hundred colors the flickering of the candle and the few shafts of light that managed to slide in through the boarded-up windows. As we crossed the ballroom, the girl began to dance by herself, gracefully, lightly, so that her full, blue and white checked gingham skirts flew out around her. She looked at herself with pleasure in the old mirrors as she danced, the candle flaring and guttering in her right hand.

"You've stopped shaking. Now what will I tell Her?" she said as we started to climb the broad mahogany staircase. It was very dark so she took my hand again, and before we had reached the top of the stairs I obliged her by being seized by another chill. She felt my trembling fingers with satisfaction. "Oh, you've started again. That's good." She slid open one of the huge double doors at the head of the stairs.

As I looked in to what once must have been Colonel Londermaine's study, I thought that surely what I saw was a scene in a dream or a vision in delirium. Seated at the huge table in the center of the room was the most extraordinary woman I had ever seen. I felt that she must be very beautiful, although she would never have fulfilled any of the standards of beauty set by our town. Even though she was seated, I felt that she must be immensely tall. Piled up on the table in front of her were several huge volumes, and her finger was marking the place in the open one in front of her, but she was not reading. She was leaning back in the carved chair, her head resting against a piece of blue and gold embroidered silk that was flung across the chair back, one hand gently stroking a fawn that lay sleeping in her lap. Her eyes were closed and somehow I couldn't imagine what color they would be. It wouldn't have surprised me if they had been shining amber or the deep purple of her velvet robe. She had a great quantity of hair, the color of mahogany in firelight, which was cut quite short and seemed to be blown wildly about her head like flame. Under her closed eyes were deep shadows, and lines of pain were about her mouth. Otherwise there were no marks of age on her face but I would not have been surprised to learn that she was any age in the world —a hundred or twenty-five. Her mouth was large and mobile, and she was singing something in a deep, rich voice. Two cats, one black, one white, were coiled up, each on a book, and as we opened the doors a leopard stood up quietly beside her but did not snarl or move. It simply stood there and waited, watching us.

The girl nudged me and held her finger to her lips to warn me to be quiet, but I would not have spoken—could not, anyhow, my teeth were chattering so from my chill, which I had completely forgotten, so fascinated was I by this woman sitting back with her head against the embroidered silk, soft, deep sounds coming out of her throat. At last these sounds resolved themselves into words, and we listened to her as she sang. The cats slept indifferently, but the leopard listened, too:

> *I sit high in my ivory tower,*
>   *The heavy curtains drawn.*
> *I've many a strange and lustrous flower,*
>   *A leopard and a fawn*
>
> *Together sleeping by my chair*
>   *And strange birds softly winging,*
> *And ever pleasant to my ear*
>   *Twelve maidens' voices singing.*

Here is my magic maps' array,
   My mystic circle's flame.
With symbol's art He lets me play,
   The unknown my domain,

And as I sit here in my dream
   I see myself awake,
Hearing a torn and bloody scream,
   Feeling my castle shake . . .

Her song wasn't finished but she opened her eyes and looked at us. Now that his mistress knew we were here, the leopard seemed ready to spring and devour me at one gulp, but she put her hand on his sapphire-studded collar to restrain him.

"Well, Alexandra," she said, "Whom have we here?"

The girl, who still held my hand in her long, cool fingers, answered, "It's a boy."

"So I see. Where did you find him?"

The voice sent shivers up and down my spine.

"In the fern bed. He was shaking. See? He's shaking now. Is he having a fit?" Alexandra's voice was filled with pleased interest.

"Come here, boy," the woman said.

As I didn't move, Alexandra gave me a push, and I advanced slowly. As I came near, the woman pulled one of the leopard's ears gently, saying, "Lie down, Thammuz." The beast obeyed, flinging itself at her feet. She held her hand out to me as I approached the table. If Alexandra's fingers felt firm and cool, hers had the strength of the ocean and the coolness of jade. She looked at me for a long time and I saw that her eyes were deep blue, much bluer than Alexandra's, so dark as to be almost black. When she spoke again her voice was warm and tender: "You're burning up with fever. One of the malaria bugs?" I nodded. "Well, we'll fix that for you."

POOR LITTLE SATURDAY

When she stood and put the sleeping fawn down by the leopard, she was not as tall as I had expected her to be; nevertheless she gave an impression of great height. Several of the bookshelves in one corner were emptied of books and filled with various shaped bottles and retorts. Nearby was a large skeleton. There was an acid-stained washbasin, too; that whole section of the room looked like part of a chemist's or physicist's laboratory. She selected from among the bottles a small, amber-colored one and poured a drop of the liquid it contained into a glass of water. As the drop hit the water, there was a loud hiss and clouds of dense smoke arose. When they had drifted away, she handed the glass to me and said, "Drink. Drink, my boy!"

My hand was trembling so that I could scarcely hold the glass. Seeing this, she took it from me and held it to my lips.

"What is it?" I asked.

"Drink it," she said, pressing the rim of the glass against my teeth. On the first swallow I started to choke and would have pushed the stuff away, but she forced the rest of the burning liquid down my throat. My whole body felt on fire. I felt flame flickering in every vein, and the room and everything in it swirled around. When I had regained my equilibrium to a certain extent, I managed to gasp out again, "What is it?"

She smiled and answered,

"Nine peacocks' hearts, four bats' tongues,
A pinch of moon dust, and a hummingbird's lungs."

Then I asked a question I would never have dared ask if it hadn't been that I was still half drunk from the potion I had swallowed. "Are you a witch?"

She smiled again and answered, "I make it my profession."

Since she hadn't struck me down with a flash of lightning, I went on. "Do you ride a broomstick?"

This time she laughed. "I can when I like."

"Is it—is it very hard?"

"Rather like a bucking bronco at first, but I've always been a good horsewoman, and now I can manage very nicely. I've finally progressed to sidesaddle, though I still feel safer astride. I always rode my horse astride. Still, the best witches ride sidesaddle, so. . . . Now run along home. Alexandra has lessons to study and I must work. Can you hold your tongue or must I make you forget?"

"I can hold my tongue."

She looked at me and her eyes burnt into me like the potion she had given me to drink. "Yes, I think you can," she said. "Come back tomorrow if you like. Thammuz will show you out."

The leopard rose and led the way to the door. As I hesitated, unwilling to tear myself away, it came back and pulled gently but firmly on my trouser leg.

"Good-bye, boy," the witch woman said. "And you won't have any more chills and fever."

"Good-bye," I answered. I didn't say thank you. I didn't say good-bye to Alexandra. I followed the leopard out.

She let me come every day. I think she must have been lonely. After all, I was the only thing there with a life apart from hers. And in the long run the only reason I have had a life of my own is because of her. I am as much a creation of the witch woman's as Thammuz the leopard was, or the two cats, Ashtaroth and Orus. (It wasn't until many years after the last day I saw the witch woman that I learned that those were the names of the fallen angels.)

She did cure my malaria, too. My parents and the townspeople thought that I had outgrown it. I grew angry when they talked about it so lightly and wanted to tell them that it was the witch woman, but I knew that if ever I breathed a word about her I would be eternally damned. Mama thought we should write a testimonial letter to the 666 Malaria Medicine people, and maybe they'd send us a couple of dollars.

Alexandra and I became very good friends. She was a strange, aloof creature. She liked me to watch her while she danced alone in the ballroom or played on an imaginary harp—though sometimes I fancied I could hear the music. One day she took me into the drawing room and uncovered a portrait that was hung between two of the long, boarded-up windows. Then she stepped back and held her candle high so as to throw the best light on the picture. It might have been a picture of Alexandra herself, or Alexandra as she might be in five years.

"That's my mother," she said. "Alexandra Londermaine."

As far as I knew from the tales that went about town, Alexandra Londermaine had given birth to only one child, and that stillborn, before she had hung herself on the chandelier in the ballroom—and anyhow, any child of hers would have been this Alexandra's mother or grandmother. But I didn't say anything, because when Alexandra got angry she became ferocious like one of the cats and was given to leaping on me, scratching and biting. I looked at the portrait long and silently.

"You see, she has on a ring like mine," Alexandra said, holding out her left hand, on the fourth finger of which was the most beautiful sapphire and diamond ring I had ever seen—or rather, that I could ever have imagined, for it was a ring apart from any owned by even the most wealthy of the townsfolk. Then I realized that Alexandra had brought me in here and unveiled the portrait simply that she might show me the ring to better advantage, for she had never worn a ring before.

"Where did you get it?"

"Oh, She got it for me last night."

"Alexandra," I asked suddenly, "how long have you been here?"

"Oh, awhile."

"But how long?"

"Oh, I don't remember."

"But you must remember."

"I don't. I just came—like Poor Sat."

"Who's Poor Sat?" I asked, thinking for the first time of whoever it was that had made the gentle bubbly noises at Alexandra the day she found me in the fern bed.

"Why, we've never shown you Sat, have we!" she exclaimed. "I'm sure it's all right, but we'd better ask Her first."

So we went to the witch woman's room and knocked. Thammuz pulled the door open with his strong teeth and the witch woman looked up from some sort of experiment she was making with test tubes and retorts. The fawn, as usual, lay sleeping near her feet. "Well?" she said.

"Is it all right if I take him to see Poor Little Saturday?" Alexandra asked her.

"Yes, I suppose so," she answered. "But no teasing." And she turned her back to us and bent again over her test tubes as Thammuz nosed us out of the room.

We went down to the cellar. Alexandra lit a lamp and took me back to the corner farthest from the doors, where there was a stall. In the stall was a two-humped camel. I couldn't help laughing as I looked at him because he grinned at Alexandra so foolishly, displaying all his huge buckteeth and blowing bubbles through them.

"She said we weren't to tease him," Alexandra said severely, rubbing her cheek against the preposterous splotchy hair that seemed to be coming out, leaving bald pink spots of skin on his long nose.

"But what—" I started.

"She rides him sometimes." Alexandra held out her hand

while he nuzzled against it, scratching his rubbery lips against the diamond and sapphire of her ring. "Mostly She talks to him. She says he is very wise. He goes up to Her room sometimes and they talk and talk. I can't understand a word they say. She says it's Hindustani and Arabic. Sometimes I can remember little bits of it, like: *iderow, sorcabatcha,* and *anna bibed bech.* She says I can learn to speak with them when I finish learning French and Greek."

Poor Little Saturday was rolling his eyes in delight as Alexandra scratched behind his ears. "Why is he called Poor Little Saturday?" I asked.

Alexandra spoke with a ring of pride in her voice. "I named him. She let me."

"But why did you name him that?"

"Because he came last winter on the Saturday that was the shortest day of the year, and it rained all day so it got light later and dark earlier than it would have if it had been nice, so it really didn't have as much of itself as it should, and I felt so sorry for it I thought maybe it would feel better if we named him after it.... She thought it was a nice name!" She turned on me suddenly.

"Oh, it is! It's a fine name!" I said quickly, smiling to myself as I realized how much greater was this compassion of Alexandra's for a day than any she might have for a human being. "How did She get him?" I asked.

"Oh, he just came."

"What do you mean?"

"She wanted him so he came. From the desert."

"He *walked!*"

"Yes. And swam part of the way. She met him at the beach and flew him here on the broomstick. You should have seen him. He was still all wet and looked so funny. She gave him hot coffee with things in it."

"What things?"

"Oh, just things."

Then the witch woman's voice came from behind us. "Well, children?"

It was the first time I had seen her out of her room. Thammuz was at her right heel, the fawn at her left. The cats, Ashtaroth and Orus, had evidently stayed upstairs. "Would you like to ride Saturday?" she asked me.

Speechless, I nodded. She put her hand against the wall and a portion of it slid down into the earth so that Poor Little Saturday was free to go out. "She's sweet, isn't she?" the witch woman asked me, looking affectionately at the strange, bumpy-kneed, splay-footed creature. "Her grandmother was very good to me in Egypt once. Besides, I love camel's milk."

"But Alexandra said she was a he!" I exclaimed.

"Alexandra's the kind of woman to whom all animals are he except cats, and all cats are she. As a matter of fact, Ashtaroth and Orus are she, but it wouldn't make any difference to Alexandra if they weren't. Go on out, Saturday. Come on!"

Saturday backed out, bumping her bulging knees and ankles against her stall, and stood under a live oak tree. "Down," the witch woman said. Saturday leered at me and didn't move. "Down, *sorcabatcha*!" the witch woman commanded, and Saturday obediently got down on her knees. I clambered up onto her, and before I had managed to get at all settled she rose with such a jerky motion that I knocked my chin against her front hump and nearly bit my tongue off. Round and round Saturday danced while I clung wildly to her front hump and the witch woman and Alexandra rolled on the ground with laughter. I felt as though I were on a very unseaworthy vessel on the high seas, and it wasn't long before I felt violently seasick as Saturday pranced among the live oak trees, sneezing delicately.

At last the witch woman called out, "Enough!" and Saturday stopped in her traces, nearly throwing me, and knelt laboriously. "It was mean to tease you," the witch woman said, pulling my nose gently. "You may come sit in my room with me for a while if you like."

There was nothing I liked better than to sit in the witch woman's room and to watch her while she studied from her books, worked out strange-looking mathematical problems, argued with the zodiac, or conducted complicated experiments with her test tubes and retorts, sometimes filling the room with sulphurous odors or flooding it with red or blue light. Only once was I afraid of her, and that was when she danced with the skeleton in the corner. She had the room flooded with a strange red glow, and I almost thought I could see the flesh covering the bones of the skeleton as they danced together like lovers. I think she had forgotten that I was sitting there, half hidden in the wing chair, because when they had finished dancing and the skeleton stood in the corner again, his bones shining and polished, devoid of any living trappings, she stood with her forehead against one of the deep red velvet curtains that covered the boarded-up windows and tears streamed down her cheeks. Then she went back to her test tubes and worked feverishly. She never alluded to the incident and neither did I.

As winter drew on she let me spend more and more time in the room. Once I gathered up courage enough to ask her about herself, but I got precious little satisfaction.

"Well, then, are you maybe one of the northerners who bought the place?"

"Let's leave it at that, boy. We'll say that's who I am. Did you know that my skeleton was old Colonel Londermaine? Not so old, as a matter of fact; he was only thirty-seven when he was killed at the battle of Bunker Hill—or am I getting him confused with his great grandfather, Rudolph Londermaine? Anyhow he was only thirty-seven, and a fine figure of a man, and Alexandra only thirty when she hung herself for love of him on the chandelier in the ballroom. Did you know that the fat man with the red mustaches has been trying to cheat your father? His cow will give sour milk for seven days. Run along now and talk to Alexandra. She's lonely."

When the winter had turned to spring and the camellias and azaleas and Cape Jessamine had given way to the more lush blooms of early May, I kissed Alexandra for the first time, very clumsily. The next evening when I managed to get away from the chores at home and hurried out to the plantation, she gave me her sapphire and diamond ring, which she had swung for me on a narrow bit of turquoise satin.

"It will keep us both safe," she said, "if you wear it always. And then when we're older we can get married and you can give it back to me. Only you mustn't let anyone see it, ever, ever, or She'd be very angry."

I was afraid to take the ring but when I demurred Alexandra grew furious and started kicking and biting and I had to give in.

Summer was almost over before my father discovered the ring hanging about my neck. I fought like a witch boy to keep him from pulling out the narrow ribbon and seeing the ring, and indeed the ring seemed to give me added strength, and I had grown, in any case, much stronger during the winter than I had ever been in my life. But my father was still stronger than I, and he pulled it out. He looked at it in dead silence for a moment and then the storm broke. That was the famous Londermaine ring that had disappeared the night Alexandra Londermaine hung herself. That ring was worth a fortune. Where had I got it?

No one believed me when I said I had found it in the grounds near the house—I chose the grounds because I didn't want anybody to think I had been in the house or indeed that I was able to get in. I don't know why they didn't believe me; it still seems quite logical to me that I might have found it buried among the ferns.

It had been a long, dull year, and the men of the town were all bored. They took me and forced me to swallow quantities of corn liquor until I didn't know what I was saying or doing. When they had finished with me I didn't even manage to reach home before I was violently sick and then I was in my mother's arms and she was weeping over me. It was morning before I was able to slip away to the plantation house. I ran pounding up the mahogany stairs to the witch woman's room and opened the heavy sliding doors without knocking. She stood in the center of the room in her purple robe, her arms around Alexandra, who was weeping bitterly. Overnight the room had completely changed. The skeleton of Colonel Londermaine was gone, and books filled the shelves in the corner of the room that had been her laboratory. Cobwebs were everywhere, and broken glass lay on the floor; dust was inches thick on her worktable. There was no sign of Thammuz, Ashtaroth or Orus, or the fawn, but four birds were flying about her, beating their wings against her hair.

She did not look at me or in any way acknowledge my presence. Her arm about Alexandra, she led her out of the room and to the drawing room where the portrait hung. The birds followed, flying around and around them. Alexandra had stopped weeping now. Her face was very proud and pale, and if she saw me miserably trailing behind them she gave no notice. When the witch woman stood in front of the portrait the sheet fell from it. She raised her arm; there was a great cloud of smoke; the smell of sulphur filled my nostrils, and when the smoke was gone, Alexandra was gone, too. Only the portrait was there, the fourth finger of the left hand now bearing no ring. The witch woman raised her hand again and the sheet lifted itself up and covered the portrait. Then she went, with the birds, slowly back to what had once been her room, and still I tailed after, frightened as I had never been before in my life, or have been since.

She stood without moving in the center of the room for a long time. At last she turned and spoke to me.

"Well, boy, where is the ring?"

"They have it."

"They made you drunk, didn't they?"

"Yes."

"I was afraid something like this would happen when I gave Alexandra the ring. But it doesn't matter. . . . I'm tired. . . ." She drew her hand wearily across her forehead.

"Did I—did I tell them everything?"

"You did."

"I—I didn't know."

"I know you didn't know, boy."

"Do you hate me now?"

"No, boy, I don't hate you."

"Do you have to go away?"

"Yes."

I bowed my head. "I'm so sorry. . . ."

She smiled slightly. "The sands of time . . . cities crumble and rise and will crumble again and breath dies down and blows once more. . . ."

The birds flew madly about her head, pulling at her hair, calling into her ears. Downstairs we could hear a loud pounding, and then the crack of boards being pulled away from a window.

"Go, boy," she said to me. I stood rooted, motionless, unable to move. "*Go!*" she commanded, giving me a mighty push so that

POOR LITTLE SATURDAY

I stumbled out of the room. They were waiting for me by the cellar doors and caught me as I climbed out. I had to stand there and watch when they came out with her. But it wasn't the witch woman, my witch woman. It was *their* idea of a witch woman, someone thousands of years old, a disheveled old creature in rusty black, with long wisps of gray hair, a hooked nose, and four wiry black hairs springing out of the mole on her chin. Behind her flew the four birds, and suddenly they went up, up, into the sky, directly in the path of the sun until they were lost in its burning glare.

Two of the men stood holding her tightly, although she wasn't struggling but standing there, very quiet, while the others searched the house, searched it in vain. Then as a group of them went down into the cellar I remembered, and by a flicker of the old light in the witch woman's eyes I could see that she remembered, too. Poor Little Saturday had been forgotten. Out she came, prancing absurdly up the cellar steps, her rubbery lips stretched back over her gigantic teeth, her eyes bulging with terror. When she saw the witch woman, her lord and master, held captive by two dirty, insensitive men, she let out a shriek and began to kick and lunge wildly, biting, screaming with the blood-curdling, heart-rending screams that only a camel can make. One of the men fell to the ground, holding a leg in which the bone had snapped from one of Saturday's kicks. The others scattered in terror, leaving the witch woman standing on the veranda supporting herself by clinging to one of the huge wisteria vines that curled around the columns. Saturday clambered up onto the veranda and knelt while she flung herself between the two humps. Then off they ran, Saturday still screaming, her knees knocking together, the ground shaking as she pounded along. Down from the sun plummeted the four birds and flew after them.

Up and down I danced, waving my arms, shouting wildly

until Saturday and the witch woman and the birds were lost in a cloud of dust, while the man with the broken leg lay moaning on the ground beside me.

MADELEINE L'ENGLE *(1918–)* won the Newbery Medal in 1963 for *A Wrinkle in Time,* as well as an American Book Award in 1980 for *A Swiftly Tilting Planet.* Her other noteworthy books for young people include *A Ring of Endless Light* (1980), *The Arm of the Starfish* (1965), *The Young Unicorns* (1968), *Dragons in the Waters* (1976), *Meet the Austins* (1960), and *Summer of the Great-Grandmother* (1974).

LOIS LENSKI

THE CHRISTMAS FAKE

A poor family can't have a rich Christmas. But a poor Southern girl can demonstrate a richness of spirit. . . .

THE RIDLEYS' HOUSE STOOD all alone back in the great piney woods. From the blacktop highway, a shady road wandered in and out around pine trees and palmettos to get to it. Sometimes trucks and wagons got stuck in the loose sand and had to be jacked up before they could be pulled out.

Two old live oak trees stood near the house, with broken branches and streams of Spanish moss hanging. The unpainted house, built of vertical battens, had turned a dull gray from the ravages of wind and weather. It had a porch across the front and four rooms inside. Under the house, several wild hogs were rooting. Tangled, torn curtains hung at the windows and the front door stood wide open. Blocking the entrance lay three hound dogs outstretched. Their names were Trixie, Patches, and Jerry. Daddy insisted they were good watchdogs, but Mom said they were lazy and good-for-nothing.

Letty was ten, the oldest; Mike, seven; and little Punky, three. Besides Mom and Dad, there was Mom's sister, Aunt Vi, who spent most of her spare time with them. Mom didn't like living out in the backwoods so far from town, but the owner let them rent the house for almost nothing, so she tried to make the best of it.

The days were still as hot as midsummer. The only way anyone could tell that winter was coming was by the shortness of daylight. The sun seemed to set earlier every night. Just as soon as the big red ball slid down into the horizon, the dark dropped down like a heavy black curtain. The short days meant December, and December meant only one thing to the children. Christmas came to them in hot weather, not in cold. Christmas was green to them, never white. Having lived all their lives in the sunny South, they had never seen snow.

"How many days till Christmas?" asked Mike.

Letty, his sister, answered. First it was ten, then only seven, and now it was only one. Christmas was tomorrow.

"I want a doll and a buggy to ride her in," said little Punky.

"I want a bicycle and a BB gun and a football," said Mike.

"Forget it!" said Letty. "You won't get 'em."

"How do you know?" asked Mike.

"I asked Mom," said Letty. "She said there's no money for presents. I asked her if we could have a tree, and she said no money for a tree, either."

THE CHRISTMAS FAKE

"I'll ask Santa Claus," said Mike.

Letty stared at her brother. Mike was seven now. Did he still believe in Santa Claus?

"Mom said she's gonna take us to town to see Santa Claus," Mike went on. "He's coming in a helicopter, landing right in City Park. I'll ask him for what I want."

Letty felt sad. She hated to tell Mike the truth. Let him believe in Santa as long as he could.

"Don't you remember when the man came and took our TV away?" she began. "'Cause Daddy only made the first payment?"

"Yes, and I fought him," said Mike. "Then he told us we could have it back after . . . Daddy got a job."

"Daddy got a job," said Letty, "but it's way over on the east coast. He can't even get home for Christmas. We never got the TV back, either. Don't you know that, Mike?"

"Yes, but we will," said Mike. "Daddy told me so, the last time he was home."

"He's got a job, but still there's no money for anything," said Letty bitterly.

"I know that," said Mike. "So I'll just ask Santa Claus . . ."

It was hopeless, so Letty said no more.

Mom said they could all go to town that afternoon to see Santa Claus. She made them wash their faces and necks and ears and arms and put their feet in the tin tub to get them clean. She got out clean clothes for them and they put shoes and stockings on. Letty's dress was patched, but it held together.

The Ridleys did not have a car. Daddy drove to his new job on the east coast with a neighbor who worked there, too. They left early Monday morning and did not return till late Saturday.

It was only a mile to town, not too far, except when Punky went along and got tired and had to be carried. Today Aunt Vi came by in her Ford and picked Mom and the children up. Aunt

Vi had a job in an office in town. She typed letters for a real-estate man. She was having a few days off for Christmas.

When they got to town, Mom went with Aunt Vi to the beauty shop. Aunt Vi was to get a permanent, and Mom had to go to the supermarket for food. The children jumped out at Main Street. "Meet me at the bench at the corner," said Mom, "after Santa Claus leaves." It was too early for Santa Claus now, so Letty took Punky in the dime store. Mike saw some boys and went off with them.

How festive the little town looked! The light posts along the street were trimmed with tinsel and red paper bells. All the stores had Christmas decorations in their windows. From several, loudspeakers were blaring Christmas music. There were many shoppers going in and out. Everybody was happy because Christmas was coming.

Letty started down Main Street, pulling Punky by the hand. Punky broke loose and dashed on ahead. So Letty had to skip along fast to keep up. Inside the store, Punky ran down the aisle and picked things off the counters. Letty made her put them back and slapped her hands.

Letty had two dollars of her own in her pocket. She had earned it baby-sitting for the Boyers. They had four little ones under six and she often sat with them. She went to the jewelry counter. She wanted a pretty brass pin to wear on her shoulder. There were so many it was hard to choose. They were only twenty-five cents. If there wasn't going to be any Christmas at home, at least she could buy herself a present. She'd still have $1.75 left to help pay for that new coat she needed.

"Is that your little sister?" asked the clerk.

Letty heard a child crying but did not look up.

"Yes," she said. "She bothers the daylights out of me. Keeps me runnin' my legs off. I get mad at her. I take her by the arm and jerk her."

"Better watch her now," said the clerk. "She's helping herself to a doll. Guess she's too little to know you have to pay for things in here."

"Do you know what I do to make her mind?" asked Letty.

"No," said the clerk, "but you'd better do it quick."

"I spank her," said Letty. "Not when my mother's around, of course. I spank her with my hand—hard, too!"

She rushed over to Punky, took the doll out of her hand, and spanked her. Punky screamed and stamped her foot.

"Now you keep still," said Letty, "or I'll take you home."

Letty dragged her back to the jewelry counter.

"Does spanking make her better?" asked the clerk.

"Well, no," said Letty. "The more I spank her, the more I have to spank her."

Punky ran back to the doll counter. She picked up the doll again.

"She really wants that doll," said the clerk.

"Oh, she wants everything she sees," said Letty. "She's always saying 'gimme, gimme. . . .'"

Punky called out: "I want it, Letty, I want it. . . ."

"Well, you can't have it!" answered Letty. She bent over the jewelry counter again. Should she get the flying bird or the butterfly? The brooches were all so pretty, she could not decide which one she liked best.

"Has she got a doll at home?" asked the clerk.

"No," said Letty. "She's had dozens, but she breaks 'em all up."

"She ought to have one," said the clerk. "Why don't you buy that doll for her? Then maybe you could keep her quiet. A little girl like that needs a doll to love and play with."

Letty looked up, startled. What business was it of the clerk's? She opened her purse. In that moment, she had an important decision to make. She looked across to the toy counter, where

Punky was holding up the doll. It was just a cheap one. She saw its price tag—49¢. Then she looked down at the butterfly brooch in her hand.

"I'll take this," she said. She handed the clerk a quarter.

The clerk made no comment. She put the brooch in a small paper bag and rang up the money.

Letty rushed over and jerked Punky away from the toy counter. Punky began to cry. "I want a dolly. . . . I want my mama . . . . I wanna go home. . . ."

The clerk came over and spoke again: "Do you ever read her a story? Or take her for a ride in her little wagon?"

"What wagon?" Letty stared at the clerk. "Punky hasn't got any little wagon."

"She'd be a pretty little girl," said the clerk, "if you'd wash her face."

"She bothers the daylights out of me," said Letty.

Out on the sidewalk, Punky was still crying. Letty leaned over and wiped her tears away.

"Do you want to see Santa Claus?" Letty asked.

"Yes," said Punky.

"We'll go see Santa Claus, and you can ask him for a dolly," said Letty. "Tell him you want a great big doll as big as a baby . . . ."

Punky smiled. "As big as a baby," she said.

The little City Park was crowded now, with children of all sizes and ages. Men from the Jaycees were herding them into a long line.

"Get in line! Take your turn!" the men shouted.

Overhead, a loud buzzing sound could be heard. The children's eyes all turned toward the sky. There, coming closer and closer, was a helicopter. It slowed up, then came straight down in a roped-off open spot. The door opened and Santa Claus stepped out. He was very fat, dressed in a bright red suit, and he had a white mustache and a long white beard. The children screamed with delight.

Letty looked over the crowd and finally spotted Mike. She called to him. Mike made his way over to her and they waited their turn, holding Punky tightly by the hands. Once Letty lifted Punky up so she could see Santa Claus.

The children in the line asked for everything under the sun from bicycles, typewriters, and pianos to parakeets, rabbits, and turtles. The line moved slowly toward the big fat Santa Claus.

"We're next!" said Letty, pushing Mike forward.

Mike never forgot for a minute.

"I want a bicycle, a BB gun, and a football," he said in a loud voice.

Santa patted him on the back.

"I'll do what I can for you, son," he said and shoved him along. "Who's next?"

Now it was Punky's turn. She stared at the big fat man and his white whiskers, half frightened.

Letty leaned over. "Say what you want, Punky," she prompted. "Tell him you want a buggy and a doll...."

"I want..." began Punky. "I want *a great big doll as big as a baby!*"

Santa laughed. "You be a good girl, now," he said, "and I'll try to get it for you, honey."

Then he turned to Letty.

"You're too old..." he began.

"I want a watch!" said Letty emphatically. "Not a Mickey Mouse one—I'm too big for that. A real one, I want this time. That's the only thing I want. I don't care if I get candy or anything else—just a wristwatch!"

Santa eyed her coldly.

"What if you don't get it?" he said.

Letty shrugged. "I'll be satisfied with what I get, even if it's nothing. That's all I can do, I reckon."

But Santa was not listening. He had shoved her quickly aside. He was beaming and smiling and making rash promises to all the children coming behind.

When they got out of the crowd, Letty said to Mike, "Oh, I hate that guy!"

"Who?" said Mike.

"That fool of a Santa Claus," said Letty.

Mike's eyes opened wide.

"Why, he's going to bring us"—Mike began—"the things we asked for!"

"Oh, no, he's not!" cried Letty angrily. "He's tellin' lies—to all the kids in town, makin' them believe he'll bring them anything they ask for!"

Mike's face turned white. "You mean . . . ?"

Punky began to cry.

Letty did not stop there.

"Santa Claus is just a fake—a big Christmas *fake!*" she said. "I don't believe anything like that. Three years ago I knew it. I got up that Christmas Eve night to see Santa, and it wasn't him. It was Grandma. I saw her—not even Daddy—puttin' presents out."

The sparkle in Mike's eyes faded as they filled with tears.

Then suddenly Mom and Aunt Vi came up and Aunt Vi told them where the car was parked.

"Did you tell Santa what you want?" asked Aunt Vi.

"Yes," said Punky. "He said he's gonna bring me a dolly."

"I asked for a bike," said Mike, soberly, "but he don't have to bring it if he don't want to."

Letty lagged behind.

She looked around sharply. Mom and Aunt Vi had no pack-

THE CHRISTMAS FAKE

ages under their arms and she saw none in Aunt Vi's car. They had gone shopping but had bought nothing. Santa Claus was just a fake, and so was Christmas. Now she was sure of it.

"I'm gonna walk home," she told Mom.

"Okay," said Mom. "Better get there by supper time if you want anything to eat."

Letty walked slowly home, with a heavy heart. She hated the decorations on the street now and the sound of the Christmas music. What good was it all? There would be no Christmas at home. Mom had told her so. The only promise Mom made was, if Dad got the day off, they might eat out and go to a show. Whenever they ate out, Letty took two hot dogs and ice cream. What fun was that?

Letty came to a vacant lot where Christmas trees were being sold. A young man came rushing out and tried to urge her to buy a tree.

What good was a Christmas tree?

Then Letty stopped in her tracks. Maybe . . . maybe they could have a tree, at least. It would be better than no Christmas at all. There was a box of shiny balls and a string of electric lights left over from a couple of years before. She knew just where they were, on the bottom shelf of the kitchen cupboard.

Why not have a tree . . . with lights on it?

It would be better than nothing. Especially if there were no presents. Punky would like the pretty lights if she couldn't have a doll-baby.

But the trees were not cheap.

"Two dollars each," said the man, holding one up.

"It's too big," said Letty. "Have you got a smaller one?"

The man found a smaller one, but it was two dollars, too.

Letty looked in her purse. All she had left was $1.75. If only she hadn't bought the brooch.

"You got a car?" asked the man. "Where'll I take it?"

"I'm walking," said Letty. "I'll carry it."

The man laughed as if it was a big joke.

"Carry it?" he cried. "A skinny little kid like you?"

Now he was more friendly.

"I'll tell you what I'll do," he said. He found a nice tree for her. "This one's a little lopsided, but you can have it for one-fifty. That'll leave you twenty-five cents for a taxi. Here's a taxi now."

A man got out of the taxi and Letty got in with her tree. The man called, "Merry Christmas!" after her. The taxi driver took her and the tree home for twenty-five cents.

It was nearly dark when she got there. Days were short now in December, and night clamped down early. The three dogs were on the porch as usual, Trixie, Patches, and Jerry. They slept on the porch to keep burglars away.

Now they thought Letty was a burglar. They barked and barked as she came up, pulling the tree behind her. Now everybody would see it. Letty had hoped supper would be over and Punky and Mike in bed and, of course, Dad not home yet. Dad was not coming home for Christmas! She wanted to set the tree up in the front room and surprise them all.

But they were all there eating supper—Aunt Vi, too; of course, not Dad. Punky had fallen asleep on the couch. Mom called to Letty but Letty was too excited now to eat supper. She put up the tree all by herself. She found Dad's hammer and fixed a brace at the bottom to keep it from falling over. She found the lights and the cord and put them on. She tied the shiny balls on. She turned the switch and the tree looked beautiful.

Then Punky woke up. How surprised she was to see a tree with lights on it! On Christmas Eve, too!

Punky danced around the tree and tripped over the light cord. She grabbed the cord and pulled it. The lights went out.

Punky pulled the colored balls off. She dropped one of them and broke it.

Letty took Punky and spanked her.

She plugged the cord in again and put the balls back on.

At least it was something for Christmas.

Letty was tired now and felt like going to bed. She reached for a hot dog off the table and gulped it down. It was all she wanted to eat. She wasn't hungry.

She and Mike looked at each other. They looked round the house. There were no signs of Christmas—except the tree.

"I paid all my baby-sitting money for it!" Letty bragged.

Mom scolded. "You were saving for a new coat. You need a coat more than we need a tree."

Letty turned to Mike. "Tomorrow's Christmas. No presents anywhere. Didn't I tell you?" she whispered.

It was in the middle of the night when Daddy came and wakened them. That is, it seemed like the middle of the night. It was really six in the morning.

"Merry Christmas! Merry Christmas!" shouted Daddy. When did he come? How did he get there? Did he get an unexpected day off?

Dad was wheeling a bike. Where had it come from?

"But, Mom!" cried Letty. She rubbed her eyes as if she'd been dreaming. "You said there was no money. . . ."

Mike was so happy, he did not ask where the bike came from. He did not notice that it was scuffed and secondhand. It was a bike at last.

Mom was opening a big box beside her. She took a small one out and handed it to Letty. Letty opened it. There lay a wristwatch —a real one, not a Mickey Mouse one. Letty could not believe her eyes.

"So you won't miss the school bus," said Mom.

Letty threw her arms around Mom's neck. Then she hugged Dad.

"You are both *fakes!*" she cried. "Mom said there was no money . . . and that Dad couldn't get home. . . ."

Best of all was Punky's doll. It had blue eyes that closed, yellow curls, and white teeth. It was as big as a baby, as big as Punky could hold. She walked up and down, patting the doll and singing to it.

Letty plugged in the lights on the tree. Dad stared. "Where on earth did *that* come from?"

Letty still could not understand. She looked from Mom to Dad. How did they find out about the bike and the watch and the doll? She forgot that she and Mike and Punky had been talking about what they wanted for weeks in advance.

Mike had the answer.

"Santa Claus brought them," he said.

Suddenly Letty thought of something. She ran into the bedroom and came out with a little box. She took out the beautiful butterfly brooch. She had wanted it for herself, but now it was Christmas, so she knew what she wanted to do. She'd give it to Mom.

She turned to Mom and pinned it on her shoulder.

"Merry Christmas, Mom!" she said.

"What! For *me?*" cried Mom.

Mom kissed her and they all said, "Merry Christmas!"

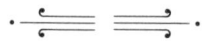

LOIS LENSKI (1893–1974) won the Newbery Medal in 1946 for *Strawberry Girl*. Her other honors include the Child Study Association of America Award in 1948 and the Regina Medal in 1969.

Enormously prolific, she wrote dozens of popular books, including *Indian Captive: The Story of Mary Jemison* (a Newbery Honor Book in 1942), *Phebe Fairchild* (a Newbery Honor Book in 1937), *Cowboy Small* (1949), *Prairie School* (1951), and *Lois Lenski's Christmas Stories* (1968).

CORNELIA MEIGS

THE SAMPLER

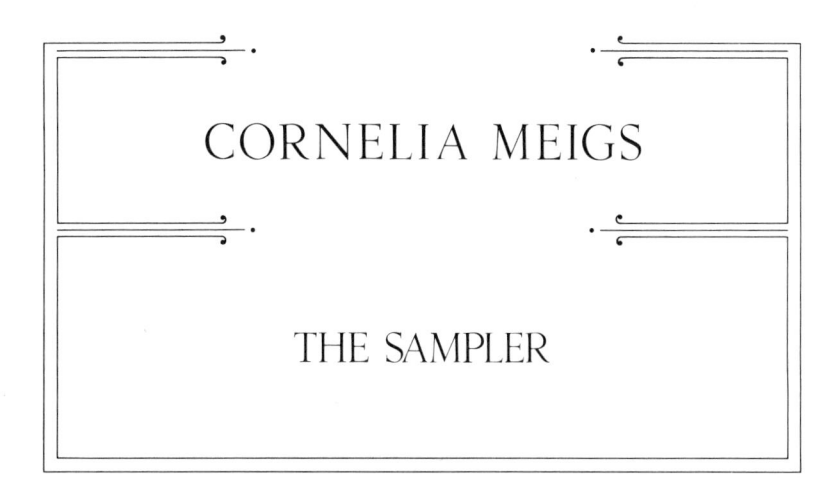

Sometimes it is more of a challenge to prove you are an adult than to become one. But fourteen-year-old Elizabeth has all kinds of courage....

BECAUSE THE LLOYDS' household was a very regular one, Elizabeth sat down every afternoon at exactly the same hour to sew on her sampler. Sewing was no easy task for an active girl who liked to be doing other things. But nobody, of course, ever thought of excusing her from it or ever dreamed of her growing up without having covered at least one square of linen with neat letters and figures.

The sampler was supposed to give her practice in all the different stitches of embroidery. Below the alphabet and the figures up to ten it showed a small, carefully outlined picture of a willow tree and a tombstone. It was to be finished with her name and a motto such as THE GOOD DIE YOUNG or WASTE NOT, WANT NOT.

There was so much to do in that thick-walled stone house, looking from its low hill out upon the bay, that there was no real time during the day when any older person could say with reason, "Elizabeth, you should be at your sewing." But when candlelight came—when the baking and sweeping, the dressing of chickens, and the curing of hams could not go forward so quickly by the dimmer light, then it was that her mother always said, "Now, Elizabeth," and the girl knew the sampler could not be avoided. It never occurred to her to hate it; she only knew that she liked doing anything else a great deal better.

She had sat down to it this October evening, with a wild wind swinging about the house and making the waves crash upon the shore below the hill. Elizabeth was alone, or almost alone; for her father and mother had driven five miles to the nearest town for the weekly marketing and had left Elizabeth with only deaf old Nora, the cook, who as everyone knew would fall asleep in her rocking chair in the little room above the kitchen the moment the last of the work was finished.

Not even the wind that blew in around the deep-framed windows, setting the candles to flickering—not even the slamming of the shutters—could rouse her. But as Elizabeth paused to slip the end of a thread into the slim eye of her needle there came a sound that, it seemed, would wake any sleeper on earth. *Boom!*

The great crash sounded from out on the water, where just at twilight she had looked out to see the smooth surface of the bay with not even a fishing boat in sight. *Boom!* This time all the windows in the house rattled and the glasses clattered on the dresser. *Boom!* the sound came a third time.

Elizabeth jumped up and ran to the window. What could it

be? This was a time of peace, the year of 1810. It had been thirty years since the guns of the Revolution had echoed along those shores, and it would be two more years before another war was to break out between England and America.

She wondered for a puzzled minute if it could be pirates. It was quite true that pirates had landed on this coast within the memory of people not very much older than herself. She pressed her face against the pane, trying to peer out. How black it was outside!

Yet there beyond the point was the ghostly form of a ship, dark against the duller darkness of the water. It was a bigger ship than those that usually came up the bay. She saw a great flash of red flame as once again a cannon crashed, and against its light she could make out, near the shore and struggling on the top of a towering wave, the dark shape of a small boat with three men in it.

The blackness shut down again and there was nothing to be heard except the roaring of the wind. Then in a moment of brief calm there came a sound more surprising than any she had yet heard—a voice, little and distant, calling out, calling her own name.

"Elizabeth! Elizabeth Lloyd!"

She rushed to the door, lifted the latch, and immediately felt the wind snatch it from her hand and swing it wide, letting in a driving splatter of rain. Old Nora had actually been awakened by the cannon shots, which shook the house, and was thumping down the stairs. Elizabeth stood on the sill, holding back the door so that all the light that was possible would come shining out upon the darkness of the night.

The men in the boat needed a signal to guide them to the strip of beach just below the house. Her flash of light seemed to have shown them the direction; for she was almost certain that she heard, in another quiet moment, the sound of the bow on the gravel. She waited. How the wind roared!

Again there was a crash of the ship's cannon, its report followed a moment later by the splitting of wood. Voices and the tramp of feet were coming up the path. Somebody said, "They got our boat that time." And a deeper voice answered: "It's lucky we were no longer in it. Go easy there, mate; he's too tired to move another step." Three figures came out of the darkness, two of them supporting a third. The little group stumbled across the doorstep and stood blinking in the light of the warm kitchen.

Elizabeth closed the door against the rain and, as is always the duty of a hostess when guests come in out of the cold and wet, bent to put another log on the fire. One did that and then asked questions. But when she straightened up to look at the unexpected visitors, she had no need to ask. She cried out quickly, "Why, it's Cousin Nathaniel!"

"We thought this must be my uncle's house and that you at least would hear our hail."

Her cousin Nathaniel Holmes was only a year or two older than her own fourteen years; but he looked like a man indeed with his tall figure, his white, tired face, and his rough seaman's coat.

The broad-shouldered man beside him said in a big, friendly voice, "'Tis a shame to frighten you, young mistress, but men who are fleeing for their lives will take shelter anywhere."

"You did not frighten me," she answered bravely.

They were helping their comrade into the armchair in which she had been sitting. When once the tall man with graying hair had dropped back on the cushions, her cousin Nat stooped, picked something off the floor, and handed it to her.

"Your sampler, Elizabeth," he said with a broad smile. "I know how you love to sew, and I see how prettily you have made the tombstone. I fear you are to be badly interrupted in your favorite work this night. You wonder why we are here? Have you ever heard men speak of the custom of the British Navy—that of taking seamen by force?"

She had indeed, and her cheeks colored angrily as she thought of it. All America was excited over this same matter, which was to end by leading two friendly nations into war with each other. England had need of sailors and gunners for her warships, and since the life on board was hard, cruel, and dangerous, very few men would offer themselves for it. As a result the officers were ordered by their government to take men where they could, and take them they did.

They had fallen into the way of stopping American vessels at sea, searching them, and declaring that certain able seamen were really British and must be carried on board English ships to serve in His Majesty's Navy. It was of little use for the American captains to fight against them. The English battleships always had a row of cannon with which to back up their demands. Many a good man was rowed away and taken on board a proud, tall-sailed English vessel, each looking back to his own ship and to his comrades, whom perhaps he was never to see again. But here it seemed were three, at least, who had dared to refuse and had made this bold effort to escape.

"Yes," Nat said, looking up to answer the question in Elizabeth's eyes, "they took us all three, though Bo'sun Leonard here is an old sailor, and though I am not yet a real seaman, for I sailed only six months ago. We swore to one another that we were not going to fight for the British king."

He held out his thin, cold hands to the blaze, saying no more, for he did not seem to think it was necessary to tell just what they had done. It was the broad-shouldered man, Dan Peters, who finished the account. He gave it in the most matter-of-fact way in the world. It was plain to see that all three were too weary to think of much of anything except that they were warm and safe here, at least for a few minutes.

Peters told of how they were carried away in a boat with four British sailors and a lieutenant, all armed with pistols and heavy swords. They made Peters pull an oar in the middle of the boat; but as they came near the towering side of the British vessel he saw, to his amazement, that Nat had leaped up to seize the officer around the middle, pinning his arms so that he could not draw his sword. The brief, hard struggle ended in the lieutenant's being flung overboard, while the two older Americans each fought with the sailor nearest him.

"We swung them over the side like sacks of gravel," Peters related cheerfully. "They were so taken by surprise that they had no time to fight. The last one jumped to save us the trouble, and we caught up the oars and slipped away into the twilight, for it was just beginning to get dark. All those we dropped overboard got to the ship, and before she could get her cannon aimed at us we were in among the islands. But we didn't dare land anywhere along these swampy shores."

The war vessel had followed, most of the shots from it going wide in the dark, but a few of them were good guesses that almost hit their mark. Higher and higher up the bay they had come, the men in the boat fighting so hard against wind and tide that Leonard, the old sailor, was fainting at the oars, and even the other two could scarcely lift and dip the heavy blades.

"Then we saw your light."

Old Nora, like Elizabeth, had without a word turned herself to caring for the comfort of the guests. She brought a great bowl of stew from the cupboard, poured it into a big iron kettle, and hung the kettle on the swinging hook. Nat helped her to lift it, and she nodded thanks and greeting to him, but she asked no questions. She had been deaf so long that she was used to the idea of not having things explained to her. She trotted back and forth, casting curious looks at the weary and dripping guests, but she stirred and seasoned the soup, cut bread from the long loaf, and said nothing. Elizabeth, however, kept no such silence.

"What will you do next?" she asked, looking from one to the other.

They were all three quiet, so that the beat of the rain outside and the harsh voice of the wind were the only sounds. The storm roared, then dropped an instant, and in the stillness there came to all of them the sound that no person who lives by the sea can ever fail to recognize—the creak of oars in their oarlocks. Even Bo'sun Leonard, sitting with closed eyes in the big chair, heard it and raised his drooping head.

"It's only a matter of minutes before they'll be here." It was the first time he had spoken, but his words were quick and very clear. "They can't fail to visit the only house that's in sight. You're to go on, you two. Do you hear me? That's orders. I can't move; but you're to get away, and I will stay here."

It is the habit of every sailor to obey the commands of his superior. Nat and Peters hesitated a minute. Then Nat turned suddenly to the door of the bedroom opening from the kitchen. "Carry him in there," he said. "There's no time even to get him upstairs. And by some chance they may not search the house."

They lifted Leonard, bore him into the room, and laid him on the bed. He did not speak again or even open his eyes, but he made an impatient motion with his hand. They were to go.

"If we could get across the hill to the Mallorys' house," Nat said, "we could get Ephraim Mallory and his three sons to stand by us, that I know. We could make a dash back and get Leonard away safe, even if the British had already laid hands on him. But if harm should come to you, Elizabeth—"

"No harm will come to us—two women who have done

nothing," Elizabeth answered boldly, more boldly than she felt. "We will keep them back as long as we can." She put her mouth close to Nora's ear and shouted. "We are going to have still more guests. Pile up the fire and bring out the biggest ham."

Nat hesitated a moment in the doorway. Peters said, as he went through the door, "And if they do follow us, little mistress, would you try to flash a light at the window, maybe, if you could do it without danger? Then we would know where to make a stand." The door banged, and Elizabeth was left in the kitchen, listening.

The wind, roaring over the hill, drowned the noise of their retreating steps, but in the shelter of the house another sound began to be very plain, the heavy, orderly tramp of marching feet coming up from the landing—many of them, it seemed, oh, very many. Then there were voices, a thundering knock, and a command, "Open, in the king's name."

They all came in together—a tall officer wrapped in a dripping cape, a file of men behind him, their shoes, their hair, their rough blue coats streaming with the rain.

Elizabeth made her most polite curtsy, just as she had seen her mother do when important guests arrived. "My parents are from home," she said calmly, "but we shall do our best to make you comfortable. You—you look as though you might be in need of refreshment."

The officer—it might possibly have been the same lieutenant whom Nat had thrown out of the boat—swung his rapid glance about the room. The big, spotless kitchen was bright with the leaping fire and its reflection in the polished copper pots and pans. Elizabeth was laying a white cloth on the long table. Nora had unwrapped the ham and was already cutting delicate, rosy slices. The officer looked, hesitated, and then sat down in the big chair.

"The men will march better if they have some food," he said.

"That was a long row we had, searching along the shore. Dobbs, go out and see that guards are placed around the house. If there is anyone hiding here it will be impossible to get away while they are watching. We may as well give ourselves the relief of a little warmth and food and look for those runaway rascals later on. Well, young woman, let me see what your house has to offer."

It was a splendid feast that the old farmhouse gave its guests that night. The whitest linen out of the great chest in the parlor, the glass dishes and the blue plates that had come from England with Elizabeth's great grandmother, the polished silver spoons were all brought forth. The choicest preserves, the last vegetables from the garden, the ham cured by a recipe a hundred years old made a supper fit for King George III himself instead of one of his lower and lazier officers. "Have you this?" the blue-uniformed man would ask now and again. "Do you not have that?"

"In a minute, sir; in just a minute," Elizabeth would answer. She lingered over the serving as long as she dared, she ducked curtsies when she received an order, she did everything to make the meal last a little longer.

Nora went back and forth, waiting on the men who sat humbly upon the benches by the fire while their commander dined alone at the long table. It was fortunate that farmhouses of that day had generous supplies in their storerooms. A large company it was, ten men, with even larger appetites.

The minutes went by, oh, so slowly. Nat and his comrade would be across the farm, Elizabeth was thinking; they would be climbing the hill; once over the top they would be within reach of the Mallory's house. How long, how very long it took to reach shelter on this stormy night. But time was passing. Triumph colored her cheeks. They were growing safer every minute, safer. . . .

"And now," ordered the British officer, pushing his chair

back suddenly, "I have even a mind to lay me down to take a little rest before I start out in the storm again. Light me a candle. I will go into the bedroom yonder and sleep a little."

No! Oh, no! Elizabeth had almost cried out the words in her terror, but she put her hand over her mouth and held them back. "We have better rooms above," she managed to say, her voice shaking, "if it would please you just to walk up the stairs."

"In an American farmhouse the best bed is always in the spare chamber below," he answered stubbornly. "I have been on shore often enough to learn that." He yawned widely and got up. "In our wandering life we must learn how to sleep comfortably when we can."

He walked across the kitchen. Elizabeth had lighted the candle and stood shaking, holding out her arm to bar the door. How, how could she stop him? She looked hopefully past him to old Nora beside the fire. Could not Nora think of something? But no, what did she understand?

The officer stopped, staring at her as she barred the way. His heavy brows drew together in a suspicious frown. "What is this? You have, after all, something hidden in that room? Out of my way!" He stepped forward.

Old Nora dropped a spoon with a great clatter. She took one limping step across the floor and flung the kitchen door wide open. "Don't waste time," she cried in her trembling old voice. "It was that way they went. Can't you see the marks of their feet beyond the doorstone? Go, if you have any hope of catching them."

There was a thump of heavy feet, a clash of swords drawn, a hail of orders as the men jumped up, seized their arms, and swung toward the door. The officer snatched up his cloak. "Why did you not tell me this before?" he roared at Nora.

"Eh? I'm so deaf, how was I to know your errand? Nobody

tells me anything." He was over the sill, but he swung around on the doorstep to give a final order.

"Dobbs, stand here and do not let either of these women pass. Keep three men to guard the windows so that they cannot make a signal. Do not follow us until we are well away." He was gone, and the door slammed behind him.

Elizabeth stood for a second trembling, wondering what she should do next. Then she seized a lantern from its hook on the wall, lighted it at the fire, and sped up the stairs. The door as well as the windows was guarded, but the men would not be watching that little round opening, hardly a real window, just above the roof of the kitchen.

She was beside it; she had wrapped her skirt about the lantern to hide its light; and she had climbed out through the space, which was little bigger than the porthole of a ship. The shingles on the roof below were wet and slippery, but she knew how to run across them, knew that she must keep running or she would fall. She ended, with a bump, against the great stone chimney. Steadying herself with one arm against the warm, rough stones, she made her way around the chimney and was on the peak of the kitchen roof, facing the distant hill.

Fearlessly she swung the lantern once, and again and again. A deep voice below shouted to her to stop. She took no notice, and suddenly a humming bullet went past her and hit against the chimney. The crash of the big pistol would give warning, even if the swinging light was not enough. Nat and his companion would know that the British were coming behind them. The lantern fell from her hand and broke on the stones below, but she had given her wild signal of danger and could do no more.

It had taken but a few seconds to run across the roof, but now it was slow minutes as she crawled back in the wind and the wet. Once inside and downstairs, she stood close to Nora by the fire.

Her knees felt suddenly like water and her voice was trembling.

"Nora," she said close to the old woman's ear, "how could you tell them where Nat had gone?"

"It was better to give the old one a chance, even at the cost of a bit of danger to the young ones," answered Nora. "Yes, you told me nothing, but it did not take me long to guess what was going on. I saw the Revolution; I've been by before this when hunted men were hiding from their enemies." She drew a great breath and smoothed her apron. "Sakes, but we have a lot of dishes to wash up. Men do be great ones for messing a kitchen!"

Elizabeth was not of much help in setting the place to rights. Again and again she stood at the back door, straining to hear any sound that the wind might carry. Was that a distant shout and another? What was that? Voices that were far-off. They were nearer; they were coming this way. Had they taken her cousin? Would they in the end lay hands on poor Bo'sun Leonard, lying helpless within? Oh, Nat! Oh, Nat!

There was shouting and stumbling before the door. It swung back, and a dripping figure, sword in hand, was on the doorstep. Here was no blue coat or gold lace; here was no heavy British seaman. This thin, long figure could be only one person—her cousin Nat!

Nathaniel threw his weapon down upon the table, where there were still standing the dishes and glasses that had been used for the lieutenant's dinner.

"'Tis the wrong men who have feasted in this house tonight," he said. "Such a dinner! And we out there in the dark, hungry! May the Mallory boys come in?"

There was enough left; for the farmhouse could feed one company and still have plenty remaining for another. Nora, smiling broadly, brought them more and more food; the fire leaped on the hearth, and everyone together tried to give an account of what had happened. Nat and Peters were just coming over the hill with the Mallorys behind them when they saw Elizabeth's signal and found a favorable place to make a stand against the advancing British.

"They could not guess our numbers in the dark, and they decided, after the first attack, to retreat to their boat," Nat said. "They will have a pretty row out to their ship, for she has had to stand offshore in this wind. Here's a pleasant journey to them, and may they take profit by the lesson they have learned. It is not well to lay hands on American seamen."

"The whole British nation may learn an even better one in time," Dan Peters added; but most of his remark was lost in the hollow of the cup of cider he had raised to his lips.

It was easy to see by looking at Bo'sun Leonard that he must stay where he was for many days. Perhaps, indeed, he would never be able to go to sea again. But the other two stood up at last and said good night.

"We have to join our ship," Nathaniel said. "Our skipper will be in need of sailors, and he was to stop at Norfolk, where we can meet him." The night's adventures seemed to mean little to men whose days and hours were passed among the dangers of the sea. "No, we can spend no more time except to offer you our thanks, Elizabeth Lloyd."

Two hours later Elizabeth's father and mother came home. Their daughter was sitting by the table, quietly stitching away at the task that she had begun so much earlier. She looked up as her parents came in.

"There is a guest in the spare chamber," she remarked calmly, "and there have been others here to supper. And see, Mother, I have finished my willow tree. Instead of the verse at the bottom I am going to embroider LIBERTY FOREVER. And then I am never going to sew another sampler. I think, now that I am fourteen, that I have other things to do besides stitching pictures of tombstones."

CORNELIA MEIGS (1884-1973) won the Newbery Medal in 1934 for *Invincible Louisa*. Her other honors include a Drama League Prize in 1915 and the Jane Addams Award in 1971. Her many books for children include three Newbery Honor Books: *Windy Hill* (1922), *Clearing Weather* (1929), and *Swift Rivers* (1933). She also wrote an important survey book, *A Critical History of Children's Literature* (revised edition, 1969).

EMILY CHENEY NEVILLE

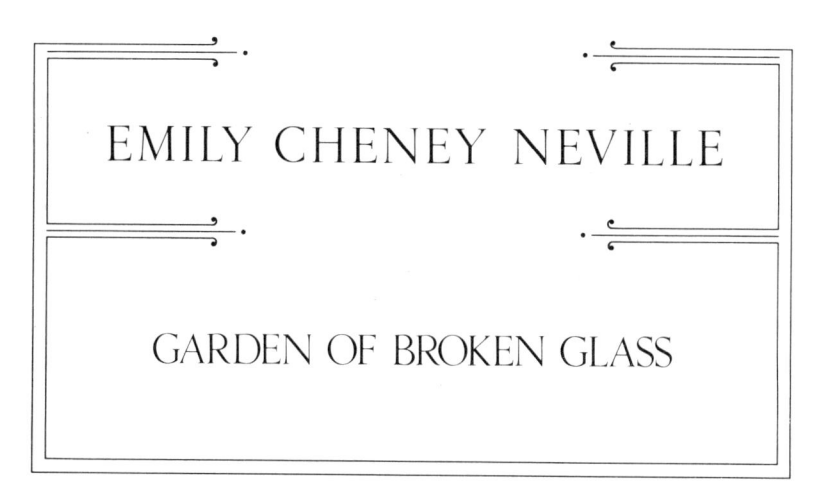

GARDEN OF BROKEN GLASS

In a world of drugs and violence, the aftermath of a moral mistake is often worse than the act. . . .

A<small>FTER SCHOOL</small> let out, Dwayne got down to painting the part of the house he and Brian had scraped. His father said, "Where yo' skinny little friend? He need another meal—you better get him to help you."

"I didn't see him in a while," Dwayne said. "I don't know where he live. Jus' have to wait till he turn up again." Actually, he didn't mind painting alone, and he wanted to earn as much money as he could. By the Fourth of July weekend, he had the job all done. The ladder and paint were put away and the yard all raked.

"There! Now it be lookin' pretty when your gran'mama come," his mother said.

His father paid him ten dollars and offered to drive them all to Six Flags Park on Sunday. Melvita came along, and for once Dwayne could spend money freely. By the end of the day, he'd spent it all, but he didn't let Melvita know that.

Melvita had never been out of the city in a car before. She exclaimed over everything—the interstate highway, and the billboards and factories, and train cars alongside the highway piled high with automobiles. As they came back into the suburbs close to St. Louis, she sat up straight and pointed. "Man, lookit all the parks they got and all them big houses!"

"That ain't no park, girl! It jus' the backyard go with that house."

"Backyard? They playin' baseball in there!"

"So? They rich folks, don't you know that?"

"Mmm, that what I want when I get my house. I'm goin' to have me a big backyard, and you can play baseball in it, and I look out the window, and I know where you be, all the time!"

"Them houses ain't for people like us."

"I know." She sighed and leaned against him and closed her eyes.

After a few minutes, she opened her eyes and looked at Dwayne. "Hey—how they figure out who goin' to get the big house with the baseball field, and who goin' to get the house with the plaster cracked and the broken glass out back? How they decide that, huh?"

Up front, Dwayne's father laughed shortly. "Some cats make all the rules. They the ones get the big houses, don't you worry, girl!"

Melvita sat up straight and set her chin. "Well, then, when I grow up, I goin' to be there when they make the rules."

"They don't let chicks make laws," Dwayne scoffed.

"You wait. They didn' see me yet!"

Dwayne, in spite of himself, looked at her admiringly. "Yeah, they see you comin', they better get under the seat!"

"Right on, brother!" Melvita settled back comfortably in the seat again. "What you goin' to do next week, Dwayne?"

There it was, the same old question. Automatically, Dwayne answered, "Hunt me a job."

The next week passed, and he did a few jobs for neighbors, raking a yard, hauling some trash, repairing a back step, but he hardly made more money than he spent every night at Happy Jack's. On Saturday, his mother kept him busy around the house all morning, and then she gave him two quarters. He went away scowling, thinking, *That ain't pay, that jus' a handout.* Then he felt bad, because she was his mother, and he knew she didn't have money to spare.

He walked away from home, over toward the park. The boys were playing ball in there, but Dwayne walked past stiff-faced. He was still angry about the hassle the day before. They had ruled him out on a base, when he knew he was safe. He was the pitcher, and they should have known he was right. They could just see who they'd get to pitch now—he wasn't going to play.

He saw Melvita and Martha sitting on a bench in the playground. He could always tell Melvita's funny hair sticking up, with a piece of yarn tied in it. He felt good, thinking she was his girl. He jingled the two quarters in his pocket—at least he'd have something to spend with her that night.

Meanwhile, there was all day to spend, and he wasn't going to spend it sitting in the park baby-sitting. He walked on past the city hospital and the project houses. He looked up at them, with all the broken windows gaping or boarded up, and he was glad he didn't live there.

They had a big new recreation building down there, though, on Twelfth Avenue. *Maybe I get in a game down there,* he thought. *I can pitch better than them project dudes.*

He sauntered alongside the field, as if he wasn't much interested, and yelled to a boy he knew, a little guy built like a monkey, "Hey, Calvin! You winnin'?"

"What else? Man, I don't lose! You wanta play?"

"I don't care. Ain't got my glove."

"Wait till next inning. I tell Mole."

Calvin used to live near Dwayne, and they used to hang out together then. Calvin used to catch when Dwayne pitched.

Mole was the dude pitching on this team. Dwayne knew him by sight. He was a couple of years older, and ba-ad! Dwayne felt the skin on the back of his neck prickling, and he thought, *That one cat I won't never mess with. I don't tell him I be the pitcher.*

At the end of the inning, Mole's team was gathered in their dugout. Mole stood there, slapping the ball into his glove, but his eyes ranged over the field, the other players, and Dwayne. Dwayne let their eyes meet but kept his own bland and expressionless while he joked with a boy near him. Mole could think what he wanted about him.

"Hey, Willie!" Mole called. It was an order. "This cat Dwayne going to play third base for a while. Loan him your glove."

"Good, I done been out in this sun long enough," Willie said, and he tossed his glove to Dwayne.

Third base, Dwayne thought, *that ain't my spot.* But when they went out in the field, he got the picture: Mole could watch him all the time. A runner got to second and Mole's eyes bored in on him, testing, seeing if he would get nerved up. Mole pegged the ball to him, hard, but Dwayne caught it easily, tossed it home, kicked his base carelessly. On the next play, he got the runner out.

They played a few more innings, and Mole's team won. Everyone was hot, so they went into the rec building for drinks. Dwayne got a soda and a candy bar, and then he and Calvin played Ping-Pong.

"Pretty nice joint you got here," Dwayne said.

"Yeah, we going to have us a basketball team in winter. You play?"

"I might. I see if I can fit it in!" Dwayne grinned and served the Ping-Pong ball. He won the game.

Mole sauntered up and watched the last few points. Calvin laid down his paddle, and Mole said, "You settin' up to be champ?"

"If you say so," Dwayne said.

"I ain't sayin'—you got to show me."

They started playing and right away Dwayne knew Mole could beat him. He played along easily, winning a few points but losing more. Once he got Mole way back from the table and then dropped a soft one just over the net.

Calvin laughed and Mole threw him one of those squinty looks, and after that Mole didn't miss any more points. He put his paddle down and said, "You might come along, boy. With practice. Like, you might get to be second best!"

"Man, I don't practice to be second best. This just ain't my game, dig?"

"What yo' game, man?"

"Oh-h—" Dwayne rocked back on his heels and cupped the one quarter in his pocket, then walked jauntily over to the soda machine and got another soda. Now he only had a dime left—Melvita would be out of luck tonight. He walked back to Mole.

"I ain't got a particular game—I'm jus' an all-round player. I go for the chicks, and they go for me. Then they is the supermarket I work for some days, when I got the time."

Mole's eyes flicked from Dwayne to Calvin, and he nodded his head to Calvin and the two walked a little bit away.

Mole said, "You know that cat? He solid?"

Calvin said, "Yeah, I know him. He be together."

"He got no brother with the pigs or nothin'?"

"Nah. He don't know no pigs."

Mole said, "We need a third. It good to have a cat don't live in the project."

"Dwayne solid on solid. You could ask him."

Mole got a soda out of the machine and strolled back toward Dwayne. "What you into tonight, man?"

"I ain't into nothin' special." Dwayne didn't want to get maneuvered into a spot where he'd need to spend money, so he took his dime out of his pocket and spun it in the air. He joked, "Look like me and my dime goin' to have a thin time tonight."

"Hang around, man, we could use you."

"Yeah? Like how?"

"Just hang loose, man, we show you. Calvin and me got us a little business. You ain't got to be livin' on one thin dime. Right, Calvin?"

"Right on!" Calvin winked.

"They's a dude here I got to straighten out," Mole said. "I see you over to your place later."

"Okay, man. Me and Dwayne be together."

They fooled around the rec building and then went to Calvin's apartment, which was on the second floor of one of the project buildings. Mole turned up in a little while. Calvin said, "See, my mama work at the hospital nights, so we got the place to ourselves. This is our headquarters."

"Cool. My mama work at the hospital, too, but she work days. She on my butt all evening."

"You just tell her to switch to nights, man," Mole laughed. "What you got to eat here, Calvin?"

Dwayne watched Calvin get out some bologna and pickles, and he thought uneasily about his mother waiting for him for supper. The phone was sitting here. He could call. But she'd want to know where he was, and he couldn't see trying to make something up with Mole and Calvin listening. There'd be cracks about his calling Mama up, like a little boy.

He put his bologna and pickle between bread and sauntered around the apartment.

"What building we going to?" Calvin asked.

"Next to the end, down on Twelfth."

"Good. I don't like to work too near home. Cats get to know me."

"We take the top floors. They ain't so suspicious up there."

"Mink comin' with the stuff?"

"What you think we working for?"

"What time?"

"'Bout ten. We be through then."

"How many bags?"

"Many as we got the bread for."

Dwayne turned the radio dial to another station. His back was to them. He thought, *Bags . . . horse, the real stuff.* His palms turned cold and sweaty. He'd seen pushers on the street. Never inside. Never talked to one. Maybe there was still some way he could get out of this.

He turned around and got a grin onto his face. "What time you cats goin' to yo' office? I don't want to be too late—my old man bust me."

"Boy, you got to ed-u-cate your mama and daddy! Don't

worry, man—we get you home ten, eleven o'clock. That ain't past your bedtime, is it?" Mole looked at him, and Calvin laughed.

"Nah," Dwayne heard himself say. "I got time." Now there was no way out.

When it was almost dark, they left Calvin's apartment. Dwayne looked up at the shoe-box buildings. Lights shone in some windows. Others were dark, some were broken, and whole rows of ground-floor windows were boarded up with bright orange-painted plywood. Living in those apartments must be like living in a shooting gallery. Some buildings were entirely empty, deserted, no more targets.

They turned into a building just as a project guard was coming out. Calvin nodded and murmured, "Hey, man." The guard walked on past. They got into the elevator and Mole pushed the button for the top floor. The elevators only stopped every third floor.

"Hey, you watch *Surf Boys* last night?" Calvin said.

"Man, that cat hit the other cat with the surf board. . . ."

Their voices were loud and chatty, and Dwayne realized the conversation was just for show, just to sound natural, in case anyone else got on the elevator.

They got off and walked down one flight. Mole took Dwayne by the arm and went one way, and Calvin went the other. Mole said, "You stay with me. Stay cool, man. You don't do nothing this time—Calvin doing the work."

They watched Calvin walk to the far end of the corridor. He rang the first doorbell. No answer. He went to the next, listened at the door, then moved on. He rang at the third. Someone inside called, "Who that?"

"Ma name is Jai-mes Bufor', ma'am. Ah huntin' for ma

gran'mama, and ah cain't tell which do' is which, ma'am." Dwayne grinned at Calvin's voice, which sounded straight out of the Deep South. The lady inside shouted something back, but she didn't open the door. Calvin moved two doors down.

Suddenly Mole bumped into Dwayne and started walking down the corridor. In a high-pitched, nasal voice, he said, "She is one slick chick if I ever see one! Man, she got big legs, she got big—" Mole gestured, grinning back at Dwayne and then looking over his head. "'Scuse me, sir!" He nudged Dwayne aside and let an old man go past them. He went on talking loudly. "I sure am going to ring her number . . ."

As Mole talked, his eyes aimed like needles at the old man's back. When the man stopped at a door and took out his key, Calvin came up from the other side and started in. "Ah'm from Miss'sippi, sah, and ah be huntin' for ma gran'mama. . . ."

Mole grabbed the old man from the back, one arm crooked around his face, and the other yanking his jacket down. Calvin's hands darted like cockroaches into the man's pockets, and then Mole hooked his foot around the old man's leg and dumped him on the floor. He didn't struggle, didn't move. Everything was silent.

Mole turned and the others followed him to the stairs. They ran down two flights of stairs, and then Mole sauntered along the hall, talking baseball. At the other end of the hall, when they knew no one was watching them, he said to Calvin, "What you get?"

"Twelve is all."

"You drop the wallet down the trash chute?"

"Sure, man."

Dwayne asked, "Ain't we going to get out of the building?" He was scared, and he looked it.

"Cool it, man. If that old cat call the guard, he be looking for us to run out of the building. 'Sides, we got work to do.

Twelve bucks don't buy beans." He looked right at Dwayne. "Get yourself together, man. Your turn coming up."

"What you want me to do?"

"Me and Calvin stand lookouts, and you knock on . . ."

"I can't do that corn-patch talk—I can't pull that off!" Dwayne's voice went up and it wasn't steady.

Mole looked at him with that squinty grin that had no laughs in it. "Okay, boy—I got a line for you. You be scared, see?"

"Huh?"

"You is scared right now, but what I mean—you going to knock on the door, and you going to sound scared. You be this little dude with a high voice, and his mama—oh, she had a fainting spell, I guess. You gotta get help. You knocking on the door and yelling, 'Please, ma'am, come help ma mama!'"

Mole stopped and his face went flat, expressionless. His eyes fixed Dwayne and he grabbed hold of his shoulder. "You got it, man? 'Cause you better have it. You better not make no mistake!"

Dwayne's hands went into fists in his pockets, and his fingers pressed sweat against his palms. He nodded.

Mole went on. "Me and Calvin, we on the stairs either side. Anyone come, we yell out, 'Okay, Mama, I be home ten o'clock!' That the signal, see? You hear that, you go along with Calvin. If you get somebody to open the door, me or Calvin be with you, whoever be the nearest. Got it?" His eyes checked Calvin and lingered a little longer on Dwayne. Then Mole and Calvin left him.

Dwayne was alone in the middle of the hall. He thought, *This ain't me, it must be some other cat. My mama didn' have no boy like this. She just got that Dwayne—he be a good boy.* In crazy flashes before his eyes, he saw his mother's wide mouth smiling, and then his father's eyes and high, shiny forehead, with the hair going gray.

Mole whistled a snatch of "Dixie," and Dwayne jerked

around to look at him and got an icy look back. Mole pointed one jabbing finger. Dwayne went to the first door on the corridor. He listened and heard a babble of kids' voices and a TV going. That was no good—too many people. He wiped his hands on his jeans, saved for a moment.

He went to the second door. Silence. He knocked, knocked again, remembering he was supposed to sound frantic and scared. There was no answer. He went to the next door and knocked some more. Still no answer. He began to hope—maybe no one would open a door.

His knuckles rattled on the next door. From inside he could hear soft gospel music.

"Who that?" It was an old lady's voice, and the music was turned down.

Dwayne sucked in his breath and felt himself trembling. "Please, ma'am! Help me, please, ma'am! Ma mama done fall down! She layin' on the floor.... You gotta come help me! Please, ma'am!"

"Wait a minute, boy!" He heard shuffling footsteps, then a snicking sound at the lock. Instantly, he heard Mole coming down the hall, still whistling "Dixie."

He was scared—it wasn't hard to make his voice convincing. "Oh, hurry, ma'am, please. . . ." There, the door wiggled, started to open. Before there was even a crack, and before the old lady could put the chain on, Mole crashed past Dwayne and hit the door. The door flew open, and there was an awful thump.

"Get in! Shut the door!" Mole ordered.

They were inside the apartment, and suddenly there was silence. Dwayne turned, and his stomach flipped. She was lying on the floor, an old lady with a fuzz of white hair haloing her black face. She hadn't even had time to look frightened. She just lay there, her face nice and peaceful, except for one thing. Her false teeth half hung out of her mouth, and a dribble of pink saliva ran out of the corner of her mouth.

Mole was moving. He grabbed the old lady's purse off a table and emptied it on the floor beside Dwayne. "Go through it! Just get the money!" He whirled and started pulling out bureau drawers.

Dwayne turned away from the old lady, but a sick, yellow taste hung in his throat. He picked at the litter from the pocketbook. He didn't really want to touch it, but he opened the change purse and took out a dollar and some change.

Mole swooped back toward him, jerked the pocketbook from his hands. "She gotta have more than that!" He put his foot on the purse and yanked out the lining. Bills tumbled out. "Get that! Look under the mattress and pillow!" Mole barked, and he disappeared into the closet and started throwing clothes and boxes out.

Dwayne looked under the bed pillow and moved the mattress a little. Mole came back and took the bills from the pocketbook and fanned them out in his hand quickly. He looked over at the limp old woman and winked. "That a good granny! I knowed you have somethin' for me! How 'bout your Holy Bible, granny?" He seized it from the bedside table and shook it by the cover. A twenty-dollar bill floated out. Mole pocketed it and said, "You a real good granny!"

Dwayne stood helplessly in the middle of the room. He couldn't stop his eyes' going back to the old lady. She still looked peaceful, except for those teeth and the pink trickle, which was bigger now. He looked away.

Calvin's voice sounded from the hall. "Okay, Mama, I'll be home ten o'clock."

Mole's hand reached out to the bedside radio and turned the gospel singer up a little louder. Then the two of them stood motionless.

There was a knock on the door. "Hannah, you there?"

Dwayne held his breath.

"Hannah?" the woman's voice again.

A man said, "Likely she fell asleep already. Don't be waking her."

"She musta doze off and left her radio going. She do that," the woman said.

Dwayne heard the footsteps moving away and let out his breath. Mole turned the radio down and listened at the door. As soon as he heard the other door open and close, he beckoned to Dwayne. "Walk out nice and easy, see? Just be cool." He looked past Dwayne at the old lady and jeered, "Sweet dreams! You be cool, too, granny!"

He closed the door softly. As soon as they were in the stairwell, he started talking and laughing. "You know what that chick say to me? She say, 'Mole, you is the mellowest. . . .'"

Dwayne felt as if his whole body was stiff, battered, and inflexible. He managed to bend his knees to get down the stairs and to get out a "Yeah!" or "Man!" when Mole paused. All he could see in front of him was that black face with the white hair, and the teeth.

They got to Calvin's apartment, and Mole beat a tattoo on the door. Calvin opened and said, "How you do, man?"

"We do all right, man!" They went inside and closed the door, and Mole tossed the money on the table. Calvin put his twelve down and started dividing it all up. He looked at Mole and jerked his head briefly toward Dwayne. "What he get?"

Mole looked at Dwayne, looked at him as if he was a Ping-Pong ball. He said, "Ten." His eyes dared Dwayne to question it.

Calvin handed Dwayne the ten, and Dwayne's cold hand stuffed it down in his pocket. He heard himself say, "Okay, you cats. Seeya around."

"You goin', man? What your hurry?" Mole mocked. "Ain't you want a coupla bags—Mink be here any minute."

"I get it some other time. I gotta be goin'."

Mole winked at Calvin. "That cat look like he seen a ghost! You b'lieve in ghos's, boy? Run 'long to Mama now!" He laughed, that low, icy laugh. "And keep your mouth shut, or you be a real ghost!"

Dwayne didn't even care. He went home, blown along the dim streets like a shadow. He still had the yellow taste in the back of his mouth. He came to his own street and saw the light on his porch. The ball that was his stomach tightened. Vaguely, he noticed a strange car parked in front of the door.

He pulled open the door and stumbled inside. Three people stared at him. "There he is—praise the Lord!" said his mother.

"Boy, come here!" his father shouted.

The third was his grandmother, a little old lady with a black face and white hair. The yellow taste would not be swallowed again. Dwayne clapped his hand over his mouth and ran for the toilet.

He sat on the bathroom floor, panting, his forehead resting against the cool porcelain of the toilet. He sat there quite a while. He began to overhear them talking outside.

"Boy be sick—that why he so late," his gran'mama said.

"What he sick from, that what I want to know!" said his father.

His mother opened the bathroom door. "You all right now?" He nodded, kept his eyes closed. "Where you been? What you eat to make you sick like that?"

Dwayne knew he couldn't speak. His stomach was still churning, and he clutched it and stumbled into his room. He plunged onto the bed and buried his face in the pillow. He felt his mother pulling off his tennis shoes, and she covered him with a blanket. The door closed. The dark lit up with faces, all kinds of faces, spinning crazily. Mole's face, his mother's, Melvita, his father's voice came roaring as through a tunnel, his gran'mama, and then with every spin of the wheel that other face, the one with the blob of teeth.

Dwayne groaned, jumped up, and made for the bathroom again. Nothing really came up, just the yellowness. He got back to bed, and once in the night he felt someone pat him gently on the back. Sometimes he must have slept, but when he woke up, the faces were still there. They came toward him and retreated, instead of spinning.

He heard his mother come in to see how he was, but he kept his eyes tight shut and breathed deeply. His stomach felt all right now, but how could he get up and talk to them? If he didn't have to talk about it, maybe the whole thing would go away, it wouldn't have happened.

"Git outa that bed, boy! Stand up here and look at me!"

It was his father, and there was no way to play sick anymore. Dwayne swung his feet around to the floor and stood up. His eyes met his father's for an instant, an instant only.

"Where you been last night?"

"Mmm . . ."

"Answer me! And look at me!"

Dwayne's eyes tracked across his father again and he mumbled, "Out with some kids."

"You gone got yourself drunk, that it?"

Dwayne was about to shake his head, and then he thought, *That would do. That ain't so bad.*

He nodded, not looking up, and was unprepared for the fast smack across the face, first right cheek, then left.

"You look at me, boy! What you do that for?"

Dwayne looked, said nothing.

"You just stupid, that right?"

Dwayne nodded.

"Say it!"

"Yessir, I just stupid."

"You get in any other trouble?"

Dwayne shook his head and prayed he wouldn't have to speak. His father stared at him, a full minute. He said, "You get in any trouble, you better tell me 'bout it now. I don't want to hear 'bout it from nobody else, hear?"

Dwayne stared at the floor, swayed a little. He couldn't tell his father. There were no words. Only those faces.

"Well, you in trouble with me, boy, that for sure! You be home five o'clock every evening, and you not going nowhere after that. Not for a month. You got me?"

"Yessir."

"Now you get washed up and dressed, and you come out and don't give your mama or your gran'mama no more grief, y'hear?"

Dwayne went in the bathroom and shucked off his clothes and got under the shower. When he came out, he felt better. He balled up the dirty clothes and was about to stuff them in the laundry basket when he remembered. The money. As if something might bite him, he slid his hand into the pocket and pulled out the ten. He stood bare naked and looked at it.

There was nothing he could do with it. No place to put it, no way to spend it without someone asking where it came from. Slowly, in sort of a daze, he stretched out his arm and dropped it in the toilet and flushed it away.

All gone, all over, he thought. He looked at himself in the mirror, but it was all still there. It would always be part of him.

Somehow he got through breakfast and lunch and the day. His mother had gone to work, and his father stayed outside working on his car. His gran'mama clucked over him, made him a soft-boiled egg and dry toast for breakfast for his stomach, and asked him about school and baseball and Melvita. She thought his father had been hard on him, so she tried to be extra nice. The nicer she was, the worse he felt.

She asked what he wanted her to cook for supper. "I dunno!" he answered irritably. "I be all right—don't keep askin' me what I want!"

She looked hurt, and he felt ashamed. He turned on the TV and stared through the screen. *I ain't never goin' to be able to tell anyone,* he thought. *No one know how evil I be. I ain't never goin' to that project again. I can't look at that Mole—Calvin neither.*

On the evening news that night, the announcer said an elderly woman from the Darst-Webbe Project had been taken to the hospital, after burglars broke into her apartment and knocked her down. Dwayne realized suddenly that he heard news like that on the TV every day, and he never listened to it. His mother and father were hardly listening now.

Only his gran'mama said, "Poor soul! Maybe she don't have nothing worth taking, anyway. Who would do a thing like that?"

No one looked at Dwayne.

EMILY CHENEY NEVILLE *(1919–   )* won the Newbery Medal in 1964 for *It's Like This, Cat,* and the Jane Addams Award in 1966. Her other novels for young readers include *The Seventeenth Street Gang* (1966), *Traveler From a Small Kingdom* (1968), *Garden of Broken Glass* (1975), and *Berries Goodman* (1965).

ROBERT C. O'BRIEN

THROUGH THE VALLEY

There are things worse than being alone. Ann believes herself to be the last person alive on earth— until the stranger comes and with him, evil. . . .

May 20

I am afraid. Someone is coming. That is, I think someone is coming, but I pray that I am wrong. I went into the church and prayed this morning. Then I put some flowers on the altar, violets and dogwood.

But on the horizon there is smoke. It is a thin column, like smoke from a camp fire.

It has appeared for three days, and each time it is nearer. At first it was behind Claypole Ridge, and I could see only the top of it, the smallest smudge. When we used to go there in the truck, Claypole Ridge was fifteen miles away. Behind Claypole Ridge there is Ogdentown, about ten miles farther. But there is no one left in Ogdentown.

I know, because after the war ended and all the telephones went dead, my father and my brothers, Joseph and David, went there to find out what was happening. They left early in the morning, and it was dark before they came back. Mother had been worrying—they took so long—so we were glad to see the truck lights finally coming over Burden Hill, six miles away.

"What did you find?" my mother asked.

Father said, "Bodies. That's all."

We went inside the house and my father sat down. "Terrible," he said, "just terrible. We drove around, looking. We blew the horn. Then we went to the church and rang the bell. You can hear it five miles away. But nobody came. I went in a couple of houses—the Johnsons', the Peterses'—they were all dead."

My brother Joseph began to cry. He was fourteen. I think I had not heard him cry for six years.

MAY 21

The smoke is coming closer. Today I know where it is: at the crossroads, where the east-west highway crosses our road. He has stopped there and is deciding whether to follow the highway or come over the ridge. I say *he* because that is what I think, though it could be *they* or even *she*. But I think it is he. If he comes to the top of the ridge, he is sure to come down here, because he will see the green leaves. On the other side of the ridge, even on the other side of Burden Hill, there are no leaves; everything is dead.

There are some things I need to explain. One is why I am afraid. Another is why I am writing in this composition book, which I got from Klein's store a mile up the road.

THROUGH THE VALLEY

I took the book and a supply of ball-point pens back in February when I discovered I was forgetting when things happened. Another reason I got it is that I thought writing in it might be like having someone to talk to.

At first I hated being alone, and I watched the road all day and most of the night hoping that a car, *anybody*, would come over the hill. Then the weeks went by and the radio stations went off one by one. When the last one went off and stayed off it came to me, finally, that no one, no car, was ever going to come.

The man on the last radio station kept repeating his latitude and longitude, though he was not on a ship, he was on land—somewhere near Boston, Massachusetts. He said some other things, too, things that I did not like to hear. And that started me thinking. Suppose a car did come over the hill, and I ran out, and whoever was in it got out—suppose he was crazy? Or suppose it was a murderer? What could I do? The fact is the man on the radio, toward the end, was afraid; there were only a few people left where he was and not much food. He said that men should act with dignity even in the face of death, and I knew something terrible was happening there. Once he broke down and cried.

So I decided, if anyone does come, I want to see *who it is* before I show myself. It is one thing to hope for someone to come when things are civilized, but when there is nobody else around, then the whole idea changes. This is what I gradually realized. There are worse things than being alone. It was after I thought about that and watched the smoke coming closer that I began moving my things to the cave.

I haven't seen my family since the day after my father and brothers came back from Ogdentown. The next morning my father decided to explore some more. This time there were two cars—our truck and Mr. Klein's, the man who owned the store. They thought that was better, in case one broke down. Mr. Klein and his wife went, too, and finally Mother decided to go. I think she was afraid of being separated from my father. Joseph was to stay with me.

They planned to go south, first through the gap to where the Amish lived and then west to Dean Town, a real city of 20,000 people, much bigger than Ogdentown. My father put his hand on my head when they left, the way he used to when I was six years old. My mother hugged me hard when she kissed me, but David just waved. They had been gone about an hour when I discovered that Joseph was nowhere to be found, and I guessed where he was: hidden in the back of Mr. Klein's panel truck. I should have thought of that. We were both afraid of being left behind, but my father said we should stay to water the farm animals and to be there in case anybody came.

My family never came back, and neither did Mr. and Mrs. Klein. I know now there weren't any Amish left alive, nor anybody in Dean Town.

Since then I have climbed the high hills on all sides of this valley, and when I look beyond I see all the trees out there are dead, and there is never a sign of anything moving. I don't go out there.

MAY 23

I am writing this in the morning, about 10:30, while I rest after finishing some things I had to do. I hated doing them, but if I had waited until he came over the ridge, it would have been too late.

First I let the chickens out of the chicken yard. Then I chased the two cows and the calf, the young bull calf, out through the pasture gate. They will be all right for a while. There is good grass in the fields down the road and water in the pond, and the calf will keep the cow fresh in milk. Generally I have had good luck with the animals. Only the dog—David's dog, Faro—ran off. I suppose he followed David out of the valley and died.

The last thing I did this morning was to dig up the vegetable garden, everything I'd planted. I covered the ground with dead leaves. I minded that the most, because everything was growing so well. But I have enough canned and dried stuff to live on; and if he had seen the garden all in rows and weeded, he would have known someone was here.

Now I am sitting at the entrance to the cave. From here I can see most of the valley—my own house and barn, the roof of the store, the little steeple on the old church, and the road where it comes over Burden Hill. But I do not think he will see the cave, since trees and bushes hide the small opening. Joseph and David and I did not find it for years, and we played near it every day, or nearly.

It's early; I'm not really sure of the time. My wristwatch runs all right, but I have nothing to set it by except the sun. I'm not really sure of the date, either. I have a calendar, but it is hard—really hard—to remember to check off the dates. It isn't important, I suppose, except that my birthday comes June 15. I will be sixteen.

I remember, after the others left and didn't return, I realized how lucky it was that the store was there, and that it was a general store, well stocked because of the Amish trade. Another lucky thing was that the war ended in the spring (it began in the spring, too, of course—it only lasted a week) and the bombs fell far enough away so we only heard a booming and felt the earth shake. But, as it was, I had all summer to understand how things were, to get over being afraid and to think about how I was going to live through the winter.

Heat, for instance. The house had an oil furnace, but it couldn't run without electricity, and the tanks for the gas stove were soon empty. But the house has two fireplaces, one in the living room, one in the dining room, and there was plenty of wood in the woodshed. I cooked in the fireplace, but I kept remembering the old wood-coal stove in the barn that my mother used to use before we got gas. This summer I'm going to try—that is, I *was* going to try—to take it apart and haul it to the house.

Now it is afternoon and the smoke has come again. It is definitely closer.

Tomorrow morning I may go up near the top of Burden Hill, climb a tree, and watch. I won't go on the road. There is a path that goes in the same direction but it is in the woods, higher up the hillside. If I go I will take one of my guns—the light one, the .22. I am a good shot, better than Joseph or David, though I have practiced only on cans and bottles.

Tonight I have to get some more water into the cave and to cook some stuff before he reaches the valley. I have six empty cider-jugs for water.

That was another thing I had to decide about when the electricity went off: water. There was—there is—a drilled well near the house, with an electric pump. You can't lower a bucket into a drilled well, the hole is too small. So that left me a choice of two brooks. The one that flows past the cave, the one I can see from here, widens into a good pond—a small lake, really, with bream and bass in it. The other, named Burden Creek (after my family, like the hill) flows parallel to the road and out the valley through the gap at the south.

Since Burden Creek was nearer, I had planned to carry water to the house from that but, just in time, I noticed a dead fish floating past and I found a dead turtle on the bank. This stream flows into the valley out of a sort of cleft in the rock ridge to the left of Burden Hill. The water comes from the outside—and it was poisoned. There was nothing left alive in it at all, not even a water bug.

I was scared. I ran all the way to the pond, and I was never so glad to see a bunch of minnows in my life. The water was all right, and it still is. It rises from a spring inside the valley, and its source must be confined to the valley. I still catch fish in the pond, one of my best food supplies.

MAY 24
It is a man, one man alone.

This morning I took the .22 rifle and the binoculars. I climbed a tree on the hill and saw him coming up the road. He is dressed —entirely covered—in a sort of greenish, plastic-looking suit. It even covers his head, and there is a glass mask for his eyes—like the wet suits that skin divers wear. And he has an air tank on his back. He is pulling a wagon, a thing about the size of a big trunk. It is covered with the same green plastic as his suit. It must be heavy, because he has to stop to rest every few minutes.

Now it is night.

He is in my house.

Or possibly not in it, but just outside it, in a small plastic tent he put up. I cannot be sure, because it is too dark.

He came over the top of Burden Hill this afternoon. When he got to the top of the hill he dropped the shaft of the wagon and just stared for about a minute. Then he ran forward, clumsy in his plastic suit, tearing off leaves from the trees and holding them close to his glass face-mask.

All at once he ran back to the wagon. He unsnapped the plastic cover and took out something like a big thermometer with a dial or gauge on it to read. He held it in front of his mask and turned it slowly, studying it. He held it down close to the ground, then up to the tree. I knew it must be some kind of Geiger counter.

He tested the whole area around him for a long time, very carefully.

Then, without warning, he took off the mask and shouted.

It startled me so that I jumped back. He was cheering—a long *haaay* sound, the kind they make at football games. Then he called out: "Anybody here?"

The sound of his voice was nice, a strong sound. For a minute I wanted to run down the hill through the woods and call, "I'm here." But I caught myself in time and stayed quiet. He turned, and I saw his face.

He had a beard, and his hair was long and dark brown. What I noticed most, though, was that he was extremely pale. I have seen pictures of coal miners who work all day underground. He looked like that.

He came back to the wagon, looking over his shoulder a lot, in the direction of my house. I supposed he was thinking, *There might be someone there; they might not hear from here.* Then he did a surprising thing. He took out a gun and laid it on top of the plastic cover as if he wanted it handy. He kept the Geiger counter out and checked all the way to the house. I watched him through the binoculars.

When he got to the house he looked cautiously in every window. Finally he opened the door and went in. Fortunately, I had not dusted the house recently, but I wondered if I had overlooked anything. A half bucket of fresh water? An egg on the shelf?

About twenty minutes later he came out, looking puzzled. It was getting dark when he went back to his wagon and opened its plastic cover. This time he pulled several things from it, including a bulky square that he unfolded and set up—the tent.

He got wood from the woodshed and built a fire. I could not see very well by then—it was completely dark—but I could tell he was cooking a meal of some kind. Then he ate and got into the tent. He could have slept in the house, but I suppose he didn't trust it. I think that green plastic stuff—the suit, the tent, the wagon cover—is something that stops radiation.

I will go in the cave now and sleep. I am still afraid. And yet it is—what is the word I mean?—*companionable* to know there is someone else in the valley.

MAY 25

This morning he made a mistake. It worries me.

When I woke at dawn this morning, he was already up. He had folded his tent and was putting it back in the wagon, when one of the hens crowed. And from the distance, as if it were answering, one of the cows mooed, a real bellow. He looked around, amazed, as if he could not believe it.

After a minute he got quite busy. He pulled out his Geiger counter and looked at it. He was still wearing his plastic suit, though without the helmet or glove parts. He picked up his rifle and went toward the chicken sound. The barn was in the way, so I couldn't see, but I soon heard the rifle crack, and a couple of minutes later he came back carrying a dead chicken. One of *my* chickens!

He put the chicken down on top of the wagon and then, without waiting to pluck or clean it, started out immediately down the road in the direction of the church and the store. He took the rifle and the Geiger counter.

I thought I had better keep him in sight as much as I could so I followed along a path I know in the woods, about two-thirds of the way up the hillside. I took my binoculars and my own rifle.

He soon saw the cows off by the pond, in the far field. He started toward them, then caught sight of movement—minnows, I suppose—at the edge of the pond. He stared into the water and after a moment held his Geiger counter close to the water. Finally he put his hand in the water and tasted it. It tastes fine, I know, and I could tell he felt like cheering.

He went on. He passed the church and went on to the store.

When he came out he was carrying a box of something—canned stuff, I thought. From the store he headed back toward the house.

It was now nearly eleven o'clock, the sun was high and bright, and the day had turned warm. Wearing the plastic suit and carrying all that stuff, I could tell he was getting too hot; he stopped twice to rest and put the carton down. And that was why, when he got back to the house, he made the mistake. He took off his plastic suit, got some soap from the carton, and took a bath in the dead stream of Burden Creek.

He had been so cautious up till then, but I can understand how he was careless. Not knowing the geography of the valley very well, he must have thought that it was the same stream that fed into the pond where he had seen the fish. He did not know there were two streams.

I don't know how bad a mistake it was. That's because I don't know what is wrong with that water. The stream merges with the other one, the pond-stream, down at the end of the valley, and they flow out the gap as one. Downstream from where they merge they are both dead—I have looked many times. But I don't know what the poison is. On the radio at the end of the war, they said the enemy was using nerve gas, bacteria, and "other antipersonnel weapons." So it could be anything. All I can do is wait and watch. I hope it doesn't kill him.

STILL MAY 25

It is night again, and I am in the cave with the lantern lighted.

An inexplicable thing: the dog, Faro, has come back. How that is possible I don't know. Where has he been? How has he lived? He looks pitiful—as thin as a skeleton, and half the hair is gone from his left side. He was—he is—a mongrel, but mostly setter, and he loved to hunt. When we went hunting, when he even saw a gun come out, he would get so excited you would never believe he would freeze on a point, but he always did. When the dog disappeared, I had assumed he had gone looking for David. But apparently he did not go through the gap. He must have been waiting for David in the woods up near the gap, living on what he could catch.

I suppose he heard the gunshot, and that's what brought him back. I was watching at the time. It was about 1:30 and the man was cooking the chicken on a fire he had made. The dog came up very cautiously, watching and sniffing. When the man saw him he took a step toward Faro, and Faro backed away. The man whistled, but again Faro backed away.

The man ignored him then, but when the chicken was done, he put some on a plate for Faro. It took Faro a long time to approach the plate, but at last he did and finished the food in two gulps. Then he began circling the yard, sniffing as he went, still keeping away from the man. Then, to my horror, he began wagging his tail and headed up the hill toward the cave. He had found my tracks.

The man started to follow, but the dog soon outdistanced him and disappeared into the underbrush. I crept back into the cave, and soon Faro came bounding in.

Poor dog. He looked terrible, even worse close up. He gave two short, creaky little barks and ran to me. But I was scared. Inevitably, if he stayed around, if the man made friends with him, Faro would betray me. He would come up here, and the man would follow.

I suppose it seems wrong to be so afraid of that. It is just that I can't be sure of what the man will do. There's no way to tell what he's like. Suppose I don't like him? Or worse, what if he doesn't like me?

I have been here alone for so long. I have hoped and prayed for someone to come, someone to talk to, to work with. I dreamed that it would be a man, for then, sometime in the future—it is a dream, I know—there might be children in the valley. Yet, now that a man has actually come, I realize that my hopes were too simple. All men are different, but the man on the radio station, fighting to survive, saw people that were desperate and selfish. This man is a stranger and bigger and stronger than I am. If he is kind, then I am all right. But if he is not—what then?

MAY 26

A sunny day. According to my calendar, it is Sunday. Ordinarily that would mean I would go to church in the morning. I did not pretend to have any real service, of course, but I would sit and read something from the Bible.

There never were any real services in the church—not in our time, anyway—nor any minister. It was built a long time ago by one of our ancestors—"an early Burden," my father used to say—when they first settled in the valley, and I guess they thought it would grow into a village. It never did—just us and the Kleins and the Amish south of the gap. When we went to church, we drove to Ogdentown.

But this morning I had to forget about church. The man got up early and cooked his breakfast, still on the fire out in front of the house. He clearly intended to explore the length of this valley and take a look beyond. He still did not know how far the green part extended.

I followed the man, staying on my high woods path. When he got to the store he went in, and when he came out he was dressed in a whole new outfit—khaki slacks, very neat, a blue work shirt, even new work shoes and a straw cap. He had shaved by now and looked like a different person—and a lot younger, maybe thirty or thirty-two.

He walked on down the road, heading south toward the far

end of the valley, toward the gap. He looked around him as he went; he was curious about everything, but he did not slow down much until he reached the culvert. At that point the small stream, having flowed into the pond and out again and meandered along through the meadow, runs into Burden Creek.

He stopped there. I think it dawned on him then for the first time that there were two streams, and that the pond was not formed by Burden Creek. And here, if you look at them closely where they join, the difference between them becomes plain.

I think it was then he started worrying, maybe even feeling sick. Still, after studying the water, he walked on. In another fifteen minutes he was approaching the end of the valley and the beginning of the deadness beyond, where the road leads on to the Amish farms.

He could not see that, of course. In fact, unless you know about it, it is hard to believe that there is any way out of the valley at the south end. That is because the gap is in the shape of a very large S, and until you are right on top of it you think you are coming to a solid wall of rock and trees. Then the road (and the stream beside it) turns sharply right, left, and right again, cutting through the ridge without even going uphill.

With Burden Hill on the other end, the result is that the valley is completely closed in. People used to say it even has its own weather; the winds from outside do not blow through it.

When he reached the gap I lost sight of him—but I knew he would reappear shortly. When he saw the dead land outside he would turn and come back; he could not go farther without his plastic suit.

I sat down in the sun to wait. Behind me some blackberry bushes gave off quite a sweet smell, and there were bees humming in the blossoms. Soon he came walking back, moving somewhat more slowly now.

About halfway to the house it happened; he stopped, sat

down quickly in the middle of the road, and was very sick to his stomach.

He was sick again three times on the way, and after the third time he was barely stumbling along, dragging the rifle. When he reached the tent he crawled in; he has not come out again. He did not make a fire tonight, nor eat any supper.

MAY 27

I am writing in the morning, sitting at the entrance to the cave with my binoculars, watching the house and the tent for a sign of life. So far there has been none. I know the man is sick, but I do not know how much. It may be that he just doesn't feel very well and decided to stay in bed.

Or he may be so sick he can't get up. He may even be dying. That idea makes me feel quite desperate. I must go there.

MAY 28

I am back in the house, in my own room.

The man is in the tent. He is asleep, most of the time at least, and so sick he cannot get up. He scarcely knows I am here.

Yesterday when I took my gun and went down to the tent, I went very cautiously, but there was no need. He was very sick. His eyes were closed, his breathing fast and shallow. Beside him lay a green plastic water-bottle, knocked over and spilled; beside that was a jar of pills, large white ones, with the top off.

The tent roof was only about four feet high. I knelt down and went in, just a little. The smell was terrible. I touched his hand. It was dry and hot with fever. At my touch, he opened his eyes.

"Edward," he said. "Edward?"

He was not looking at me but at my gun, which I was still holding. The next thing he said was, "Bullets. It won't stop...." His voice sounded thick, as if his throat and mouth were swollen.

"You're sick," I said. "You have a fever."

He moaned. "Water. Please give me water."

I got a pail and a cup from the kitchen and ran to the good stream. He was asleep again when I got back, so I touched his shoulder. "Here," I said, "drink this."

I lifted his head a little while he drank. He fell back and went to sleep again instantly.

I thought that since drinking the water had not made him sick again, perhaps he should eat something. Soup, I decided, since that is what my mother usually gave us when we were sick. I had left some cans in the house—it would have looked odd not to—when I moved to the cave.

When I took the hot soup to him, he was awake. His voice was very weak. "Who are you?"

"I'm Ann Burden," I said, "of Burden Valley. You've been sick."

"The valley," he said. "I remember now. All the green trees. But there was no one there."

"I was here" I said. "I stayed in the woods." (I thought it better not to mention the cave.) "I made you some soup," I said and started to feed him. He ate seven spoonfuls and then said, "No more." Then he fell asleep again.

I went back up to the cave, got my alarm clock, a lamp, this notebook, and some other things, and came back to the house. I set and reset the alarm through the night. Each time it rang, I went out with a flashlight and gave him water.

This morning I crumbled some corn bread in milk and took it to him for breakfast. (I had to use powdered milk because the cows are still out. I will have to catch them now and bring them back in. Also the chickens.)

This time he seemed very much better, and his eyes had lost their dazed look. After he finished eating, he said, "I need to find out what made me sick."

"I think it is because you swam in Burden Creek," I said. "Nothing lives in it."

"I discovered that. It was stupid to be so careless, after all this time. I had not been in water for a year. I was too eager. Still, I should have tested. But that other water, in the pond, was all right. So I thought. . . ." He stopped. Then he said, "I might as well know. Could you—do you know what a Geiger counter is?"

"That instrument you have?"

"Yes. Can you read one?"

"No. That is, I never have."

He showed me how, and I took it to Burden Creek. In the tent and while I was crossing the road, the needle stayed quiet. But when I got near the water, it began to go up. At the edge of the creek, it shot up almost as high as it could go. I did not stay there, but ran back to him.

When I told him what the needle showed, he groaned and covered his eyes with his hand. Finally he said, "I have radiation poisoning. Very bad."

"But you're getting better."

"It comes in stages."

He told me about radiation sickness. The first part, getting sick to your stomach, lasts only a day or so, then goes away. Then the radiation causes real damage. In a few days he was going to get much sicker. He would get a very high fever, and since his blood cells were damaged he would also get anemic. Worst of all, he would have no resistance to germs and infection.

I said, "You must tell me what I should do. Do you have medicine to take?"

He looked at the jar of white pills, still on the floor where I had left it. "Those won't help, not now. No, there's no medicine. In a hospital they give transfusions."

I can't do that, of course, but I can try to keep him from developing some kind of secondary infection like pneumonia or dysentery. I will boil and sterilize everything he eats and eats from —just like a baby. And if he is strong enough to walk a little tomorrow, I will try to help him into the house. He can sleep in Joseph and David's room, on a bed, and it will be easier for me to take care of him.

I just realized that after all this I still do not even know his name.

MAY 29

His name is John R. Loomis. He is a chemist from Ithaca, New York, where Cornell University is, or used to be. He knows a lot about radiation poisoning. In fact, that is, in a way, how he happens to be alive at all, and how he was able to make his way here.

I learned this when I brought him breakfast. Last night before I went to bed I went out to the chicken yard, opened the gate, and scattered some corn on the ground. So this morning, sure enough, the chickens had come back in, and there were two fresh eggs. I boiled them, toasted the last of the corn bread, made some coffee, and opened a can of tomato juice. I put it all on a tray and carried it out to him.

To my surprise he was sitting up. "You're better," I said.

"For the moment," he said. "At least I think I can eat something."

I put the tray down in front of him and he stared at it.

"Amazing," he said. He just whispered it.

"What?"

"This. Fresh eggs. Toast. Coffee. This valley. You, all by yourself. You are all by yourself?"

It was sort of a key question, and he looked a little suspicious as he asked it.

"Yes."

"And you managed to stay alive and raise chickens and eggs and cows?"

"It hasn't been so hard."

"And the valley. How did it escape?"

"I don't really understand that. Except that people always used to say the valley had its own weather."

"A meteorological enclave. Some kind of an inversion, I suppose."

I said, "You'd better eat. It will all get cold."

He finished his breakfast and then he told me his name. And I repeated mine.

"Ann Burden," he said. "But weren't there other people living in the valley?"

"Just my family," I said. "And the people who owned the store, Mr. and Mrs. Klein."

And I told him about how they drove away and never came back.

"I suppose they kept going too long," he said. "It's hard not to, especially at first. I know. You keep hoping."

He said it had taken him months to get from Ithaca to the valley, and all the way, all that time, he had seen no living thing —no people, no animals, no birds, no trees, not even insects—only gray wasteland, empty highways, and dead cities and towns. He had been ready to give up when he finally came over the ridge and saw, in the late evening, the haze of blue-green.

He drank the last of his coffee, and I helped him into the house and into Joseph and David's room on the ground floor next to the living room. He lay on David's bed and went to sleep.

He slept until about noon, and during that time I went down

to the far field to get the two cows and the calf. When I came back to the house, Mr. Loomis was awake, but he stayed in bed. I fixed some lunch, and then he told me some more of his story.

It began when he was a graduate student at Cornell, an organic chemist doing research on plastics and polymers. (He explained that these are very long molecules used in making nylon, Dacron and the stretchy kind of plastic wrap.) The head of the department in which he worked, a very famous scientist who had once won a Nobel prize, asked him to help on some research in a secret laboratory in the mountains about twenty miles away.

In time, they made an important breakthrough—a method of magnetizing plastic. Mr. Loomis called it "polarizing," but that just means making it magnetic.

That did not sound like too exciting a discovery to me, but when he explained what it was for, I could see that it was. The point was that magnetism can stop, or at least turn aside, radiation. Mr. Loomis reminded me (I had learned it in school) that it is the earth's magnetic field that keeps us all from being killed by cosmic rays. So a magnetic plastic could be used to make a radiation-proof suit.

That was what the government—the Army, of course—wanted. So that troops could live on (*fight* on!) in places that had been nuclear-bombed. But the project was more complicated than just making a plastic suit. Next they had to make an air filter and then a filter that would provide safe water.

These were, I now realized, the things Mr. Loomis had brought with him—the greenish suit he was wearing when I first saw him, the air tank on his back; the water filter and a supply of purified water had been in the wagon trunk. The tent, of course, was the same stuff as the suit and so was the trunk itself.

They had designed all these in the laboratory, and they finished a single pilot model of each just before the war began.

They had sent their report to Washington, and a team was coming from the Pentagon to test them.

But the men from the Pentagon never got there. It was all too late.

On the night the bombing began, Mr. Loomis was working late in the laboratory. He heard the news on the radio, and he decided it was safer to stay there. The professor had gone back to Ithaca, and Mr. Loomis never saw him again.

Like me, Mr. Loomis heard the radio stations go off one by one. He stayed in the laboratory for three months before he dared venture out. The suit had been carefully tested in the laboratory, but it had never actually been used "in the field," so he was cautious, and it was lucky he was. His first impulse, for instance, was to get into his car and drive to Ithaca. Before he did, he checked the radioactivity inside the car and discovered it was *ten times* as high as in the open air. The level was too near the theoretical limit of what the suit could handle, and he decided not to risk it. So he ended up walking and hauling his supplies in the wagon trunk.

His first trip was to the west, to where he knew there had been an underground Air Force command post supposedly self-sustaining for months. He found the air base all right, but with signs of riot, and all dead.

When Mr. Loomis finished telling all this I could see that he was getting tired. I went to get him some water, and while I was taking it back I remembered one more thing I was really curious about.

I handed him the glass and asked, "Who was Edward?" That was the name he had called me when he first saw me in the tent, when he was delirious.

For a second I thought the sickness had come back on him, because his eyes got a wild look again, as if he were seeing a nightmare, and he dropped the glass. "How do you know about Edward?"

"When I first saw you," I said, "in the tent, you called me Edward. Is something wrong? Are you sick?"

He relaxed. "It was a shock," he said. "Edward was a man who worked in the laboratory with me. But I didn't think I had mentioned his name."

JUNE 3

Four days have passed. I have been very busy. With Mr. Loomis in the valley—in the house—I decided I should cook better meals than I did when I was by myself. For one thing, if he was going to be sick he ought to build up his strength.

So I made several trips to the store for supplies. It was all canned stuff, of course, or dried. There would not be anything fresh except milk and eggs until I could get the garden going again. Since it was already June, that was the most urgent thing.

I got the spade and the hoe and went to work. It was easy spading, since the dirt had already been turned up once; also, the manure was still in it, so I did not have to haul that again. But after I had turned up the whole patch, I realized that it was not really big enough. With two eating we would need twice as much of everything, and I wanted some left over for preserving. The canned stuff in the store is not going to last forever. So I started to double the size of the garden. There were lots of seeds in the store.

For the new part, I had to spade through turf, which was much harder digging. I had made pretty good progress when I looked up and saw Mr. Loomis watching me. It was late in the afternoon, almost time to stop and get dinner.

I called, "Is something wrong?"

"Nothing wrong," he said. "I just got bored. That's hard work for a girl."

"I'm used to it." I started to tell him that most of it had already been dug before and was therefore easy, but then I decided not to. I did not want him to know how afraid I had been when I first saw him coming.

He looked puzzled. "But do you have to do it all by hand? Didn't your father have a tractor?"

"It's in the barn."

"Can't you run it?"

"Yes, but there's no gasoline."

"But there are two gasoline pumps at the store. There must be gas there."

"That's true," I said. "But the pumps need electricity."

"And you've been doing all this with a shovel. Don't you realize it would be simple to take the motors off the pumps and work them by hand?" He smiled, but it made me feel stupid.

"I don't know much about electric motors and pumps," I said.

"But I do," he said. "At least enough to do that."

"When you're well again," I said.

It turned colder that night, so after we had eaten dinner I built a fire in the living-room fireplace. Since the living room adjoins his—Joseph and David's—room, I opened the door so the fire would warm it, too. He did not go back into the bedroom immediately, however, but sat down in the chair my father always used.

"Would you like me to get you a book?" I asked. "I can put the lamp on the table by the chair."

He said, "No, thank you. I only want to look at the fire a few minutes. Then I'll get sleepy. The fire always does that."

Still, it bothered me. There was absolutely nothing for him to do. I wished there was a radio station to tune in, or that the phonograph could work. It was quite a good one, and we had a lot of records. But it would not play without electricity, so I did something I would be embarrassed to do under ordinary circumstances. I said, "Would you like me to play the piano?"

To my surprise, he seemed extremely pleased. Almost excited. "Could you?" he said. "I haven't heard music for more than a year."

I can play hymns better than anything else, because I used to play them for our Sunday-school singing. I played two of my favorites, *How Great Thou Art* and *In the Garden*. When I looked around he had fallen asleep, so I stopped, and when I did he woke up.

"Thank you," he said. "That was beautiful."

He went to bed then; I told him to leave the bedroom door open, and I put some more wood on the fire. Then I went upstairs to my bedroom. For some reason, playing the hymns had made me feel sad, as if I were homesick even though I was at home.

I was just drifting off to sleep when I heard Mr. Loomis shout. I jumped up and opened my door. He was dreaming, a bad dream, I could tell, a nightmare.

He said, "In charge. In charge of what, Edward?"

Then he said, "What good can it do? We know they're dead. There isn't a chance. Can't you grasp that? Mary is *dead*. Billy is dead. You can't help them."

Then he shouted again, a very urgent shout. "Get away. I warn you. Get away from—" The last word I could not understand. And after that he gave a terrible groan, so painful I thought he must be hurt.

And then silence.

I crept downstairs and listened. He was breathing regularly and deeply. Whatever the nightmare had been, it was over. The rest of the night was quiet.

In the morning, I woke early and decided to pick some wild

greens. My mother always gathered field cress and dandelions and poke greens in early June. I was hungry for a salad and thought Mr. Loomis must be even hungrier, since he could not possibly have eaten anything like that in a long time, while I at least had had last summer's garden. He seemed to be sleeping peacefully, so I decided it was safe to go. I got a basket from the shelf, drank a glass of milk, and went out. I would cook breakfast later.

It was cool, but still and pleasant. Faro came with me, sniffing everything. At the pond I heard a big bass jump, and I thought, *After I get the greens, I will cook breakfast and then go fishing. A bass or two would make a good dinner with the salad.*

In half an hour I had picked enough greens to fill the basket; and then I was aware of a beautiful, sweet perfume. There, twenty feet ahead of me on the edge of the woods, was a crab apple tree in full bloom.

I had known the tree was there, of course; but I had never known the tree to look so beautiful or smell so nice. I sat down, right in the wet grass, to stare. I thought if I ever got married, apple blossoms were what I would like to have in the church. Which meant that I would have to get married in May or early June.

I got to thinking about it. In June next year I would be seventeen, and though that was young to marry, it was not *too* young. I knew there could be no minister, but the marriage ceremony was all written out in the Book of Prayer. There *should* be a ceremony; I felt strongly about that, and it should be in the church, on a definite date, with flowers. I thought I might even wear my mother's wedding dress. I knew where it was, folded up in a box in her closet.

That thought made me feel lonesome for my mother, a feeling I have tried hard to avoid, so I stood up to change the subject. I got out my pocketknife and cut a bunch of apple blossoms. Mr. Loomis could have a bouquet for his sickroom.

At the house I put the flowers in a vase and the greens in the cold cellar—they would be for dinner. Then I cooked breakfast—eggs, canned ham, and some pan biscuits. I went to call Mr. Loomis and learned why the house was so quiet—he was not in his room.

Immediately I was worried, very worried. I realized that it was stupid of me to have left him alone, knowing that he had had the nightmare, knowing that it might have been the start of the high fever. I placed the breakfast near the fire, where it would stay warm, and ran outside.

I saw him immediately, across the road not far from Burden Creek, sitting on a large stone. He was staring at the creek, looking upstream.

When he saw me, he said, "I thought you had run away."

"Are you all right?" I was still worried.

"Yes," he said. "In fact, I woke up feeling so much better that I decided to take another look at this water. I've been thinking about it."

"Thinking what? That it's all right?"

"Oh, it's dangerous, there's no doubt about that. But that's no reason it shouldn't be useful. Up there"—he pointed to a place a hundred feet upstream, a rocky place where a big boulder blocked the creek and made a little waterfall—"there's a sort of a natural dam."

I nodded. "My father said that my great grandfather had a small mill there, a flour mill. We thought the stone you're sitting on was part of it. It's worn smooth."

"What I was thinking about was not a mill, but electricity. If I could build that dam up a few feet higher—there's a good flow of water. It could run a small generator."

"But if we tried to build a dam, we'd get the water on ourselves. It's too risky."

"Not if I was wearing the safe-suit, and if I was careful. And you can always make a generator from an electric motor. Your father must have some around."

It would be wonderful to have electricity again. But the thought reminded me that his breakfast was drying up by the fire. We started back to the house, but after a few steps, he began walking very slowly; then he stumbled. He had turned extremely pale, a bluish color. He looked terrible.

"It's the anemia," he said. "I should have known. It's the dependable part of the disease."

Somehow we got him back to the house, and after he'd rested his color improved.

"It came so suddenly," I said.

"No. I knew it had started a little."

I persuaded him to eat, and then he went to bed.

After he was asleep, I milked the cow and planted potatoes. Between times, I checked on Mr. Loomis. He stayed asleep, so I went down to the pond and caught three bass.

When I got back to the house he was awake. He seemed better and even got up and sat at the table for lunch, though I noticed that he moved slowly and rather cautiously, and after he had eaten he lay down again immediately. When I looked into the bedroom a little later, he was asleep. He slept all afternoon.

In spite of everything, dinner that night was festive, with the bass and the salad. It is incredible how good fresh green things can taste when you have not had any for months. After dinner, I built up the fire again. I had found Mr. Loomis some books that interested him. They were a set called *The Farm Mechanic* that were on a shelf in my father's workshop in the barn. The books were full of diagrams of motors, wiring systems, pumps, silos, balers, and so on. Mr. Loomis studied them for a long time.

The next morning, amazingly enough, I got the tractor running. That was a direct result of *The Farm Mechanic*. After breakfast, Mr. Loomis showed me a set of diagram-drawings of the inside mechanism of a gasoline pump—almost identical to the ones at Mr. Klein's store.

Mr. Loomis explained the diagrams to me, and they were surprisingly easy to follow. All I had to do was open the front of the pump, disconnect the electric motor and belt, and then take a handle (handle H, it was called) from its place inside the door, and I should be able to pump gasoline.

I went down to Klein's, and it was all as the book said. At last I was ready. Quite excited, I took handle H from its clamp and inserted it into its slot. In ten seconds I was pumping gasoline.

I got a five-gallon container from the store and filled it. With the can bumping my leg every step, I carried it to the barn and filled the tractor's gas tank. I checked the oil—it was all right. There was a self-starter, but the battery was dead, of course. That had happened many times before, however, and I knew how to start it with the crank. We all knew how to run the tractor, starting about age eight. I cranked hard and the motor started immediately, with a loud, sputtering roar.

I climbed up to the seat, put it in reverse, and backed it out. Though I was sure Mr. Loomis had heard the motor, I wanted him to see it, too, so I drove the tractor up to the house and ran it past his window.

I took the tractor back down to the barn and hitched on the plow. I had already decided what I was going to do. Beyond the garden is a small field of about an acre and a half. I wanted to plow that field and plant it in corn, with maybe a few rows of soybeans and pea beans. Corn could be eaten by us, by the chickens, and, if there was any left over, by the cows—shucks and all.

As I started plowing, the sun was pleasant and warm on my back. Faro had followed me to the field, looking astonishingly healthy; even his hair was growing back. After I'd worked about a half hour, I looked up and saw crows, sharp and black against the sky, wheeling in a circle over the field. I realized they had remembered the sound of plowing; they knew there would be seeds to follow. My father used to call them pests, but I was glad to see them. They were probably the only wild birds left anywhere.

I had half the field plowed by lunchtime. I finished it in the afternoon and planned to harrow it in the morning, and then seed it. But as it turned out, I had to change my plans.

That night Mr. Loomis's fever went up to 104°.

That is why, after these days of being too busy, I now have time to write down all that has happened.

I do not dare to leave the house for more than a few minutes at a time. This morning I ran down to the barn to milk the cow, and though I hurried as fast as I could, I was gone about fifteen minutes. When I came back he was sitting up in bed, shivering and blue with cold. He was calling me, and he had become frightened when I did not answer. The fever makes him afraid to be alone. I got him to lie down again, re-made the bed, and put some extra blankets on it. I filled a hot-water bottle and put it under the blankets. I am afraid he will get pneumonia.

Once I had him settled and into a fresh pair of my father's heaviest pajamas, I took his temperature. It had gone up—it was 105°. It looked strange to see the mercury stretched almost to the end of the thermometer.

I persuaded him to swallow a few bites of boiled egg. Then he fell asleep again.

But now I face a problem. I have to go to the brook for more water, and sometime soon I am going to have to go to the store, since I am running out of several things, including flour and sugar. But how can I go when he is afraid to be left alone? And I will have to milk the cow again this evening.

Perhaps if I wait until he is awake and I tell him where I am going, he will be all right if I do not stay too long. I will have to try that. There is nothing else I can do.

I went, both to the brook and to the store, and it was a bad business. I am writing this in the living room; it is night, and I have a lamp lit. Everything is quiet now, at least for the moment.

This is what happened. At about four o'clock this afternoon I knocked on his door and went in. He was asleep (he sleeps about ninety percent of the time now) but woke up and seemed calm enough. I explained that I had to go out, and he did not seem at all bothered or upset; in fact he was surprised that I was worried about it. Still, I said, "I will take the tractor and the utility cart, so I can go faster and carry more."

"A waste of gas," he said.

I had thought of that, but I decided to do it anyway. It was an emergency.

Despite his reassurance, I rushed to the barn and hitched the cart to the tractor as quickly as I could. I put three large milk cans into the cart—they would hold enough water for a week or more. I put the tractor into high gear (it can go about fifteen miles an hour in high) and headed first for the brook.

After I got water, I went on to the store and loaded a lot of food supplies, including canned stuff, sugar, flour, cornmeal, dog food, and chicken corn.

I was hurrying toward the house, still in high gear, when I saw the front door fly open, and Mr. Loomis came out, trying to run but staggering. He stumbled down the steps and across the yard toward the wagon trunk.

By this time I had reached the driveway. I turned in and shut off the motor. Mr. Loomis, moving in a groping kind of way, opened the end of the trunk and—to my horror—drew out a gun, a big carbine. I jumped down and ran toward him, but before I reached him he had fired three shots. He aimed them at the second floor of the house at my father and mother's bedroom, and I could see puffs of white paint fly off where the bullets hit.

I shouted—I may have shrieked; I cannot remember—and he turned toward me, swinging the gun around so it was aimed at me. To my own surprise I stayed calm.

"Mr. Loomis," I said, "you're sick. You're dreaming. Put the gun away." After a long moment, he lowered the rifle.

"You went away," he said.

"I told you," I said. "I had to go. Don't you remember?"

"I went to sleep," he said. "When I woke up I heard—"

"Heard what?"

"I heard . . . somebody . . . in the house. He was upstairs."

"Who was upstairs?"

But he was being evasive. "Someone moving."

"Mr. Loomis, there was no one in the house. It's the fever again. You *must* stay in bed." I took the gun from his hands and put it back in the trunk. He did not resist, but he began to shiver violently, and I saw that he was soaked with sweat.

I got him back into the house and onto the bed. I pulled the blankets over him and went upstairs to get him some dry pajamas.

In my father and mother's room I saw where the bullets had gone. Fortunately, except for breaking the windows and knocking down plaster, they had done no real damage.

When I went back downstairs I realized he had still not quite lost his illusion. He said, "Is he gone?"

I said, "Is who gone?"

"Edward." he said.

"You were dreaming again."

He shook his head, and then he said, "Yes, I forgot. Edward is dead. He couldn't have come all this way."

So it was Edward again. But I am worried. If he is dreaming

about Edward, who was, I suppose, a friend of his, why does he want to shoot him?

I think I had better sleep downstairs on the sofa. He sleeps very restlessly, muttering and groaning.

JUNE 4

This is a terrible day.

I do not know how high his fever has gone because it has reached 106°, and beyond that the thermometer does not show. I do not think he can live on very long with such a high temperature. I keep sponging him with alcohol.

He still sleeps most of the time, and when he wakes up it is into a dream, a nightmare. Only for a few minutes now and then does he seem to recognize me or even see or hear me. The rest of the time he is delirious, and often he is terrified, always of the same thing: He thinks Edward is here and is threatening him with something.

I am beginning to realize that something bad happened between Mr. Loomis and Edward (I do not know his last name), and that they were not friends at all, but enemies, at least at the end.

Sometimes Mr. Loomis acts as if he thinks *I* am Edward, but more often he stares beyond me, as if he is looking at someone over my shoulder. At times he thinks Edward is here in the valley, in the house; other times Mr. Loomis is back with him in the laboratory.

This morning when I knocked and went into his room with a tray, he said, "Stay back, Edward, stay back. It's no use."

I said, "Mr. Loomis, it's me. I've brought you some breakfast."

He rubbed his eyes, and they came into focus. But his voice was blurred. "No breakfast. Too sick."

"Try," I said, and I persuaded him to eat a little. He was very thirsty.

But then he stared at the door again. "Edward?"

I said. "Mr. Loomis, Edward is not here."

"You don't understand," he said. "He's a thief. He'll steal. . . ." To my dismay he gave a terrible groan and tried to get out of the bed.

I caught his shoulders and held him back.

"Poor Mr. Loomis," I said. "You're dreaming. There is no Edward, and nothing to steal."

"The suit," he said, his voice hardly above a whisper. "He'll steal the suit."

I said, "Mr. Loomis, the safe-suit is in the wagon, in the trunk. You put it there. Remember?"

"In the trunk," he said. "Of course! That's where he's gone."

It was obviously the wrong thing for me to have said, because now he tried again to get up. I held him down; it was not so hard, because he is so very weak, but I must now stay in the room with him, at least until he gets through this nightmare.

But I have an idea. When Mr. Loomis calms down a little, I will get the safe-suit. I will bring it in and put it by the bed where he can see it. It will make him less worried.

This afternoon I got the suit and brought it in, but in a few minutes he was in another, even worse nightmare, perhaps brought on by the sight of the suit. He was back in the laboratory having a desperate quarrel with Edward. I am glad it was only a dream, because it sounded as if one of them was going to murder the other. I suppose when two men are shut up together in a confined area the tensions grow terrible.

Mr. Loomis said, " . . . not for just twenty-four hours, Edward. Not even for twenty-four minutes. If you want to find your family, go ahead. But the suit stays here."

A pause. He was listening to Edward's reply.

Poor Edward. It was not hard to understand the situation. Edward was married. He had a wife named Mary and a son named Billy, and he was frantic with worry about them. Apparently he had been working late—along with Mr. Loomis—when the bombing started. At first, Edward was afraid to go out—they had real exploding H-bombs in that area, not just drifting fallout. But after the first few days, when things quieted down, he wanted to go and find them, and that is when the fight began.

One suit and two people. That was the situation. In his dream, Mr. Loomis kept reminding Edward that his wife and son were dead, and I suppose Edward had a wild hope that some people might have survived, that they might be alive in a shelter.

Mr. Loomis did not want Edward to take the suit. What was the use, if they were dead? In the dream he said, "How do I know you'll bring it back? Suppose something goes wrong?"

And later: "Of course they're dead. You heard the radio, Edward. And even if you found them alive—what then?"

A pause.

"You mean you would leave them to bring the suit back? You're lying, Edward."

And again: "The suit, Edward, the suit. Think about it. It may be the last useful thing anybody ever made. You're not going to waste it on a visit to your dead wife."

Poor Edward. He kept pleading. I wondered why Edward did not just take the suit, or at least try. For instance, I thought, Mr. Loomis would have to sleep some of the time.

And then I learned that is just what Edward did do. And that led to the worst part of the nightmare, because Mr. Loomis was holding, or dreamed he was holding, a gun. "You're a thief and a liar, Edward, but it's no use. Stand back from the door."

A pause.

"No, I warn you. I will shoot. The suit will stop radiation, but it won't stop bullets."

I remembered. That was the first thing he had said to me when I found him sick in the tent, when he saw my rifle. The sight of it had brought him back to this moment, and now he was in it again. He was threatening to shoot Edward as he had in the laboratory, where he had been guarding the door leading out.

In a few more seconds it was over. Mr. Loomis gave a desperate groan, a deeper sound then before, and then a series of strangling noises. I thought he must be trying to cry. Then he closed his eyes and lay still, except for his breathing, which was very fast and light, like the breathing of a small animal that has been running. I tried to take his pulse, but all I could feel was a fluttering, so faint I could not count it.

I wondered if he really had shot Edward, and if so, how badly he had injured him. I went to where I had put his suit, on a chair beside his bed. I unfolded it and took it to the window, into the light.

What I feared was true. There were three holes spaced about two inches apart, across the middle of the chest. They had been patched—that is, new plastic had been welded over them so that they were airtight—but from the inside you could see that they were bullet holes, round and quite large. If Edward was inside the suit when they were fired, then he had certainly been killed. I folded the suit and returned it to the wagon trunk.

Now it is night, about ten o'clock. His dreams seem to be over, but I do not know if he will live until morning. His hands and feet are ice-cold; his breathing is faint, almost undetectable. There is nothing more I can do for him.

There is not even any use in my staying with him continuously, since he can no longer get out of bed or even fall out. His face is pale blue, his eyelids almost purple and translucent.

This afternoon I thought of something that might do him some good. I checked his bedroom one more time, and then I left the house and walked to the church, taking the Bible with me. I do not want to make it sound as if I am extremely religious, but I did not know what else to do, so I thought I might pray. I said it might do him some good; maybe what I really thought was that it might do me some good. I cannot be sure. But I knew he needed help and so did I.

I sat and read the Bible for half an hour, and I prayed for Mr. Loomis. Even though he may be a murderer, I do not want him to die.

JUNE 5
He has lived through the night.

I could not really sleep any length of time, but I dozed now and then. I kept the fire going and changed the hot-water bottle every hour.

Morning finally came, and during the day everything remained the same. I nodded by the window between times of tending him. Now and then I speak to him very softly. I just tell him I am here. He does not wake up or even flicker his eyelids. Yet I have a feeling he hears me, even if unconsciously, and that it is good for him to know someone is here.

In fact I am so convinced of this that I read to him quietly, sitting by his bed so he can sense where I am. I decided poetry would be soothing but, again, I am not too sure for whose benefit I am really doing it.

I suppose I have to accept the idea that Mr. Loomis shot Edward and killed him, and that is a terrible thought, because of what I hoped and because he is the only other human being I am ever likely to know.

But from what Mr. Loomis said, in a way it was self-defense.

If Edward had taken the suit, and left, and had never come back, he would, in effect, have doomed Mr. Loomis to stay in the laboratory until he ran out of food, or water, or air, and died. So in a way Edward was, when he tried to steal the suit, threatening to kill him.

Also, Mr. Loomis may have been concerned about more than just staying alive. In his dream he said that the suit was too important to waste. He called it "the last useful thing." At that time he surely still believed that there might be groups of people alive in sophisticated shelters—underground Air Force bases, and so on—and the suit, the only one of its kind, might be the only answer to their survival.

In a way it depends on knowing what Mr. Loomis was like —*is* like. I really do not know that, not yet.

JUNE 6

This morning I just about gave up hope. He had lain absolutely motionless, with no flicker of life except the faintest of breathing, for more than thirty-two hours. I began to feel as if I were alone again, after all. It was hard to think of him as a person; the belief that he could talk and think began to slip away. Yet I did not want to give up. I feel that if I do, he would, too. That is why I played the piano—the same hymns—hoping the music would penetrate to wherever he was.

JUNE 7

He is better.

He still does not wake up, but his respiration is more regular and his color has come up from blue to white. And he *looks* better. I have not yet taken his temperature, but I can tell that it is not as high as it was.

Taking advantage of this improvement, I changed his sheets,

blankets, pillowcase, and pajamas, gently easing him from one side of the bed to the other.

I have a big wash to do, and I know now that I was not cut out to be a nurse. I did consider it at one time. From a distance it seemed like a good profession, since your whole occupation is helping people who need help. But I had decided on teaching instead; it is also a job of helping people, though perhaps not so much as nursing.

It is still hard for me to realize, even after all this time, that I am not going to *be* anything, not ever have a job or go anywhere or do anything except what I do here. I had chosen teaching because I like books and reading more than anything else.

I miss having new books. We always depended on the Ogdentown public library, and I have so few here that I have read them twenty times or more.

Thinking about that set me to wondering. Having traveled all this way, Mr. Loomis could easily—with the safe-suit—make a trip to Ogdentown to get some books.

But would they be dangerous to bring into the valley? Or would it be possible to set them out somewhere—up the hillside, with a cover over them to keep the rain off—until they lost their radioactivity? Mr. Loomis would know, though he might not be interested. He clearly is not much of a reader.

Then I thought, *If it could be done, if the books would become safe to handle, and Mr. Loomis did not want to go, I could go. That is, if he would lend me the safe-suit.*

And that—with a jolt—brought me back to remembering Edward.

JUNE 8

He opened his eyes this morning, but they were blank and unfocused, the eyes of a newborn animal.

I fed him some water with a spoon. I knew he was not really conscious. But it was progress. A little later I also took his temperature—103—*much* better.

But he is skin and bones. Now that he could swallow, at least fluids, I thought about the most nourishing liquids I could concoct. Soup, of course. But even better, I decided, was boiled custard. I made some—milk, egg yolks, sugar, salt. While I waited for the milk to boil, I wished again for the stove.

And I thought—*well, why not?* I had the tractor now.

So, while I waited for the custard to cool, I ran to the barn, backed the tractor and cart to the loading platform, and lowered the tailgate. The cart and the platform are the same height—my father planned it that way. I got to work.

Unloading at the back porch of the house was equally easy and by afternoon the stove was reassembled and in place. I often took time out to check on Mr. Loomis. When his custard was cool enough, I tried feeding it to him with a spoon, a sip at a time. Again he did not wake up, but he did swallow it, gulping each spoon with an effort.

JUNE 15

A week has passed, and Mr. Loomis has become more improved in health.

Today is my birthday. I am sixteen, and for dinner we had a roast chicken and a cake, both baked in my wood-stove oven. I will not say it is the first cake I ever made, but it is the first I have baked alone—without my mother around—and the first in this oven.

We were celebrating not only my birthday, but also Mr. Loomis' recovery, which has been astonishing, though it is still not complete. He still cannot walk; his legs are weak and buckle under him.

So we had the birthday dinner on a folding card-table that I put beside his bed. When the table was all set, with the good china and silver, Mr. Loomis looked at it and said, "It seems like a miracle." And in a way it really did—a week ago he was nearly dead, and I had almost given up hope. But I think he was talking about the table.

His recovery had already begun when his breathing slowed down, though I was not sure of that at the time. I felt surer the next day, late in the afternoon, when he finally woke up. I had just walked into the room and, to my amazement, he spoke, very faintly. "You played the piano."

"Yes. I didn't know if you could hear."

"I heard. It faded away. . . ." His eyes closed again, and he did not finish the sentence.

The next day he seemed twice as strong. His temperature was only 101°, and he kept his eyes open longer. "I thought I was a long way from . . . from everything. Someplace cold. Floating away. It was hard to breathe. But I heard you playing, and then sometimes reading, and the floating stopped as long as I listened."

I fed him about every two hours, custard and soup, and on the third day I switched to solid food.

My worry over him grew less each day, and as always with worries (mine, at least), when a big one fades away smaller ones start creeping in. I went out to the garden I had been neglecting (I had scarcely looked at it for two weeks) and the field I had plowed but never planted. I hoped I could salvage both and, of course, did not intend to say anything to Mr. Loomis about it, sick as he still was.

But he began questioning me. "How is the planting? Has the garden come up? And the corn?" His tone was nervous, almost suspicious.

I confessed. "The garden is all right. It needs hoeing. But the corn . . ."

"Yes?" Very impatiently.

"I haven't planted it yet."

At that he acted very disturbed. He tried to raise himself on his elbow. "Not planted it? Why not?"

"You were so sick," I said. "I didn't dare leave."

"You mean you never left the house?"

"Not at first, except a few minutes to milk the cow," I said. "I was planning to plant the corn today. Maybe I can finish by afternoon."

He tried to explain. "I worry about food. I even dream about it."

But there was more to it than that, when I got to thinking about it. I had been regarding the field, the tractor—the *valley*—and the planting and garden, all as things of *mine,* to do or to worry about. But he had begun thinking about them as *his,* too, feeling the valley as much his as mine. I would have to get used to the idea.

JUNE 22

During the week since my birthday he has learned to walk again. But only very weakly, while holding on to something. He is secretive about it; I do not know exactly why. Probably because he feels foolish when he falls. He must practice when I am outside working, but I also hear him trying to exercise his legs when I come into the kitchen.

I do not want him to think I am eavesdropping, so when I brought him a tray this noon, I said, "I thought I heard you walking."

He was by this time back in the bed. "A little."

"How far can you walk?"

"Four steps, holding on to the bed."

"As soon as you can do a little more, I could fix a chair for you outside on the front porch."

"I had thought of that. And on the back porch, too, where I can see the planting."

"The corn is beginning to come up," I said. "The peas and beans are in but not up yet."

"How about beets? And wheat?"

"Well, I had not planned. . . ."

"You must plan. Not just for next year, but beyond. Beets make sugar. Wheat makes flour." His voice had grown edgy again.

He went on. "I've been lying in the bed for a long time now, with nothing to do but think. And I realized that we've got to plan as if this valley is the whole world, and we are starting a colony, one that will last permanently."

It was the same thought, or nearly the same, as the feeling I had had earlier, but now it made me uncomfortable. I do not know why.

JUNE 24

In these few days my uneasiness has grown worse.

At Mr. Loomis' urging, I planted wheat and beets, but that had nothing to do with my feeling uneasy. It was caused by something else.

As I had said I would, I put a chair out for him on the front porch—a small, upholstered armchair I got from my parents' bedroom. I also put a chair on the back porch, and yesterday morning he said that was where he would like to sit.

It was the first time since his sickness that he had ventured so far, but he did quite well. I had found a cane my father once used when he had a sprained ankle. With that, plus leaning heavily on my shoulder, Mr. Loomis made it to the porch and into the chair.

He sat there all morning—rather like an overseer—watching while I planted the beets.

After lunch he slept in his room while I started on the wheat field. When I came back to the house he was awake and wanted to go out again, this time to the front porch. I helped him to the chair, and then went inside and started dinner.

What happened after that was, I suppose, partly my own fault. Having put the food in the oven and the kettle on to boil, I got a chair, took it out on the porch, and sat next to him.

I had a reason for doing this, besides just wanting to rest a few minutes. It was a feeling I'd had, since he first began to recover, that I did not know him at all.

He had told me only the barest account of his life before. From his nightmares I had learned about his murder of Edward. But that was all I knew.

I did not want to discuss the thing about Edward (I decided probably not ever) nor the laboratory, but I wanted to get him talking about the times before that. I sat down beside him, but I did not know how to do it. In books and movies they say, "Let's talk about you," so I asked, "Where did you grow up?"

"A town in New York. Nyack." He did not elaborate.

I tried again. "Before you went to Cornell, what did you do?"

"What everybody does. Went to school, worked in the summers."

"Is that all?"

"After college, four years in the Navy."

That seemed to open a door. "On a ship?"

"No, in a naval ordnance laboratory in Bristol, New Jersey. I was a chemistry major in college. The Navy needed chemists. That's where I got started in plastics."

"I see." The conversation was steering into a circle.

"And when I finished there, I applied to Cornell graduate school." End of circle.

It seemed hopeless and I should have given up, but I did not. Instead I said. "But were you ever . . . did you ever get married?"

He looked at me in a queer way. He said, "I thought you were coming to that."

And then it happened. To my absolute astonishment. he did not even smile but reached over and took my hand. *Grabbed* would be a better word. He took it very quickly and hard, jerking me toward him so that I almost fell over. He held my hand between both of his.

He said, "No, I never got married. Why did you ask that?"

I was so startled that I just stared at him. All I could think of at first was that somehow he had misunderstood something I had said.

After that I felt embarrassed, and awkward, and afraid, in that order. Because of the way he held me, I was leaning off balance. When I tried to pull away he just tightened his grip. There was no expression at all on his face. "Why did you ask that?"

I said, "Please let go."

He said, "Not until you answer."

I said, "I asked because I was interested." I felt myself beginning to tremble; I was really frightened.

He said, "Interested in what?" And instead of letting go, he tightened his grip, pulling me farther off balance.

I could not help what happened next. I felt myself falling from the chair, and quite instinctively I threw up my right hand (he was holding my left one) to catch myself. It hit him in the face, near his left eye. In that moment he relaxed his grip. I snatched my left hand away.

In a very quiet voice he said, "You should not have done that."

Why should I have apologized?

"I'm sorry," I said. "I didn't mean to. I was falling." In my confusion I even tried to smile. I went back to the kitchen, thinking I was going to cry.

He walked back to the bedroom himself. I heard the sound of his cane and the dragging thump of his feet: he was holding himself up by leaning against the wall. Eventually I heard the bed creak as he reached it, and when I carried in his food he took the tray calmly, as if nothing had happened. I ate in my usual place at the card table, but we did not talk.

As I was doing the dishes, I realized that when he was holding my hand he didn't care about me—he was just taking charge, or possession—I do not know how to put it. Just as he had, in his way, of the planting, the use of gasoline, the tractor, and even of the store. And of the suit. And, in the end, of Edward.

For that reason his walking back to the bed without help, which should have been something to celebrate, instead made me uneasy.

JUNE 30

I am living in the cave again, and I am glad now that I never told Mr. Loomis about it or where it was. I moved up here two days ago, not because I wanted to, but because of what happened.

On the night after the hand-holding, I went to bed as usual with Faro beside me. I was still extremely nervous and could not get to sleep for a long while. When I woke, it was bright daylight—later than usual for me—and I still had the worried feeling. But I had my work to do, so I got up, did my morning chores, and got breakfast ready. When I took his tray into his room, I was strained and tense, but if he had any such feeling he did not show it at all. He took his tray, started eating his breakfast, and talked about what I would do that day. I had planned to fertilize the corn and the garden, too, if there was time.

It was relaxing working in the field and I felt normality returning. And then, turning at the end of a row, I glanced up at the house. There on the porch sat Mr. Loomis in his chair, leaning forward, watching me.

That made me feel nervous again, but lunch was about as usual, and then I went out again.

All in all, a fairly routine day until dinner time.

It was 6:30. I was in the kitchen and had almost finished cooking when I heard the sound of his cane and the thump of his footsteps (somewhat brisker than before) coming out of the bedroom. I listened, standing quiet, and heard him go into the dining room and sit down. When I looked in, he said, "I don't need to eat in bed anymore. I am still weak but not sick."

I put away the tray and set the table instead. We ate together, he at one end of the table, I at the other. He even tried to create conversation.

"I thought the corn looked good." He was paying me a compliment.

I said, "It's okay. So are the beans."

"And the vegetable garden?"

We were, in fact, eating radishes from the garden for dinner, and soon we would have lettuce.

He kept up a sort of inconsequential chatter, and I joined in as well as I could. I even felt relaxed after a while, which I suppose was what he intended.

After dinner I washed the dishes as usual. I was yawning, feeling quite tired, having worked hard all day and scarcely slept the night before. When I came out of the kitchen, I saw that once more he was in the big chair my father used to sit in in the evenings.

He said, "Do you remember when I was sick—something you did?"

I was alarmed, wondering what he was thinking of. "What do you mean?"

"You read to me. Could you do it again? Read whatever you want."

I did not *want* to read anything, but the fact is I did not know how to refuse, which I suppose he knew.

So I ended up reading to him from *Pride and Prejudice* by Jane Austen. But I soon discovered that he was not listening at all.

But why should he ask me to read to him if he did not want to listen? It was as if he were playing some kind of a trick on me. And that idea made me feel more nervous than ever.

The next night was worse. He asked me to play the piano. Again he was in my father's chair, which meant I had to sit with my back to him, and I felt uncomfortable about that.

I scolded myself. Did I expect that he would come creeping up on me from behind? That was ridiculous, but as I played the first piece I had a terrible urge to look over my shoulder. I played very badly, and I resolved to do better on the next one. It was going well—when all at once I heard his cane tapping behind me. I whirled around on the bench. He was still sitting in the chair. He had not moved at all.

He said, "Is something wrong?"

"Your cane," I said. "It startled me. I thought. . . ." I stopped.

"My cane slipped," he said, "but I caught it."

I turned and tried to play again, but by now my hands were shaking so badly I could not really do it. His cane had not slipped. It had been hooked over the arm of his chair with his hand resting on it. I turned around.

"I'm sorry," I said. "I can't play anymore. I guess I'm just too tired after working all day." Of course that was not why at all, and I was pretty sure he knew it.

The next night he did not ask me either to read or play the

piano. In fact, after dinner he did not sit in my father's chair at all but disappeared into his room.

I cleaned up the kitchen and then went for a walk with Faro. We ambled down the road to the church, and I felt peaceful again at being away from the house. Faro seemed to feel the same way —at least he did not scurry and sniff but just plodded along quietly. When we reached the church I did not go in but sat on the edge of the small white porch outside the front door; Faro lay on the step and rested his chin on my feet.

I waited until it was fully dark before I walked back. The house was unlighted and quiet. Mr. Loomis had left the cane on the porch. He had been out, apparently, while I was gone . . . and he no longer needed the cane. I went up to my room and Faro came with me.

I lit a candle, wound the clock, and sat on the edge of the bed thinking what I must do the next day. I felt sleepy after my walk, but uneasy. I kicked off my shoes but decided not to undress, at least for a while.

The next thing I knew I woke up in pitch darkness; the candle had burned out, and Faro was growling. The growl changed to a short *yip* of surprise. I heard him run out. I wondered what had startled him and then, in the next second, I knew. Mr. Loomis was in the room.

I could not see anything at all, but I could hear his breathing. I knew in the same second that he could hear mine. So I tried to breathe normally; perhaps if he thought I was still asleep, he would go away. He moved, very slowly and quietly—he *did* think I was still asleep. But I was never more wide awake.

He crept forward until he was just beside the bed. Then, suddenly, both his hands were over me, not roughly, but in a dreadful, possessive way. I knew what he was planning to do, as clearly as if he had told me. One hand moved upward, brushed my face, and then came down hard on my shoulder to pin me to the bed. At that instant, pretense ended. I whirled to one side, sprang to the floor, and made a dive for the door. In the same second, his whole weight landed on the bed where I had just been.

But I had tripped over his leg in my dive and his hand, grabbing blindly, caught my ankle. His grip was fiercely strong and his other hand caught the back of my shirt. I pulled forward desperately, heard the shirt rip, and felt his fingernails tearing the skin of my back. I hit back with my elbow as hard as I could.

By good luck I hit him in the throat. He gave a gasp and relaxed his hold. In an instant, I was out the door and running, my shirt rent down my back.

I did not sleep any more that night. After I got out of the house I ran, trying to get away as fast as I could. As it happened, I headed down the road toward the store and the church; I have never been so afraid. I ran at top speed for a minute or more. Then I slowed down enough to look over my shoulder. Although there was no moon, the sky was bright and I could see the road plainly. There was no sign of him. I slowed to a dogtrot, breathing so hard I was dizzy. When I reached the store I stopped and sat down where I could still watch the road.

Faro was nowhere to be seen and I knew where he was. He had hidden under the porch. He always did that when there was any friction among people. I trembled again. If Faro had not been there in the room to wake me up in time, I do not know how it would have ended.

I finally realized I was very cold. I went into the store, groped my way to the shelf where Mr. Klein kept the matches and candles. By candlelight I found sneakers my size and picked out two shirts —one cotton, one flannel.

I went to the cave—I had not been there for weeks—and all was as I had left it. I put a blanket around my shoulders and sat in the entrance, in my usual place, where I could lean back against the rock wall and look down on the house. There was no light in any window that I could see.

I sat there all the rest of the night, watching. I was sure he did not know where I was, or where the cave was, or even that there was a cave. I did not think he could climb the hillside. But I watched anyway.

In the early morning the scene below slowly took shape and color and I got my binoculars from inside the cave.

The first movement was Faro walking around hesitantly, looking for his breakfast. Almost immediately, Mr. Loomis came out the front door, carrying the dog's dish, full of food. He put it down, and as Faro began to eat it I could see that Mr. Loomis had something else in his hand. He fastened it to Faro's collar. Through the binoculars it took me a while to figure out it was a long electric cord, a heavy-duty one with a plastic covering. Mr. Loomis finished attaching it to Faro's collar and tied the other end to the porch rail.

Poor Faro! After Mr. Loomis went back in the house, Faro tried to chew himself free. But the tough plastic coating was too much for his teeth.

As I watched, I thought about all the things I should be doing—milking the cow, feeding the chickens and collecting the eggs, weeding the garden. Could I just live up here, keeping my distance, and continue to do them? Cooking the meals I could not do, since that would mean going into the house. Mr. Loomis would have to cook his own. I could bring him supplies, though.

I decided that somehow or other we would have to work out a compromise, a way that we could both live in the valley even though not as friends. There was enough room, and he was welcome to have the house. Thinking that, I fell asleep.

When I awoke in late afternoon, I took stock of what I had in the cave: a few pounds of cornmeal, some salt, three cans of meat, three of beans, one of peas, two of corn. That was all the food—not very much. I had the two guns and a box of shells for each. One book, *Famous Short Stories of England and America*, which we had used as a text in high-school English. And the empty bottles for water.

The sun was going down, and I decided before it was fully dark I would see about arranging to make a fire. He would see smoke if I cooked during daylight; I would have to build a wall so he could not see flames or sparks at night.

It turned out to be quite easy, and I was able to have a warm supper. After I had eaten I felt very tired and decided not to sleep in the cave—with only one entrance, and a small one, it would be like a trap.

I took my sleeping bag and a blanket up to the small shelf where I had built the fire wall. The ground was lumpy, but it made no difference. I fell asleep instantly and did not wake up until the sunlight reached my eyes this morning.

I got up, washed, ate, took my bedding back to the cave, and set out for the house. I went the long way around, of course, so that I could approach along the road as I had left. I did not want him to have any idea as to which direction I was really coming from.

When I came up to the front yard I stopped, staying in the road, and waited. I planned to go no closer than that.

In only a minute the door opened and Mr. Loomis stepped out onto the porch. "I thought you would come back," he said. Then he added, "I hoped you would."

For a moment I was stunned. "No," I said. "I'm not coming back. Not anymore. But I thought we should talk."

"Not come back?" he said. "But why not? Where will you stay?"

It was as before, the time he had held my hand and I had struck him. He acted as if nothing had happened.

I said, "I will find someplace to stay."

He shrugged, very unconcerned. "All right. Then why did you come?"

"Because, although I can't stay here anymore, I need to stay alive, and so do you. And there is work that has to be done. There are the crops, the garden, the animals."

He said, "Of course. That's why I thought you would come back."

"I'm willing to do those things if I am left alone. I will also bring food and water as you need them. You will have to cook for yourself."

He was thinking all the time. He glanced down the road in the direction I had come from. Finally he said, "I have no choice. I can only hope you will change your mind." He paused. "And act more like an adult and less like a schoolgirl."

"I will not change my mind."

He said no more but turned and went back into the house. I walked to the barn, trying to guess what he was thinking. Then I wondered: Where had Faro been when we talked? There had been no sight or sound of him. He must be tied up inside the house. Did Mr. Loomis think, then, that I might try to untie him—to steal him? (As Edward had stolen the suit.) Then I had a really sickening thought.

It was that whatever Mr. Loomis was planning, at the end of the plan was a picture, and it was of me, too, tied up like Faro in the house.

I put it out of my mind and milked the cow. I poured half the milk into an extra pail and put it on the back porch for Mr.

Loomis. I fed the chickens, gathered the eggs, and divided them.

In short, I did my outdoor work about as usual, and he left me alone, though I had the feeling he was watching me through the kitchen window.

At four o'clock, having run the cultivator between the rows of corn and beans, I quit and walked to the store, thinking as I went that for one day, at least, the system had worked.

But as darkness began to fall, two ominous things happened. First, Mr. Loomis brought Faro out on the leash, and it was clear Faro was able to follow my track. Faro started down the road to the store, but Mr. Loomis could not walk far.

When they came back, Mr. Loomis tied him up again and then went to the barn. He was out of my sight, but after perhaps five minutes, I heard the sputtering of the tractor engine. A minute later the tractor appeared, moving cautiously as he backed out.

He had, as far as I know, never driven a tractor before, but it was not hard to figure it out for anyone who knew how to drive a car. Mr. Loomis backed it all the way out of the barn, shifted into forward, and practiced driving it in small circles in the barn lot. In a while, he drove it back into the barn and turned it off.

I wish now Mr. Loomis had never come to the valley at all. It was lonely with no one here, but it was better than this. I wish that by luck, by chance, he might have taken some other road and found some other valley than this. And I wonder: *Could* there be others? Could it be that farther south there are more valleys like this, other places that have been spared? Perhaps bigger than this, with two or three or half a dozen people still alive. Or maybe no people at all. If Mr. Loomis had taken another road, he might have found one of them.

When Faro had returned that day I was astonished and puzzled about where he had been. Could he have been living in another valley? Could he have run to it from this one and then run back? There is no way of knowing.

AUGUST 4

(I think). I am in terrible trouble. Mr. Loomis *shot* me. I haven't written in my journal for several weeks. I have been too sick and too afraid. I have to keep moving. I am now hiding in thick woods high up on the west ridge. There is a hollow tree where I can keep my things. It is all a nightmare. Here is what happened.

For about ten days we had a sort of system. In the morning I would milk, gather all the eggs, feed the chickens, work the garden, and pick the vegetables. Each day I divided the food evenly and brought him water. I saw little of Mr. Loomis except from a distance. He seemed to have given up and accepted the new order of things; and yet he had not, as I know now, and as I think I really knew then. I lived—what else could I do?—as if it were to continue this way.

Each evening he would come out of the house with Faro. They would walk, and Faro would always follow my trail, going a little farther (and Mr. Loomis a little more briskly) each time. Three or four times Mr. Loomis took the tractor out again. Once, toward the end of this period, he took it out on the road and shifted into high gear. He ran it at top speed for about 300 yards —he was obviously trying to see how fast it would go, though I did not know why.

On the morning of the tenth day, he drove the tractor down to the store and went inside. When he came out again, he had a variety of materials with him. He padlocked both the front and the back doors of the store and boarded up the windows.

Knowing his mind, knowing his compulsion for taking

charge of things, for planning with the long-term point of view, I tried to tell myself that perhaps he was only trying to protect the remaining supplies.

With that in mind, I came down and did my usual chores, and then took up my milk can and started down the road to go back to the cave. Behind me, I heard the tractor engine. I sputtered slowly at first and then suddenly smoothed out and was running fast. It got louder very quickly. He was on the blacktop and was coming after me at top speed.

I made a dash up the hill, to the right of the pond, to reach the woods behind it before he turned the bend. I found a vantage point behind a bush, set down my milk, crouched, and waited.

The tractor had come out of the trees and ran in plain view down the blacktop. Mr. Loomis sat astride, steering with his left hand. In his right, to my amazement and horror, he held his rifle. He looked like an Indian on horseback in an old Western movie, attacking a wagon train. I stared, at first not comprehending at all.

But then I realized: He was trying to follow me—to see where (and how) I was living. At the same time, I reasoned, he must think I have a rifle—most farm families do—and that is why he is armed. There are no guns in the house, therefore I have taken them. He must fear I will shoot *him!*

So, still thinking we could somehow come to accommodate each other, I left my hiding place and went back to the cave. He was still sick, I told myself—he would have a long recovery. I went to sleep that night thinking I must be cautious, but also understanding. He has been through so much and I do not know what radiation sickness does to the mind.

It was the next morning he shot me.

I woke at dawn as usual, moved my blanket and sleeping bag to the cave, and ate breakfast. As I ate I thought again about the padlocks on the store. I knew that he had a compulsion for taking charge of things, but with daylight I had a new thought—and fear. Perhaps he had thought of a simple way to force me to come back: starvation.

Feeling worried and quite depressed, I took my milk can and walked to the house, going the long way around. It seemed especially important now to keep him from finding where I stayed.

When I came in sight of the house I thought, *Should I just go about my work as usual, or should I let him know straightaway that I have seen the padlocks and ask for a key?* I decided to ask and get it settled. It was, in fact, time to bring him some more supplies.

I remember now that my father once said that great events have a way of happening uneventfully. They slip up on you and are over before you know they have happened. This could hardly be called a great event, I suppose, but it was for me an important and terrible one.

I stood there in front of the house as I had before, watching the front door. Without warning there was a sharp snapping noise. I felt a hard tug on the leg of my blue jeans and a stinging pain in my right ankle. The noise came again. Not until then did I look up and see the shiny blue rifle-barrel poking from the upstaris window.

The second shot missed, hit the blacktop next to me, and flew away humming like a bee.

I dropped my milk can and ran for my life. I dashed for the trees, expecting each second another bullet to come crashing into me—because for the next thirty yards my back was still a clear target. But he fired no more.

In the trees I felt reasonably safe. At the bend, where I could look back and see that he was not following, I sat down to examine my ankle. The bullet had gone through the leg of my blue jeans, leaving two small, round holes. The sock underneath showed a narrow, straight tear through which blood was slowly oozing.

As wounds go, it was not serious; in fact while I sat there the bleeding virtually stopped. Back at the cave, I washed my ankle. It was a most peculiar wound, and puzzling. He had fired two shots; if he was trying to hit me, both had been aimed much too low. The more I thought, the more it seemed he was not trying to hit me, but to scare me away. Nobody could be that bad a shot.

And then, sickeningly, the truth came to me.

He was not trying to miss. He wanted to shoot me in the leg so that I could not walk. He wanted to maim, not to kill me. So that he could catch me. It was a simple plan, a terrible one. It still is. He thinks starvation will force me to come to the house or the store. And the gun will keep me from going away again. He will try again and again.

At that moment I heard the tractor start. I knew by some instinct what was going to happen next. I put on my sock and shoe as fast as I could and watched.

The tractor, bright red in the morning sun, came out of the barn. Mr. Loomis was carrying the .22; he does not want to shatter my leg, only cripple it, because after I am caught he intends it to mend again. Faro was with him.

Mr. Loomis stopped at the store and climbed down, gun ready. Faro picked up my trail and started retracing my morning's route, tail wagging, backtracking easily. And finally this small, friendly dog was an enemy, leading Mr. Loomis up the hill and to the cave.

My time there was up. I hurried into the cave and threw what I could carry into a burlap sack, not choosing very well because I was, stupidly, crying. I took cans of food, this notebook, a blanket, my knife, a jug of water. That was all I could manage—that and the .22 rifle.

There was no place to go except higher up the hill and into the woods. There, waiting, ready to run again, I had a nightmarish thought: *As long as Mr. Loomis has Faro, he will find me, no matter where I hide. Therefore, I must shoot Faro.* I felt sick to my stomach.

When they came in sight, Mr. Loomis had Faro on a short leash; Mr. Loomis was going very slowly and limping. Directly below me, he stopped to listen, and I had a stationary target. I took aim, but at that moment Faro gave a small bark. It was his bark of greeting, a soft pleasure bark for me—he knew the cave was just ahead. And at the sound, so gentle and familiar, my finger went limp on the trigger, and I lowered the gun.

In a few minutes they were at the cave. I could not see them from where I was hiding, but I smelled smoke. After about half an hour, Mr. Loomis and Faro came back down the trail. Apparently Mr. Loomis had walked enough for the day. When I heard the sound of the tractor, I made my way, sparing my right foot, back to the cave.

It was hard to keep from crying again. In front of the entrance in a black and smoldering pile were the remains of all my things. My sleeping bag, my clothes, even the box I used as a table, and my schoolbook, were cinders. And the other gun was gone.

The only thing I had to be glad about was that I had not shot Faro. But in the end I did kill him, though not with the gun.

AUGUST 6

It is raining and I am sitting in the hollow tree to keep dry. I slept here most of last night, and I woke up feeling more hopeful than I have in a long time. My ankle is almost well, but the main reason I feel happier is that at last I have decided what to do. I have made a plan: *I will steal the safe-suit and leave the valley.* The idea came to me while I was sick.

For several days after I was shot, I was aware of very little. I think I had a fever, though I had no thermometer to find out, and my ankle swelled very large and looked bad—blue on one side and bright red on the other. Most of the time I lay still, wrapped in my blanket.

Mr. Loomis, if he had known it, could have caught me easily, because I could not run. But of course he did not know it, since the last time he saw me I had been sprinting at high speed. He must have assumed that he had missed his chance.

It was during these days of sleeping that a dream began, a dream I have had many times since. Coming day after day, the dream began to dominate my thoughts, so that I came to believe in what it seemed to tell. There is another place—another valley—where I can live. And I am needed there. There is a schoolroom lined with books and children sitting at the desks. There is no one to teach them, so they cannot read. They sit waiting, watching the door, and they look as if they have been waiting for a long time.

And so I decided to leave the valley. I was convinced, after the shooting, that Mr. Loomis was insane. We would never be able to live in the same place in peace. I made my plans: I would go as Mr. Loomis had before me—wearing the safe-suit, pulling the cart.

Once I realized that it was something I was actually going to do, there were many things to think about and plan. Most important, I had to figure out a way to get the suit and cart without being seen. One person, Edward, had already lost his life because of the suit, and I knew that Mr. Loomis would not hesitate to kill me for it.

Yet for almost a month, Mr. Loomis left me alone. The drone of the tractor was reassuring; it let me know where he was. Mr. Loomis seemed finally to realize that someone had to harvest the crops, and since he would not let me do it, he would have to do it himself.

How have I lived for a month? When I explain, it will seem strange that I did not choose to leave long before now, for my life during that time was more miserable than I ever thought possible. Much of the time I was hungry. I picked mushrooms and blackberries on the ridge; for anything else, I had to sneak down to the pond or garden. I did not go often. I was too terrified of walking into a trap.

And one day I did walk into one.

On a warm afternoon I went to the east ridge to pick berries. Stooping behind the bushes to keep out of sight, I glanced downward; the front door to the store was wide open.

At first I thought that Mr. Loomis must be inside the store, gathering supplies for himself. I waited, but there was no sign of him. Suddenly I thought, *What if he simply forgot to lock it?* The longer I waited, the more I became convinced that it was true. He had forgotten to fasten the padlock and the heavy door had swung open.

My mind flooded quickly with the tastes and smells of food I had not eaten for the past month: canned meat, beans, crackers, soup, cookies. I thought of supplies that I needed for the trip: flashlight batteries, a compass. Warily I began to creep forward.

I came to a place where the brush stopped, and before me was the road and the store. All was quiet. I started into the open when suddenly a rabbit exploded from underneath my feet. I leaped backward in surprise and fear. Something moved near the store and a shot rang out. I turned and ran. He fired again but missed. I made it back into the trees and cover.

I was too shaken to consider my own foolishness. It was only the rabbit, and Mr. Loomis' impatience, that had saved me. But it was not over yet, for soon he came into sight, the gun under one arm and Faro on the leash. Faro found my trail almost immediately. He began to whine and bark.

I ran and got my gun. I doubled back along my own trail and moved north. I could hear Faro's barking on the hill below me. I ran through the woods leaving a twisted trail until I reached the banks of Burden Creek. I had spent many hours here, fishing for brook trout with David and Joseph, and though it was now a lethal stream, I knew of a way to cross. I walked partway across the water on a series of flat stones, then jumped to a smooth, shallow ridge of rock that connected with the opposite bank. I hurried across the ridge and through more trees and hid behind a stone. I could see the crossing place clearly.

I did not have to wait long. Mr. Loomis suddenly appeared out of the brush with Faro straining on the leash. At that moment I aimed the gun above his head and fired.

He had not known for sure I had the gun—that had only been my supposition. I think he really could not believe he heard the shot. He stood still for about ten seconds, then he released Faro and ran into a grove of trees. I fired in the air again, but Mr. Loomis had disappeared from sight, and I guessed from the motion of the brush that he had headed downhill, back toward the house.

Faro was swimming in Burden Creek. He had found my scent on the rocks and followed it, but where I had jumped he had to swim and got caught in the current. All in all he was probably in the stream for more than five minutes. Finally he reached the bank where I was, and soon he was by my side.

I hid behind the stone until dark. Then I led Faro to my camp and fed him some dried mushrooms, but he was not much interested. He was very sick in the morning. I expected he would be sick the way Mr. Loomis had been, but I guess dogs react differently from human beings, for by nightfall he was dead.

Now I am ready. I start my plan before daybreak tomorrow morning. It may be I will not write in this journal again. I know that if Mr. Loomis catches me with the safe-suit, he will shoot to kill.

AUGUST 7

I am writing this at the top of Burden Hill. I am wearing the safe-suit. I have already taken the cart and my supplies out of the valley and left them on the road toward Ogdentown. I have come back for one last confrontation with Mr. Loomis. I cannot just walk away from him, from this valley, from all that I hoped for, without a word. I know there is danger in this. He will come searching for me and he will have a gun; but I have a gun, too.

While I wait for him, I will finish my account of what has happened.

Last night I slept in this valley for the last time. I awoke several hours before dawn, ate quickly, and reviewed the order of events to come. There was no time to waste in fear or doubt. I gathered my few things in my burlap sack and left it by the road to pick up later. Then, carrying the gun, I stole down to the house in the darkness.

When I got there, I kept to the shadows and found a heavy, round stone. I took the note I had prepared so carefully from my pocket. I tiptoed to the front porch, laid the note in front of the door, and set the rock on top to hold it down. There was no way he could miss it.

The note said:

I am tired of hiding. If you will come to the south end of the valley, I will meet you at the flat rock where the road curves. We will talk. Come on foot. Leave your gun on the front porch. I will be watching you—I will not harm an unarmed man.

Hiding in the tall grass under the willows, I watched the sunrise. I thought, *Tomorrow I will watch it from a strange place.*

Then, almost before I was ready for it to happen, the front

door opened and Mr. Loomis stepped out onto the porch. He snatched up the note and gave a hurried look around before retreating into the house. I lay in the grass with my eyes on the door. It was agony, waiting. I remembered the first time I had seen him up close, when he was sick in the tent. He looked much better now. His face had grown brown from working in the fields, and he looked stronger, yet there was still that tense quality in his face that I had first regarded as poetic, and later as a sign of madness.

But the plan worked! The next time Mr. Loomis emerged from the house, he had the gun under one arm. He laid the gun on the porch hesitantly, as if he thought he were making a mistake. Then he walked to the road and turned right, headed for the south end of the valley.

For several long moments I could not believe that he was really gone. I lay still in the grass, trembling with reaction. I looked to the south: He was walking fast and was almost out of sight. I did not think he would turn back.

Keeping under cover I ran to the wagon. It looked smaller than I remembered. I lifted the green plastic covering and looked inside. Everything I needed was there: the safe-suit, the packages of food, the air tank, the water filter, even the Geiger counter.

I decided to take another desperate risk: I spent about five minutes in the house gathering up necessities and one nonessential —a picture of my parents.

Then I went to the front of the cart and pulled it forward. It was not very heavy, after all, and the wheels rolled easily over the thick grass of the yard and onto the blacktop.

I walked on up the road, heading north; the wheels of the wagon made a dry, hissing sound on the asphalt. I wondered where Mr. Loomis was, if he were still waiting by the rock for me to come. I imagined his fury when he discovered that the cart was missing, that he had been tricked.

I was nervous, walking toward the deadness. Burden Creek

flowed past the roadside, coming from outside, having crossed, perhaps, paths that I would follow. I thought of Faro and tears came to my eyes.

For the last minutes, laboring hard under the cart's weight on the uphill slope, I did not think at all. I picked up my sack on the way, and then I reached the top of Burden Hill. I took out the safe-suit and put it on and strapped the air tank on my back. Then I took the cart quickly downhill toward Ogdentown. I came back with this notebook and the gun.

The sun is high over the east ridge now and the valley is beautiful in the morning light. Mr. Loomis is bound to come soon and I must speak to him. His may be the last human voice that I will ever hear.

AUGUST 8

From the start, the interview did not go as I had planned. Mr. Loomis came on the tractor, with the gun across his lap. I stayed out of sight. He drove to the very top of Burden Hill, jumped down, and scanned the road toward Ogdentown.

My heart was pounding but my voice came out reasonably firm. "Drop your gun," I said.

Instantly he whirled and fired in the direction of my voice. I knew it was the end. I was sixteen and I had worked so hard to keep things going and now I was going to die. A wave of disappointment swept over me, disappointment so bitter it wiped out even my fear. I stood up and faced him. I do not know why he did not shoot again.

Instead he saw the safe-suit and began to shout. "It's *mine*. You know it's mine. Take it off!"

"No," I said, "I won't."

He aimed the gun at me. I stood still. When I spoke it was without conscious thought, but I realized now the words probably saved my life.

"Yes," I said, "you can kill me . . . the way you killed Edward."

He stared at me. Then he shook his head and lowered the gun.

"No," he said, "you don't know anything about that. . . ." His voice was weak.

"You told me when you were sick," I said. "You told me how you shot him in the chest. You had to patch the bullet holes in the suit."

Now Mr. Loomis turned away from me. For a moment he just stood there, his shoulders shaking. Then he said, "He tried to steal the suit . . . the way you are stealing it now."

"I have no choice," I said. "I didn't want to die, and you wouldn't give me anything. During the winter I would have starved on the hillside. I don't want to live with you hunting me as if I were an animal, and I will never agree to be your prisoner." I felt reassured by my own voice and talked on. "I'll search for a place where there are other people, people who will welcome me. To stop me, you will have to kill me, too."

"It's wrong," he said, but he knew that I meant it, and his tone was frightened and bewildered. "Don't go," he said. "Don't leave me. Don't leave me here alone."

I spoke carefully. "If you shoot me you will really be alone. But if I find people, I will tell them about you, and they may come. In the meantime you have food. You have the tractor and the store. You have the valley." There was bitterness in my voice. And suddenly, feeling near tears, I said, "You didn't even thank me for taking care of you when you were sick."

So my last words were childish.

That was all. I adjusted the mask so that it fit tightly over my face, and cool air from the tank flowed into my mouth. I turned my back on him. I waited for the jar and the sharp pain of a bullet, but it did not come. I walked into the dead wilderness. I heard Mr. Loomis calling after me. There was something in his tone that made me stop and look back up the hill. He was pointing to the west.

"Birds," he shouted. "I saw birds . . . west of here . . . circling. I was heading that way when I found this place. I saw them."

I raised my hand to him to let him know that I had understood. Then I forced myself to turn and walk away.

AUGUST ?

I have been walking west for many days now. The deadness is terrible, and I am beginning to understand how Mr. Loomis became the way he was. It is difficult not to become obsessed with survival when everything about you—when what amounts to your whole world—is a monument to death.

There actually were times when I was tempted to turn back, when I was ready to accept the conditions Mr. Loomis offered rather than go on further into nothingness. I even feared for my sanity, but then yesterday I saw the birds. Crows, they must be— they look like specks through the binoculars.

And then last night, just at dusk when I topped this hill, I saw the line of green on the horizon. It is still there this morning; I have not imagined it.

Last night I had the dream again, the one about the children waiting.

I do not know what day it is because I have lost track, but I believe it is Sunday. This morning I heard a bell, faint, but definite. It sounds like a church bell, maybe five miles away. If there is a bell, there are people.

I wonder if they see the smoke from my camp fire; I wonder if the children are waiting.

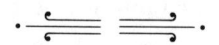

ROBERT C. O'BRIEN (Robert Leslie Conly; 1918–1973) won the Newbery Medal in 1972 for *Mrs. Frisby and the Rats of NIMH*. He also won an Edgar Award from the Mystery Writers of America in 1976, three years after his death. His other books for young readers are *The Silver Crown* (1968), *Z for Zachariah* (1975), and *Report From Group 17* (1972).

KATHERINE PATERSON

STAR OF NIGHT

Sometimes we don't realize how much we love others until they are gone. . . .

It had been raining when he left Chicago, but now as the plane circled for landing, he could clearly see the picture-postcard dome bathed in light and the Washington Monument piercing white against the black winter sky. Against all his resolutions, the beauty of the city below made Carl hope that this trip would not be as futile as all the others.

The last time word of his son had come was two years ago. And then the message had been that Jimmy was dead. Even so, Carl had gone out to San Francisco, hoping at least to bring the boy's body home for burial, but there had been no trace of it. He had talked to two persons who had seen Jimmy taken to a hospital, unconscious from an overdose. They had not seen him again, but they had both heard that Jimmy had died.

When he first returned from the San Francisco trip, none of the family would believe that Jimmy was really dead. No death certificate was ever sent. But after a year with no word, Carl noticed that the girls had begun to refer to Jimmy in the past tense, and lately both he and Miriam seemed to have come to an unspoken agreement to accept Jimmy's death as a fact.

And then suddenly yesterday, a phone call had come from one of Jimmy's high-school friends. Jimmy was alive, he said. He had seen him on the street in Washington. Jimmy had pretended not to recognize him, but there was no doubt in the boy's mind that it was Jimmy he had seen.

Somehow—a miracle, the ticket agent said—Carl was able to get a reservation for Christmas Eve on a flight to Washington. He hated to leave Miriam and the girls, but their hope that he might bring Jimmy back home with him canceled their own disappointment. Carl himself resolved not to hope. His hopes had been shattered so often in the last five years that he carried the obliteration of hope about in his body like shrapnel fragments. He could not lay his weary soul open to still another assault of hope. And yet—and yet he did hope.

From the airport he called Bill Woodson, a fraternity brother, who was pastor of a large church in the city. After a brief tussle with the clergyman's protective secretary, he got through to his friend.

"Carl Porter!" the voice boomed, deeper and more resonant than Carl remembered it. "What brings you to Washington on Christmas Eve?"

"I heard yesterday that Jimmy might be here in the city."

"Jimmy? But I thought. . . ."

"Yes, so did we. But a school friend saw him here on the street a few days ago."

"But that's wonderful news!"

"Well, I hope so. I've got to find him first. I know how busy you must be, but I just don't know anyone else in the area who might help me."

There was a long pause at the other end of the line.

"I know this must be a bad time for you."

"Yes"—another pause—"I have another service tonight, and my wife has invited an army of relatives. . . . Have you tried the police?"

"No." Carl cleared his throat. "This is between me and Jimmy. I don't want to go to the police with it. . . ."

"Hey, why don't you come on over here? We'll put our heads together. I might think of someone who could help us with this thing."

"This thing" is my son, thought Carl, but he thanked Bill and got directions to the church.

Wearily he dumped his suitcase and umbrella into the front seat of the rented car. But as he drove, there unfolded before him a city more beautiful than the one he had seen from the air. Arlington stood in majesty above the Potomac, and Lincoln looked out in compassion over yet another generation of his confused children. The tree on the White House lawn was a gigantic tower of brilliant light, and the hope that he tried so hard to deny kept pushing up in his chest.

He left the car in a lot marked "For Staff Only" and took the back steps of the building two at a time. He was met by a custodian, and when he gave his name and asked to see the pastor, he was handed a note.

"Sorry. Had to rush home between services. Try Chris Westoff at St. Thomas's. They work a lot with street people. Good luck and merry Christmas!"

Street people. He swallowed and asked to be directed to a phone. He found the number for St. Thomas's and let it ring for what seemed an eternity. His only alternative was the police, and he dreaded having to go there. That was where the trouble between Jimmy and him had begun. No, not begun. It began God knew when. When had the boy changed from a laughing, bright little child into a stubborn, narrow-eyed enemy? He had tried to get through to the boy, God knows he had tried, but all their encounters ended alike—he, in a rage of frustration, driven to punish the child far more stringently than he had intended, while Jimmy looked at him coldly through those narrow slits and refused ever to cry.

That was why, as he had tried to explain to Miriam a hundred times, when Jimmy had called from the police station, Carl had waited until morning to go and get him. He had been unable to discipline the boy; perhaps a taste of the consequences would straighten Jimmy out. . . .

"St. Thomas's Church. Merry Christmas!" The background was such a din that he could hardly hear the speaker.

"Yes. This is Carl Porter. I'm trying to reach a Reverend Westoff."

"He's at a Christmas party right now. Can I take a message?"

"No. I'll come over. I have to see him." He checked the address in the phone book and on the way out got directions from the custodian. He had no difficulty suppressing his hope now as he opened the car door.

There was a form on the backseat. Carl felt more annoyed than startled. It would mean another delay in this endless search. "Who are you?"

"Man, don't you know better than to leave your car unlocked in this kind of neighborhood?" The form straightened up. Under the curly black hair, the face looked about twelve, maybe fourteen. It was hard to tell.

"What do you want?"

"Well, mainly, man, I want a warm place to sleep. My old lady went out and left the apartment locked up. If I break that lock again, she'll give me hell. I don't know when she'll be home. Tomorrow, next day, maybe. When she celebrates, man, she celebrates."

"What's your name, son?"

"Independence Murray. In honor of a little celebrating she did one Fourth of July."

"Oh."

"I don't mind. Suppose it had been Halloween?"

Carl got into the car and shut the door. "You know where St. Thomas's Church is?"

"Nope."

"Want to help me find it?" It was a wild idea. The kid might mug him at the first dimly lit street.

"Hey, you're all right, man." Independence vaulted over into the front seat. He shoved the suitcase and umbrella toward the middle of the seat and settled himself comfortably in the corner.

Thus it was that when they finally found St. Thomas's, there were two of them. Carl was led through the din of a balloon race to a short man in a clerical collar. He was not sure how he could scream the tragedies of his life over the loud rock music and the shrieking voices and the bursting balloons. But the merciful pastor took the two of them to a closet-sized study and closed the door.

"I'm looking for my son. . . ." Carl saw at once that Westoff had heard the words a thousand times. He had not heard the name James or Jim or Jimmy Porter. The description Carl gave of the boy and the five-year-old picture must have sounded and looked like every other young boy the pastor had been asked about. It was to be another wild-goose chase. Rising, Carl tried to thank Westoff for his trouble.

"No, wait," the clergyman said. "We've just begun."

Westoff then spent about thirty minutes on the phone in a dozen undecipherable conversations. He seemed to spend a lot of time shaking his head. At last, in the midst of a conversation, he smiled and, putting his hand over the mouthpiece, turned to Carl.

"I have a lead on a boy that might be your son. Light brown hair, brown eyes, chipped front tooth. He's calling himself Brian Jones."

Carl's heart stopped as the huge poster of the Rolling Stones that Jimmy kept on his bedroom wall flashed before his eyes. "That sounds right. That could be Jimmy."

Westoff thanked the person at the other end of the line and hung up the receiver. "I think we're in luck," he said. "There's a girl here at the party who may be able to help us."

He reappeared shortly with a girl—a child, really—who wore a postage stamp of a dress. Her hair hung around her thin face and trailed almost to the abbreviated hem of her garment. She looked about twelve.

"I'm eighteen," she belligerently replied to Carl's stare.

"This is Tiny," Westoff said. "Tiny—Carl and Independence. Can you help them find Brian Jones?"

"I don't think Brian wants to be found too much."

"I just want to talk with him," Carl said.

She eyed him shrewdly.

"Come on, sister. Where's your Christmas spirit?" Independence asked.

The girl flashed Independence a sour look. "Okay," she said to Carl. "I'll get my coat."

Tiny climbed into the backseat of the car, curled her legs under her, and settled into the corner with a cigarette.

"You'll have to direct me, Tiny." Carl started the engine.

"Yeah. Well, I don't know exactly where it is, but I think it's like toward Maryland. Northeast, you know."

Carl shifted carefully into reverse. He must keep his temper. This child was his only hope. He waited while she took a long puff from her cigarette.

"Try Thirteenth or Fourteenth Street," she said at last.

Independence knew enough to get them to Fourteenth Street and headed north. "Do you remember anything special about the place?" Carl concentrated on erasing any trace of impatience from his voice. "Any landmark that might help you recognize it?"

"Yeah. Like there's this big blinking star on a building across the street from his house. If I hadn't been so stoned, it would have kept me awake all night."

Carl breathed audibly. "Good," he said. "We ought to be able to locate a sign like that."

They followed Fourteenth Street all the way into Maryland and Thirteenth all the way back. "Maybe they took it down," suggested the girl lackadaisically.

"Hey, wait a minute, man." Independence was leaning forward. "Stop at that drugstore over there."

Carl obeyed. The boy disappeared inside, and Carl had a fleeting fantasy of being the getaway man for Bonnie and Clyde. But in about ten minutes Independence reappeared, waving not a sawed-off shotgun but a piece of paper.

He forked it grandly over to Carl. "Here, man, is the name and address of the White Star Savings and Loan Corporation." He let Carl read the address and then slammed the door. "I had to go through a hell of a lot of stars in the Yellow Pages. But the way I figure it, with a big blinking star, it's got to be either a loan shark or an auto repair. Right?"

Carl started the car. "You're a genius, Independence."

The boy grinned happily. "So they tell me. So they tell me."

In less than five minutes they had found the White Star Savings and Loan. The cinder-block building seemed about to topple over under the weight of the huge star blinking on its roof.

Carl and Independence both turned to the backseat. "Well?" demanded the boy.

"Yeah," she said. "That's it. That house over there across the street—the one that's all boarded up."

"Don't look like nobody's living there."

"No, it don't," Tiny replied with light sarcasm and settled back into the corner for the return trip.

Carl got out. "You two can wait," he said. "I'm going to look around."

"In this neighborhood? You crazy, man?" Independence reached over and punched down the door lock, huddling down to make himself less conspicuous.

Carl walked around the house. He was feeling a little crazy. He had come so far across so many years and heartbreaks and had gotten so close, only to lose again. It had once been an impressive house, in an ugly late-Victorian way, with two bay windows and massive front steps. All the windows on the first floor were boarded up, the panes long ago sacrificed to vandals. In the dim light he could see obscenities and slogans painted across the brownstone. There was a large official warning to trespassers posted on the front door. He rattled the doorknob, then banged on the door.

"Jimmy! Jim! Are you there?" It was no use. Fatigue assailed him as he turned to go back to the car.

Just then Independence jumped out of the front seat and ran toward him, grabbing his arm. "Look!" the boy whispered, pointing upward.

A thin wisp of smoke was rising from the chimney. They watched the old house in silence. Once Carl thought he saw something move at one of the second-floor windows. He turned to speak to Independence, but the boy was already back at the car. "Okay, Tiny, out," Independence was saying.

He locked the door behind the reluctant girl. "You people got ways of letting each other know who you are. How 'bout getting us into that house?"

"Yeah." Tiny shrugged Independence's hand off her arm. They followed her to the back of the house and up some steps to a small, latticed back porch. "Got a credit card?"

Carl handed her one from his wallet, and she slipped it under the bolt through the crack of the screen door and yanked up. The door fell open. They followed her across the dark porch. She handed the card back to Carl and then knocked on the door in what he guessed was a code. There was a scuffling noise inside, then silence. At length the door opened a crack.

"Oh, Tiny, it's you, isn't it?" a soft voice replied. The crack was widening to reveal a girl even more pale and childlike than Tiny. Her dark hair hung almost to her waist. She wore a long, beaded dress. In her left hand she was carrying a candle, which gave her features a soft warmth, and slung over her right hip was a baby wrapped in a fringed shawl.

"Who is he?" She pointed her candle past Tiny.

"It's all right," said Carl. "He's with me."

Independence jabbed him in the ribs. "She means you, baby. Not me." Carl blushed in the darkness. Of course, the boy was right. It was Carl himself who was suspect in this setting.

"It's all right, sister," Independence said jauntily. "We're just the three wise guys following the big blinking star. How about a little shelter for dusty travelers?"

The solemn little mother smiled. "I thought they were three men—wise men."

"So? We're liberated. Right, Tiny?" By this time Independence had smooth-talked his way through the door and was standing beside the girl. With a bow he shoved the door wide and ushered Tiny and Carl into the house. The girl made no objections. They followed her and the candle through the ancient kitchen and broad hallway into what must have been the parlor. Through the cracks in the boards, the star of the loan company across the street gave a steady pulse of light. There was a large fireplace in the room, built for four- or five-foot logs. In it, a tiny, orphaned flame sputtered. The only furniture was a mattress pushed against the wall. The girl put the candle on the floor and shifted the baby to her other hip.

"Seen Brian lately?" Tiny asked finally. She pointed her nose at Carl. "Says he's his old man. Just wants to talk."

"Really, I do just want to talk with him," said Carl. He tried to keep from begging, but the tone came through all the same.

"Let's just sit down," suggested Independence, plopping himself down on the mattress.

Carl sat on the floor near the girl. She was toying with the fringe on the baby's shawl.

The baby was quiet, but the girl hugged it to her as though it needed comforting. She looked into the little face and said quietly, "Brian—Brian is dead."

He had heard it before, and he hadn't believed it then, either. So although the word "dead" bound his chest like a cold chain, Carl did not surrender to it.

"When did he die?"

"October," the girl replied. "November." She was talking to the baby rather than to him. "We don't always know the time, do we, Jason?"

"Was it drugs?"

The girl looked up quickly. "No," she said. "He's been clean since Frisco. He nearly died in Frisco."

"I heard that."

"No. He was looking for work. He was worried about me and the baby, you know. A car hit him. . . ."

The floor creaked above their heads. Carl looked up. "Rats," said the girl. The baby made a gurgling noise.

"Hey, can I hold him?" asked Independence.

"He might cry," said the girl.

"No way. Babies are crazy about me." Independence leaned over and took the child. "Hey, he's really something. How you doing, man?" The baby smiled up at the boy and made more baby noises. "See that? He's laughing." The boy began to sing under his breath, rocking himself and the baby in rhythm:

"Mary had a baby, yes, my Lord,
Mary had a baby, yes, my Lord,
Mary had a baby, yes, my Lord,
The people keep a-coming and the train has gone."

"I always liked that part about the train," Independence explained to no one in particular and resumed his quiet song.

Carl leaned toward the girl. "May I ask you another question?"

"Sure," said the girl, not taking her eyes off the boy and the baby.

"Is the baby—is Jason my . . . ?"

"He's Brian's, yes." She turned toward him with a half smile. "I don't mind if you don't."

"No, no," he stammered. "I'm—I'm very pleased—proud. . . ."

"You hear that, Jason-baby?" the boy asked. "You just got yourself a proud granddaddy. Want to hold him?"

"Well, I—"

"Hey, don't be scared, Carl-baby. Jason won't hurt you." He handed the baby to him.

Carl trembled at the touch. He looked into the baby's face, searching there for something of Jimmy. The baby smiled. *I'm going to cry,* thought Carl. *When have I ever cried?*

"Hey"—Tiny was on her feet—"hey, can we go now? I got you here like I said."

Carl opened his mouth to reply but shut it again as a huge rat emerged from the darkness and raced across the floor toward them. They all drew back as it ran over the mattress and into a hole in the wall on the other side.

"Wow," said Independence respectfully. "They grow 'em big around here, don't they?"

"Yes," said the girl. Carl could see that she was shivering.

"Come with us," he said. "Let me find you a warm place to stay—without any rats."

"We don't stay here all the time, you know." Her jaw was out. "Just until we can get enough for key money on a decent place."

"I know," said Carl. "But let me help you just for a few days, anyway."

"No, I can't leave."

"Are you waiting for Jim—for Brian, I mean?"

"Didn't I already tell you Brian is dead?" She wouldn't look at him.

"You're waiting for someone else?" he asked gently.

"No."

"Please, come with us—for Jason's sake."

"I can't leave." She reached out, so Carl reluctantly gave her the baby. She hugged him close.

Carl turned to the boy. "Independence, would you get my things from the car?" He handed him the keys. "We'll spend the rest of the night here."

"What a hell of a way to spend Christmas," grumbled Tiny.

Independence flipped the keys into the air with his left hand and caught them behind his back with his right. "You can always hoof it on your own, Tiny-baby."

"In this neighborhood? You crazy, man?"

Carl distributed the clothes from his suitcase. The girls and baby lay down on the mattress covered with a ragged blanket, Carl's overcoat, and his extra suit jacket and pants. Independence lay near the fireplace on top of part of the *Chicago Tribune* and put another section over him.

At everyone's insistence, Carl himself put on his bathrobe over his suit and then propped himself in a corner with the umbrella next to him. He was determined not to sleep and was sure, in fact, that the cold would keep him awake, but despite his discomfort, exhaustion overcame him. Toward dawn his head had dropped to his chest, and he was dozing, when he heard the clicking noise of rat paws on the wooden floor. By the time he was fully awake, the rat was nosing about the mattress near the baby's face.

Carl jumped to his feet with a shout, expecting the rat to run, but the creature snarled like a vicious little dog and turned its attention once more to the child.

It was not just a hungry animal to Carl. It was some evil manifestation. It was all the evil in himself, and in everyone like him, that brought these little children to such a place. And Carl attacked it as such.

He swung the heavy handle of the umbrella down with such force that the rat gave out an almost human shriek and then lay stunned. Carl kicked it away from the mattress. He tried to stab it with the point of the umbrella, but the flesh was soft and gave way under his blows, so he raised his foot and stamped down again and again with his heel until dark blood gushed from the rat's head and ran onto the floor. The creature twitched, then was still. With the point of his umbrella, Carl pushed the rat's body into the fireplace.

Panting, the sweat rolling from under his bathrobe, Carl fell back into his corner.

"Jesus"—Independence was staring at him respectfully—"you're in the wrong line of work, man."

They were all staring at him. Carl wiped his sweating hands on his bathrobe. He was ashamed for them to look at him like this.

There was a noise on the stair. Oh, God, he wasn't up to another battle, but he staggered to his feet and raised his umbrella against this new intruder. This one was human, with shoulder-length brown hair and a beard.

"Take it easy, Dad." The speaker had a chipped front tooth.

"Jimmy?" Carl lowered the umbrella.

The young man went over to the mattress and bent over the girl, who was now holding the screaming child. "Is he okay?" he asked.

"Yes," she said.

"It's all right, Jason, boy," Jimmy said soothingly, stroking the tiny cheek with his forefinger. "It's all right."

"I think he's just hungry," said the girl. She unhooked her dress and began to nurse the baby.

"We thought you were dead, Jimmy," Carl said.

"I was, in a way. I'm all right now."

"Why couldn't you let us know? Would it have been so hard just to call your mother?"

"Not hard to call Mother. No."

"Oh, God." Carl turned away. He was sobbing.

Strong young arms came about his shoulders. "Sh-sh. It's all right. You came to look for me, didn't you?" Jimmy held Carl tightly. "I saw you fighting for my baby," he said softly. "I was watching through the floor."

"Well," said Independence. "This is a nice little scene, but I gotta move on to the next act. Come on, Tiny. Hand me those things." He started to pack Carl's suitcase.

"Come back home with me, Jimmy."

The young man shook his head. "Not now," he said. "In the spring we'll come."

"Would you let me lend you the deposit for an apartment?"

Jimmy looked quickly at the rat where it lay in the cold fireplace. "That would be good, Dad. I'd appreciate it. Just until spring." He smiled his boyish, chipped-tooth smile.

"I'd appreciate a little breakfast," Tiny's shrill voice announced.

"He's taking us all out to breakfast, Tiny. Don't you worry. Little celebration due all round." Independence immediately took charge of herding the little group out the door and toward the car.

Across the street, the White Star Savings and Loan Corporation squatted small and dirty under its darkened star.

"Right on, guiding star!" Independence waved. "We wise guys have seen the light."

"Yeah," said Tiny. "Ho, ho, ho! Merry Christmas and all that."

Carl put his arm around the girl's thin shoulders. "Merry Christmas to you, too, Tiny," he said.

KATHERINE PATERSON (1932–) won the Newbery Medal in 1978 for *Bridge to Terabithia,* and then won the Medal again in 1981 for *Jacob Have I Loved.* She was also a recipient of an American Book Award in 1977 for *The Master Puppeteer.* Her other distinguished books include *Of Nightingales That Weep* (1974), *The Great Gilly Hopkins* (1978), *Angels and Other Strangers* (1980), and *Rebels of the Heavenly Kingdom* (1983).

ARMSTRONG SPERRY

GHOST OF THE LAGOON

Could a ghost be killed with a spear? A tense drama on a South Sea island . . .

THE ISLAND OF Bora Bora, where Mako lived, is far away in the South Pacific. It is not a large island—you can paddle around it in a single day—but the main body of it rises straight out of the sea, very high into the air like a castle. Waterfalls trail down the faces of the cliffs. As you look upward you see wild goats leaping from crag to crag.

Mako had been born on the very edge of the sea, and most of his waking hours were spent in the waters of the lagoon, which was nearly enclosed by the two outstretched arms of the island. He was very clever with his hands; he had made a harpoon that was as straight as an arrow and tipped with five-pointed iron spears. He had made a canoe, hollowing it out of a tree. It wasn't a very big canoe —only a little longer than his own height. It had an outrigger, a sort of balancing pole, fastened to one side to keep the boat from tipping over. The canoe was just large enough to hold Mako and his little dog, Afa. They were great companions, these two.

One evening Mako lay stretched at full length on the pandanus mats, listening to Grandfather's voice. Overhead, stars shone in the dark sky. From far off came the thunder of the surf on the reef.

The old man was speaking of Tupa, the ghost of the lagoon. Ever since the boy could remember, he had heard tales of this terrible monster. Frightened fishermen, returning from the reef at midnight, spoke of the ghost. Over the evening fires old men told endless tales about the monster.

Tupa seemed to think the lagoon of Bora Bora belonged to him. The natives left presents of food for him out on the reef: a dead goat, a chicken, or a pig. The presents always disappeared mysteriously, but everyone felt sure that it was Tupa who carried them away. Still, in spite of all this food, the nets of the fishermen were torn during the night, the fish stolen. What an appetite Tupa seemed to have!

Not many people had ever seen the ghost of the lagoon. Grandfather was one of the few who had.

"What does he really look like, Grandfather?" the boy asked for the hundredth time.

The old man shook his head solemnly. The light from the cook fire glistened on his white hair. "Tupa lives in the great caves of the reef. He is longer than this house. There is a sail on his back, not large but terrible to see, for it burns with a white fire. Once when I was fishing beyond the reef at night I saw him come up right under another canoe—"

"What happened then?" Mako asked. He half rose on one elbow. This was a story he had not heard before.

The old man's voice dropped to a whisper. "Tupa dragged the canoe right under the water—and the water boiled with white flame. The three fishermen in it were never seen again. Fine swimmers they were, too."

Grandfather shook his head. "It is bad fortune even to speak of Tupa. There is evil in his very name."

"But King Opu Nui has offered a reward for his capture," the boy pointed out.

"Thirty acres of fine coconut land and a sailing canoe, as well," said the old man. "But who ever heard of laying hands on a ghost?"

Mako's eyes glistened. "Thirty acres of land and a sailing canoe. How I should love to win that reward!"

Grandfather nodded, but Mako's mother scolded her son for such foolish talk. "Be quiet now, son, and go to sleep. Grandfather has told you that it is bad fortune to speak of Tupa. Alas, how well we have learned that lesson! Your father—" She stopped herself.

"What of my father?" the boy asked quickly. And now he sat up straight on the mats.

"Tell him, Grandfather," his mother whispered.

The old man cleared his throat and poked at the fire. A little shower of sparks whirled up into the darkness.

"Your father," he explained gently, "was one of the three fishermen in the canoe that Tupa destroyed." His words fell upon the air like stones dropped into a deep well.

Mako shivered. He brushed back the hair from his damp forehead. Then he squared his shoulders and cried fiercely, "I shall slay Tupa and win the king's reward!" He rose to his knees, his slim body tense, his eyes flashing in the firelight.

"Hush!" his mother said. "Go to sleep now. Enough of such foolish talk. Would you bring trouble upon us all?"

Mako lay down again upon the mats. He rolled over on his side and closed his eyes, but sleep was long in coming.

The palm trees whispered above the dark lagoon, and far out on the reef the sea thundered.

The boy was slow to wake up the next morning. The ghost of Tupa had played through his dreams, making him restless. And so it was almost noon before Mako sat up on the mats and stretched himself. He called Afa, and the boy and his dog ran down to the lagoon for their morning swim.

When they returned to the house, wide-awake and hungry, Mako's mother had food ready and waiting.

"These are the last of our bananas," she told him. "I wish you would paddle out to the reef this afternoon and bring back a new bunch."

The boy agreed eagerly. Nothing pleased him more than such an errand, which would take him to a little island on the outer reef half a mile from shore. It was one of Mako's favorite playgrounds, and there bananas and oranges grew in great plenty.

"Come, Afa," he called, gulping the last mouthful. "We're going on an expedition." He picked up his long-bladed knife and seized his spear. A minute later he dashed across the white sand where his canoe was drawn up beyond the water's reach.

Afa barked at his heels. He was all white except for a black spot over each eye. Wherever Mako went, there went Afa also. Now the little dog leaped into the bow of the canoe, his tail wagging with delight. The boy shoved the canoe into the water and climbed aboard. Then, picking up his paddle, he thrust it into the water. The canoe shot ahead. Its sharp bow cut through the green water of the lagoon like a knife through cheese. And so clear was the water that Mako could see the coral gardens, forty feet below him, growing in the sand. The shadow of the canoe moved over them.

A school of fish swept by like silver arrows. He saw scarlet rock cod with ruby eyes, and the head of a conger eel peering out from a cavern in the coral. The boy thought suddenly of Tupa, ghost of the lagoon. On such a bright day it was hard to believe in ghosts of any sort. The fierce sunlight drove away all thought of them. Perhaps ghosts were only old men's stories, anyway!

Mako's eyes came to rest upon his spear—the spear that he had made with his own hands—the spear that was as straight and true as an arrow. He remembered his vow of the night before. Could a ghost be killed with a spear? Some night when all the village was sleeping, Mako swore to himself, he would find out! He would paddle out to the reef and challenge Tupa! Perhaps tonight. Why not? He caught his breath at the thought. A shiver ran down his back. His hands were tense on the paddle.

As the canoe drew away from shore, the boy saw the coral reef that above all others had always interested him. It was of white coral—a long, slim shape that rose slightly above the surface of the water. It looked very much like a shark. There was a ridge on the back that the boy could pretend was a dorsal fin, while up near one end were two dark holes that looked like eyes!

Times without number the boy had practiced spearing this make-believe shark, aiming always for the eyes, the most vulnerable spot. So true and straight had his aim become that the spear would pass right into the eyeholes without even touching the sides of the coral. Mako had named the coral reef "Tupa."

This morning as he paddled past it, he shook his fist and called, "Ho, Mister Tupa! Just wait till I get my bananas. When I come back, I'll make short work of you!"

Afa followed his master's words with a sharp bark. He knew Mako was excited about something.

The bow of the canoe touched the sand of the little island where the bananas grew. Afa leaped ashore and ran barking into the jungle, now on this trail, now on that. Clouds of seabirds whirled from their nests into the air with angry cries.

Mako climbed into the shallow water, waded ashore, and pulled his canoe up on the beach. Then, picking up his banana knife, he followed Afa. In the jungle the light was so dense and green that the boy felt as if he were moving underwater. Ferns grew higher than his head. The branches of the trees formed a green roof over him. A flock of parakeets fled on swift wings. Somewhere a wild pig crashed through the undergrowth while Afa dashed away in pursuit. Mako paused anxiously. Armed only with his banana knife, he had no desire to meet the wild pig. The pig, it seemed, had no desire to meet him, either.

Then ahead of him the boy saw the broad green blades of a banana tree. A bunch of bananas, golden ripe, was growing out of the top.

At the foot of the tree he made a nest of soft leaves for the bunch to fall upon. In this way the fruit wouldn't be crushed. Then with a swift slash of his blade he cut the stem. The bananas fell to the earth with a dull thud. He found two more bunches.

Then he thought, *I might as well get some oranges while I'm here. Those little rusty ones are sweeter than any that grow on Bora Bora.*

So he set about making a net of palm leaves in which to carry the oranges. As he worked, his swift fingers moving in and out among the strong green leaves, he could hear Afa's excited barks off in the jungle. That was just like Afa, always barking at something: a bird, a fish, a wild pig. He never caught anything, either. Still, no boy ever had a finer companion.

The palm net took longer to make than Mako had realized.

By the time it was finished and filled with oranges, the jungle was dark and gloomy. Night comes quickly and without warning in the islands of the Tropics.

Mako carried the fruit down to the shore and loaded it into the canoe. Then he whistled to Afa. The dog came bounding out of the bush, wagging his tail.

"Hurry!" Mako scolded. "We won't be home before the dark comes."

The little dog leaped into the bow of the canoe, and Mako came aboard. Night seemed to rise up from the surface of the water and swallow them. On the distant shore of Bora Bora, cook fires were being lighted. The first star twinkled just over the dark mountains. Mako dug his paddle into the water, and the canoe leaped ahead.

The dark water was alive with phosphorus. The bow of the canoe seemed to cut through a pale, liquid fire. Each dip of the paddle trailed streamers of light. As the canoe approached the coral reef the boy called, "Ho, Tupa! It's too late tonight to teach you your lesson. But I'll come back tomorrow." The coral shark glistened in the darkness.

And then suddenly Mako's breath caught in his throat. His hands felt weak. Just beyond the fin of the coral Tupa there was another fin—a huge one. It had never been there before. And—could he believe his eyes? It was moving.

The boy stopped paddling. He dashed his hand across his eyes. Afa began to bark furiously. The great white fin, shaped like a small sail, glowed with phosphorescent light. Then Mako knew. Here was Tupa—the real Tupa—ghost of the lagoon!

His knees felt weak. He tried to cry out, but his voice died in his throat. The great shark was circling slowly around the canoe. With each circle it moved closer and closer. Now the boy could see the phosphorescent glow of the great shark's sides. As it moved in closer he saw the yellow eyes, the gill slits in its throat.

Afa leaped from one side of the canoe to the other. In sudden anger Mako leaned forward to grab the dog and shake him soundly. Afa wriggled out of his grasp as Mako tried to catch him, and the shift in weight tipped the canoe on one side. The outrigger rose from the water. In another second they would be overboard. The boy threw his weight over quickly to balance the canoe, but with a loud splash Afa fell over into the dark water.

Mako stared after him in dismay. The little dog, instead of swimming back to the canoe, had headed for the distant shore. And there was the great white shark—very near.

"Afa! Afa! Come back! Come quickly!" Mako shouted.

The little dog turned back toward the canoe. He was swimming with all his strength. Mako leaned forward. Could Afa make it? Swiftly the boy seized his spear. Bracing himself, he stood upright. There was no weakness in him now. His dog, his companion, was in danger of instant death.

Afa was swimming desperately to reach the canoe. The white shark had paused in his circling to gather speed for the attack. Mako raised his arm, took aim. In that instant the shark charged. Mako's arm flashed forward. All his strength was behind that thrust. The spear drove straight and true, right into the great shark's eye. Mad with pain and rage, Tupa whipped about, lashing the water in fury. The canoe rocked back and forth. Mako struggled to keep his balance as he drew back the spear by the cord fastened to his wrist.

He bent over to seize Afa and drag him aboard. Then he stood up, not a moment too soon. Once again the shark charged. Once again Mako threw his spear, this time at the other eye. The spear found its mark. Blinded and weak from loss of blood, Tupa rolled to the surface, turned slightly on his side. Was he dead?

Mako knew how clever sharks could be, and he was taking no

chances. Scarcely daring to breathe, he paddled toward the still body. He saw the faintest motion of the great tail. The shark was still alive. The boy knew that one flip of that tail could overturn the canoe and send him and Afa into the water, where Tupa could destroy them.

Swiftly, yet calmly, Mako stood upright and braced himself firmly. Then, murmuring a silent prayer to the Shark God, he threw his spear for the last time. Downward, swift as sound, the spear plunged into a white shoulder.

Peering over the side of the canoe, Mako could see the great fish turn over far below the surface. Then slowly, slowly, the great shark rose to the surface of the lagoon. There he floated, half on one side.

Tupa was dead.

Mako flung back his head and shouted for joy. Hitching a strong line about the shark's tail, the boy began to paddle toward the shore of Bora Bora. The dorsal fin, burning with the white fire of phosphorus, trailed after the canoe.

Men were running down the beaches of Bora Bora, shouting as they leaped into their canoes and put out across the lagoon. Their cries reached the boy's ears across the water.

"It is Tupa—ghost of the lagoon," he heard them shout. "Mako has killed him!"

That night as the tired boy lay on the pandanus mats listening to the distant thunder of the sea, he heard Grandfather singing a new song. It was the song that would be sung the next day at the feast that King Opu Nui would give in Mako's honor. The boy saw his mother bending over the cook fire. The stars leaned close, winking like friendly eyes. Grandfather's voice reached him now from a great distance, "Thirty acres of land and a sailing canoe..."

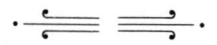

ARMSTRONG SPERRY (1897–1976) won the Newbery Medal in 1941 for *Call It Courage.* In addition, he wrote *All Sail Set* (a Newbery Honor Book in 1936) and illustrated *Codfish Market* (a Newbery Honor Book in 1937). His many other books include adventure stories and geography books.

NANCY WILLARD

THE HIGHEST HIT

A very funny baseball story...

Everybody tells me I could be old and rich when I grow up, but I'd rather be young and famous right now. I've got a plan for doing it, too. I keep a cigar box tied to the doorknob of my bedroom, and the sign on the box says:

> PROPERTY OF KATE CARPENTER SCHMIDT
> PUT YOUR MONEY IN HERE
> FOR THE PEOPLE WHO HAVE NO FOOD.

My dad puts in all the pennies that stick to the bottom of his pocket at the end of the day. My mom puts in a dime every time she brushes her teeth and thanks God she still has them. Trudy the baby-sitter can't afford to put in anything because she just bought a new set of uppers, and even though she's only twenty-five, she goes around looking like George Washington, whose uppers didn't fit him, either. My big sister, Ellen, told me that. She learned it in Sunday school, but not from the teacher.

When I've collected five dollars, I'll send it to UNICEF. Then I'll start saving for the Humane Society. And when I've saved five dollars for the Humane Society, I'll start saving for the Prisoners' Aid Association. After I've taken care of the prisoners, I'll begin on the Abused Children. By the time I'm twenty I'll have helped so many people that they'll nominate me for the *Guinness Book of World Records*. That's the only way I'll ever get in, because all the other ways have been used up.

Once in a while, I contribute a dime.

Every Friday Mom gives Ellen and me our allowances. Fifty cents apiece. Ellen saves hers because she saves everything. She has a whole drawer of old pieces of wedding cake that she's saving to sleep on when she gets up the nerve. Because when you tuck that cake under your pillow, whoever you dream of—that's who you'll marry. I tell her, "Why worry about who you'll marry? You're only fifteen."

I save a lot of stuff, too—buttons and baseball cards and bottle caps and old jars—everything except money. I always spend my allowance on baseball cards, of which I have about five hundred, including Hank Aaron, who is my number one. When Trudy the baby-sitter saw me trudging home from school with three new packs of baseball cards the day before summer vacation, she just shook her head.

"A fool and her money are soon departed," she warned me. "And keep out of my kitchen. I just waxed the floor."

"Who's coming over?"

"Nobody I know of. It's a surprise for your mom's birthday."

This year my mom's birthday came the day the new baseball cards hit the stands, which explains why I forgot all about it till that moment. Guilt and panic settled in my stomach.

"Can I help you wax the dining-room floor? It could be a present from both of us."

"No, sir. I'm wore out. Go and buy her some nice lipstick at Kresge's, or some perfume."

"I don't have any money."

Trudy put the scrub bucket on the back porch and shut the door on it as if it had insulted her. Then she pushed her long red hair out of her eyes and grabbed the dust mop and shoved it savagely under the radiator in the front hall.

"Get her something that don't cost," she said.

"Like what?" I asked.

"Draw her a picture," answered Trudy. "You got more crayons around the house than you could use up in a year."

"I can't draw anything except baseball players," I whined.

"So draw her a baseball player," said Trudy.

I know Mom hates baseball. She always complains that it makes me late for supper. I knew I could do a good drawing of Babe Ruth. I've done him about a dozen times already. Maybe it's not the baseball she hates but the bubble gum. Once every couple of months she'll buy about fifty packs of cards, throw out the gum in each pack, and fill up the old fishbowl on the piano, where she keeps the rewards. I get a baseball card each time I practice my lesson, and I generally lean the card against the music so Hank Aaron or Catfish Hunter can watch over me when I'm playing and sort of encourage me.

On the other hand, she already has so many of my drawings I knew one more wouldn't make much of a present.

"I can't draw her a baseball player," I said.

"You could rob the people-who-have-no-food box," suggested Trudy.

It so happens that Trudy married a man who robbed a grocery store while they were on their honeymoon. I could have mentioned this, but I didn't.

"My dad counted all the money in that box last night. He said I should send it in right away and not hoard it."

Trudy shrugged. "Next time you better save for the Needy Children's Fund. Then when you're down and out, you can help yourself. Did you lose that front tooth yet?"

I had a tooth so loose that I could lop it right over its neighbor. My mom made a special bag out of white velvet to hold it when it comes out and to keep the money I'd get from the tooth fairy. I wiggled the tooth hopefully, but it hung on for dear life.

"You could give your mom a tooth-wiggling lesson," said Trudy. "She's a teacher. She likes lessons."

"But she doesn't have any loose teeth."

"She might have one or two," said Trudy. "She told me her gums are going bad on her, same as mine did. Crawl down and see if you can spy my barrette under this radiator."

I scrunched myself down and peered all around but didn't spot so much as a marble. And I thought about what kind of lessons I could offer Mom. Every summer she takes the drivers' training course at the junior high where she teaches American history two nights a week to grown-ups. She still doesn't have her license, but she says she's learning a lot.

"Did you find it?" asked Trudy. "It's blue plastic, and it keeps my hair real neat. My hair is my best feature," she added, smoothing it with the back of her hand.

I left her looking under the sofa and went outside to ride my bike. I thought I'd ride around the block, but I had to pass Walter's house. He was playing in his front yard because he's not supposed to leave it, even though he's nearly ten years old. I could tell from the way he kicked his old broken soccer ball around that he had nothing important to do. So I speeded up but he saw me coming and threw himself over my back fender and hung on like a tick.

"Can you come over and play, huh? Can you come over, huh?"

Seeing that he'd gotten a good grip, I pulled over and parked my bike, and we kicked the soccer ball back and forth for a while. Then his little sister, Frances, wandered out, clutching Walter's baseball, and she dropped the ball and gave it such a mean kick that it ran into a bush and hid.

"I'll pitch," she said.

She pitched three curveballs and I struck out, and then Walter pitched, and Frances hit the first one nearly over the house.

"I'm good," she crowed. "I'm better than you."

"No, you're not," I said.

"I've been to the World Series," she said.

"When were you ever at the World Series?" demanded Walter.

"When I was six months old," she answered.

Frances is always talking about the wonderful things she did before she was six months old because she's adopted, and even her parents don't know what she was up to before they got her. For all any of us know, she might have gone on a world cruise.

"My turn to pitch," I said.

I paid great care to my wind-up, but Walter hit the ball anyway. I know I need a lot of practice because I don't belong to a regular league. On Saturday morning the kids from Holy Cross two blocks away hang around our school playground, and they'll play anyone who happens to show up. That's the only time I ever see the Holy Cross kids, except for Philip, who lives next door to us and can't hit very well and can't run very fast. He's always boasting about his cousin Tristram. Tristram can hit, Tristram can run, Tristram can pitch. Maybe Philip really has a cousin called Tristram, but I doubt it.

When I got home, Philip's mom was standing on our front steps talking to my mom.

"He's a real delinquent," she shouted. "Really incorrigible."

I wondered what awful thing Philip had done in school. He has to go to summer school because he flunked math.

"Bishop O'Hara took his gum away from him during chapel and kept it," said Philip's mother. "The amount of bubble gum he takes from kids is simply scandalous. What can a bishop do with all those packs of gum?"

"Chew it," said my dad, knee-deep in the honeysuckle. And he snapped the pruning shears at a wayward tendril.

"He's supposed to give everything back at the end of the day," she complained, "and he doesn't."

Then she caught sight of me.

"I'll bring Nellie over tomorrow," she said. "I don't know how I'm gonna hang on much longer. She's driving me nuts."

"She looks pretty healthy for sixty," said my mother.

"She's strong as a horse," said Philip's mom. "Sunday morning she broke the knobs off the TV without even turning them."

"What!" cried my mother.

"Some Baptist minister was preaching on Channel 2, and she said he jumped out of the TV and bit her."

"Who did he bite?" I hollered.

Mom shook her head at me, and I had to wait till Philip's mom disappeared through the gap in our privet hedge and crossed her own yard before she told me.

"We were talking about Nellie," said Mom. "We're taking Philip's aunt tomorrow afternoon. They've got company."

"Oh."

Suddenly a terrible thought struck me. "Do I have any batty aunts?"

"No," said Mom. "She's Philip's great-aunt. You don't have any batty great-aunts, either."

That night my dad fixed dinner. He made a big tossed salad, but he forgot to peel the cucumbers, and I was still chewing on them later when I went to bed. When Mom sat down at the dinner table, he handed her a dozen red roses and a slim package from Ellen, who was away at camp. I'd already left the envelope from me beside her plate.

Mom opened Ellen's package first, and out dropped a pair of black gloves with a little card she'd made. Mom read the message for us all to hear.

"Roses are red
Violets are blue
You can wear these gloves to church
to replace the ones you lost."

"Ellen is so thoughtful," said Mom. "I don't remember even telling her I lost my gloves in church."

Then she picked up my envelope. "I hope it's a card you made yourself," she said.

"It's not a card," I explained. "It's a present."

She opened it very carefully, just the way she'd open a present wrapped in lovely tissue that she might want to save.

A little scrap of yellow paper fluttered to the floor. Mom scooped it up and read aloud:

"THIS CARD IS GOOD FOR THREE FREE BASEBALL LESSONS."

Papa burst into a loud guffaw.

"What is this?" asked Mom.

"Free baseball lessons," I said. "For you."

"But who's giving them?"

"Me," I said.

"Oh," said Mom. Then she smiled. "That's a nice present. If I ever need baseball lessons, I'll know where to go."

"I think there's no question but that you need them," said Papa. "You can't even hit the ball with your glasses on."

Mom shot him a terrible look. "I can't learn to play baseball," she said. "I flunked gym twice in college."

"Private lessons are different," said Papa.

"Yeah," I agreed. "Private lessons are different. Remember my violin class?"

I could tell from her face that she remembered. I was five years old, and there were ten kids in the class. We met in the basement of the Episcopal church every Tuesday afternoon. The violins ordered for us never arrived. Miss Spratt, ever resourceful, made ten fake violins out of cigar boxes with rulers taped on the ends. For six weeks I bowed my cigar box with an invisible bow. Then a boy fell out of the window and broke his arm. That encouraged the other students to drop out of the class also, but not so dramatically.

My mom laughed. I knew she was thinking of Miss Spratt, too. "Okay," she agreed. "I'll take the three lessons. But we have to practice someplace where none of my friends will see me."

"The playground," I said, "early Saturday morning. That's the best time. We'll start tomorrow."

II

The next morning I wanted to leave right away, but Mom wanted me to help her clean the house for Nellie.

"I'll vacuum the guest room," she said, "and you go around the house and take down all the pictures. You can hide them in my closet."

"Why do we have to take down all the pictures?" I asked.

"Because Nellie doesn't like pictures."

I started dismantling the front hall. First I took down all my baby pictures. Then I came to the picture of my grandpa, who died last year. You'd know at a glance he wouldn't hurt a fly.

"Mom," I called, "can I leave Grandpa on the wall?"

"No," shouted Mom.

"But *why?*"

Mom switched off the vacuum cleaner. I found her in the bathroom, soaping the mirror.

"Nellie thinks all pictures are real people, right in the room with her."

"You mean she can't tell who's real and who isn't?" I asked.

"Kate, a lot of people can't tell who's real and who isn't," said Mom. "But Nellie thinks the people in the pictures are alive. And don't wipe the soap off the mirror. You can use the one over my bureau."

"Doesn't she like mirrors, either?" I asked. I couldn't believe I'd be allowed to leave the bathroom mirror dirty.

"No," said Mom. "And no TV when she's around, either."

By the time we'd covered the mirrors and hidden the pictures, it was nearly noon. Papa came in from weeding the vegetable garden, cradling two giant zucchinis.

"How's the baseball practice going?" he asked.

"We didn't have time for a lesson today," said Mom. "Nellie's coming in half an hour."

"I'll watch Nellie," said Papa. "I wouldn't want you to miss your first lesson. After all, they're free."

When we arrived at the playground, I saw Mom wince. "We should have gotten up earlier," she said.

"Oh, Mom, with this many kids around, nobody'll notice us," I assured her.

We found ourselves a spot by the fence, in the far corner of the field. I fished a couple of tin cans out of the trash basket. "The Seven-Up can is the pitcher's mound," I explained. "The Coca-Cola can is the batter's box."

"Where do I stand?"

"In the batter's box."

I was just showing Mom how to hold the bat when Olivia came by, all stooped over, concentrating on caterpillars. She had her lunch box hanging open, so I knew she hadn't caught any yet. Her little brother David was trailing after her, chewing an old washcloth tied around his hand. Usually he carries a monster puppet because he doesn't talk much, even to his sister, and sometimes he won't say a word unless his puppet says it for him. At least not on the playground, which is the only place I ever meet either Olivia or him.

Olivia ran her hand over the scarf she always wears to hide her newest home permanent. First she looked at Mom and then she looked at me.

"Is she your baby-sitter?" asked Olivia, just as if Mom couldn't speak for herself.

"Nope," I said.

I stepped onto the pitcher's mound and wiggled my loose tooth like the wad of tobacco I'll keep in my mouth when I'm a major-league pitcher. Then I pitched Mom a fast one. She swung the bat feebly and watched the ball zip past. Dropping her bat she chased it, but it beat her to the pricker bush and rolled under.

"Is she your grandmother?" asked Olivia.

I didn't answer. I made my second pitch a slow one. This time Mom didn't swing at all. She just stood there, looking injured.

"Is she your sister?" asked Olivia.

THE HIGHEST HIT

"Nope," I said. "Hey, Mom, you got to keep your eye on the ball and swing."

Olivia picked a caterpillar off her shoe and dropped it into her lunch box and slammed the lid on it.

"Is your mom gonna play with us against Holy Cross next Saturday?" asked Olivia.

I shrugged and watched the ball roll till it touched the fence. Olivia darted after it and tossed it straight to me.

"Can I be the catcher next Saturday?" she asked.

"Sure," I promised. I figured catching caterpillars had honed her reflexes and sharpened her eye. The week before she'd caught a hundred and fifty caterpillars, all brown. Then she caught a blue caterpillar, and he ate up the entire collection and died. He didn't even turn into a moth.

After twenty more pitches, Mom was all in a sweat.

"How long do your lessons last?" she murmured, leaning on the bat.

"Till you get tired and thirsty," I told her. "Are you tired and thirsty?"

She nodded, too dry to speak.

"Do you have to go?" said Olivia.

"Yeah. Mom's tired. See you tomorrow."

"See you," said David, waving his washcloth.

Olivia waved good-bye and started for home. Before I could get my baseball stuff together, she came running back.

"Does your mom know how to make a whistle out of a cough-drop box?"

"No," said Mom. "No, I don't."

"Mine does," said Olivia. "But she's moved to Toledo," she added.

"I'm thirsty," said Mom.

We crossed the street to the diner. I lugged my equipment

into a booth, and we ordered two lemonades. A man across the aisle from us ordered blueberry pie, and Mom cast a longing glance at it.

"No pie," I reminded her. "You're in training."

The minute I set foot in the front yard, I knew Nellie had arrived. I heard Papa showing someone his tomato plants in the backyard, and through the trees I saw the two of them petting the tomatoes, so green and small you'd never think they're going to amount to much. And every year the miracle happens. Bushels of tomatoes. From far off, Nellie doesn't look sixty years old. She's thin and moves as quick as I do and has a white fluffy wig that makes her whole head look like a dandelion going to seed. Philip says ten men sewed together the skins of twenty purebred poodles to make it, and it cost a whole lot of money.

"How's Mom doing?" Papa called.

"Pretty good," I lied. "She hit two out of twenty."

"Not bad for a beginner," he observed.

"Mmmmmm, mmmmmm. Yes, I do," said Nellie, but not to any of us. We eyed her uneasily.

Papa looked at Mom. "You got a call from a Mrs. Revel. She's picking you up at three and taking you to church."

Mom turned deathly white. "I promised to pour coffee at the Senior Citizens' party! I completely forgot!"

Suddenly Papa shoved a fistful of money into her hand. "You have two hours. Go and buy yourself a new dress. And don't buy anything on sale."

Mom always buys dresses on sale. And they're either too small or too big, or there's a big rip in the back, or somebody has spilled ink on the sleeve. And Mom says, "I got it for a dollar, and I can fix it." And Papa says, "All you ever do is stick on some ruffles. You always wind up looking like a turkey."

THE HIGHEST HIT

I wondered if she'd buy a new one this time. I didn't mind keeping an eye on Nellie for so worthy a cause.

"*The Flintstones* is on," I suggested. "Do you want to watch, Nellie?"

I saw Papa shaking his head at me, and his mouth shaped the words "No TV." Then I remembered how Nellie tore the knobs off the TV next door. So I said before she could answer, "I'll read to you. I know a real good book."

Everybody lay down for a nap except me. Nellie stretched out on the back-porch sofa while I read to her from the *Guinness Book of World Records.* I love that book. I get up two hours before breakfast just to read it, and I've marked the best records with colored ribbons, like the Bible in church.

"Nellie," I said, "do you want to hear about the heaviest man?"

"Mmm," said Nellie.

"He was Robert Earl Hughes of Monticello, Illinois. His greatest record weight was 1,069 pounds, his claimed waist was 122 inches, his chest 124 inches, and his upper arm 40 inches. His coffin was as large as a piano case and had to be lowered by a crane."

"What did he die of?" asked Nellie. "A virus?"

I reread the account of Robert Hughes more carefully.

"U-r-e-m-i-a. It says 'uremia.'"

A warm breeze blew over our shy, respectful silence. I didn't ask what "uremia" meant, though I was hoping she'd tell me.

"Mmmm," she said at last. "My second husband's sister died of a virus."

I began to fear the heaviest man was too depressing a subject for her.

"Nellie, do you want to hear about the official record for opening oysters?"

"All my family died of viruses," said Nellie.

"The official record is one hundred oysters in three minutes and one second by Douglas Brown in New Zealand, in 1974."

"That man behind you—tell him to go away," said Nellie.

I spun around quickly. Nobody there. But just in case she had better eyes than mine, I said, "Please go away."

Then I read to her about the largest omelette, which weighed 1,243 pounds and used 5,600 eggs. Nellie closed her eyes, and I soothed her with Trudy's story about the man who grew turnips in the shape of Teddy Roosevelt's head.

Suddenly Nellie opened her eyes and shouted, "The way these people from New York follow me around, it's enough to drive me crazy."

She jumped up and ran out the back door and across the yard so fast I couldn't catch her.

"Papa!" I shouted.

He ran out and met her at the edge of the yard, where he took her arm as if he'd been waiting impatiently all day to walk with her among his cucumbers and roses. Then I heard somebody pounding on the front door, and through the screen I saw Philip dancing up and down on the front steps. Beside him stood the biggest kid I ever saw, the opposite of Philip in every way. Philip is short and skinny and so blond that from a distance he looks bald. The big kid was tall and heavy and had lank, dark hair, parted in the middle and sleeked against his ears. I thought of muskrats and other gnawing animals that I do not like.

"This is my cousin Tristram," said Philip. And he smirked.

"Oh," I said.

"He's staying till Sunday. He's an incorrigible delinquent. He killed a guy with a curveball once."

"What a shame we can't play ball this Saturday," I said.

"Why?" demanded Tristram loudly.

I disliked him at once. "Because the junior-high kids are having their regular game this Saturday, and they use our field." I hoped this would turn out to be true.

"What time do they play?" asked Tristram.

"One o'clock."

"We'll play in the morning," he announced.

"No, we won't," I said. "They practice in the morning."

Philip's face fell. But Tristram, whose lean smile seemed engraved on his face for all time, said craftily, "We'll use the Holy Cross playground. We'll meet by the church."

"Yippee," shrieked Philip. "And the team that loses has to trash Bishop O'Hara's marigolds."

Now, I could have refused such a challenge, but Philip has it in his power to make my life miserable if he wants to, in a thousand different ways. I didn't know Bishop O'Hara because we go to the Quaker meetinghouse down the street and we don't bother about bishops. But I've had him pointed out to me on numerous occasions—a plump, pink-faced man, with a bald head and a mean squint—and once I heard Philip's father complain that the bishop had given him such a long penance he thought he'd go gray finishing it.

"Trashing a bishop's marigolds is a mortal sin," I whispered, hoping it was.

But what is a mortal sin to someone who has killed a man with a curveball? Philip and Tristram pounded each other on the head and gave rude whoops and tore home through the gap in our privet hedge, giggling.

Then I felt my dad rest his hand on my shoulder. "How about you and Nellie and me going for a drive to Baskin-Robbins? Don't you feel like an ice cream?"

III

Nellie and Papa ordered vanilla because they don't trust all the new flavors. I always get rocky road, as I have read that this is O. J. Simpson's favorite, and I can see for myself what it did for him. When we'd crunched up the last bite of our sugar cones, Papa dropped me off at the foot of our driveway and drove Nellie back to Philip's house.

Mom was already home, setting the table.

"How was the party?" I asked.

"Terrible! I had to pour the coffee, and the spigot on the urn got stuck in the open position. Then a very ritzy lady came to play the piano, and when she lifted up the lid, the keyboard was gone. Workmen had taken it away for repairs. And I got a collect call from Ellen at camp. She says somebody stole her thirty-dollar bathing suit and could I buy her another one."

"Don't forget tomorrow afternoon," I said.

Mom stopped buttering the corn. "What's happening tomorrow afternoon?"

"Your second baseball lesson," I reminded her.

"Oh, sure," said Mom.

"Saturday is your final exam, Mother."

By the time her second lesson had rolled around, a lot of kids knew about Tristram and wanted to play in the game. Walter and Frances told their mom I'd promised to take them to the playground. Today I didn't mind. Walter has long legs and runs fast, and Frances pitches well, and we needed all the help we could get.

When Walter and Frances and me and Mom reached the playground, Philip was standing in the middle of the field and pitching, and Tristram was hitting the ball right, left, and center. Theirs was a team of two, because all the kids were standing in a circle around them, watching.

"You set up the batter's box this time, Mom."

While Mom was grubbing around in the trash basket, a girl I didn't even know came over to me and said sarcastically, "Philip says your mom is a super player." She was wearing the Holy Cross jumper and navy socks. Even on Saturday.

"Super is not the word," I said. "My mom was so good when she went to college that the gym teacher wanted to send her to the Olympics."

The girl opened her eyes very wide.

"But she broke her leg," I went on, "sliding into home plate for her hundred and fiftieth home run of the season."

Then I caught sight of Olivia, wearing an old catcher's mitt and a huge strainer taped to her face. It didn't look much like a catcher's mask, but I let it pass.

We practiced for two hours. Walter and I pitched, Frances played outfield and shortstop, and Mom made four hits.

"Only one more lesson," she remarked as we left the field. Her face was shining with happiness. "When I was in college, I never even hit the ball once. Think I'll pass the final exam?"

The thought of my mother swinging at one of Tristram's lethal pitches filled me with such grief that I could hardly eat supper. At eight o'clock, I carried my grief right into bed with me and lay there. My stomach felt all crumpled. The clock struck nine, ten, eleven. Papa turned off the TV. Twelve. Everybody went to bed. Everybody went to sleep except me. One. Two.

Then I fell asleep, too. And I dreamed that Papa went away on a trip and left Mom and me alone. His train had barely pulled out of the station when Mom caught a mysterious virus that caused her to shrink till she stood knee-high to a clothespin. The day of this awful event, it was my turn to haul all the laundry to the laundromat in my wagon, five blocks away. Mom rode on top of the dirty sheets, as happy as a bee on a hayride. I tried to keep an eye on her, but she kept climbing into the dryers and falling into the washers, and Philip's mom was folding pillowcases on the folding table and shaking her head—things like this never happened to her, she said. Then she shouted, "Put butter on her feet so she can't run away. Put butter on her feet so she can't run away."

I woke up yelling, "Butter! Pass the butter!"

When the light from the hall flooded my room, I knew I'd dreamed the whole business. Still, I felt relieved when Mom poked her head in the door.

"What's wrong with you?"

"Mom," I said, "I had a horrible dream."

"That's funny," said Mom. "You haven't had nightmares since you were a baby."

"Mom," I said, "I'm scared."

She sat down at the foot of my bed. "Why?" she demanded. "Why are you scared?"

"I'm scared that tomorrow I'll have to trash Bishop O'Hara's marigolds."

Then in the dead of night, while even the crickets slept and only the owls listened, I told Mom the whole story.

She listened gravely. She didn't say a word, only picked at the rosebuds on the straps of her nightgown. Finally she stood up.

"Nobody is going to trash anyone's marigolds," my mother announced. "You wait and see."

IV

At one o'clock on Saturday, Mom and Walter and Frances and I walked the two blocks to Holy Cross. Mom looked elegant. She had gotten her hair done that very morning, partly for the game, partly because Papa told her she looked like a grasshopper and would she please cut her bangs. Now she kept touching her new curls, as if she thought they might drop off unless she reminded them not to. She had put on the white sun-back dress she wears whenever she takes me shopping.

THE HIGHEST HIT

Tristram was already there, the only player on the field, swinging his bat against invisible opponents for the fans that lounged in the grass at the edge of his kingdom. Even the gravestones seemed to be watching. Through the open windows of the church, a thin ribbon of music floated out. I wondered who was playing the organ.

The bishop's marigolds watched, too, lined up against the north wall just the way the bishop makes kids line up for everything. The Lord will no doubt call on him to line us up for the Last Judgment.

I said hi to Olivia and David and Philip and the usual gang. But who was the little group of new kids? Each time Tristram let the bat swing, they'd turn to each other and their fingers drew shapes on the air, quick as if they were knitting, and they never made a sound.

"I didn't know Saint Jude used this place," said Mom.

"Who's Saint Jude?" I asked.

"That's the school downtown for the deaf. See, they're using sign language."

We stared at them in open admiration.

"Can anyone learn sign language?" asked Walter. "It would be such a neat way to signal plays."

"I learned it when I was a baby in Paris before I was adopted," said Frances, "but of course I've forgotten it by this time."

"Maybe when you get to know some of the kids, they'll teach you," said Mom.

Suddenly Philip was waving his batter's hat and jumping all over us like a puppy. "Batter up! Batter up!" he hollered.

I tossed the quarter: heads, Holy Cross; tails, Grand Avenue Elementary. George Washington smiled up at us from the dust, and Tristram grabbed a bat and started pounding it to bits.

I threw the opening pitch.

To make a long story short, Tristram hit a home run.

The fans from Holy Cross cheered. Out of the corner of my eye, I saw the hands of the deaf children leaping like birds. Pretty soon somebody pushed Philip into the batter's box, and I pitched him a hard one. He hit a pop fly. Walter darted out from nowhere and caught it. I turned to wave encouragement to Mom, who was covering the outfield. She was sitting on a tombstone, her hands folded in her lap.

Now it was our turn to bat.

First me. I put on the batter's hat, and Tristram went into the wind-up, grinning like a pirate. The ball went right for me, as if it had some grudge against me. I jumped back.

Strike one.

Second pitch. I swung the bat, so as not to appear terrified.

Strike two.

On the third pitch I closed my eyes, heard a sharp crack, and made it to first.

When Frances came up, she made it to first, and I ran to second.

Olivia pushed Frances to second and me to third. The bases were loaded when Mom, adjusting her new curls, set the batter's hat on top of them. It didn't fit. It sat there like an apple waiting to be knocked off.

The first pitch would no doubt have killed her if she hadn't jumped backward. She frowned at Tristram. "You should never throw a ball that hard," she scolded him. "Never. It's not safe."

Tristram lifted his upper lip and showed his fangs, the wax ones he bought at the drugstore.

Whizz!

He pitched the second ball even harder.

Then you could see from Mom's face that she had discovered

the truth. He really was an incorrigible delinquent, and he deserved to be kept after school and have his bubble gum confiscated and a lot of other bad things done to him as well.

When he pitched the third ball, Mom struck. I heard a huge clap of thunder. The ball soared like a rocket over the trees, their silence ripped by a loud crash.

I closed my eyes.

When I opened them, the playing field was empty, as if somebody had erased the children and left the grass and trees. Mom was still standing in the batter's box, looking perplexed. Before either of us could run away, the chapel door opened, and a plump, pink-faced man in a cassock rushed toward us.

"Forty Paternosters for all of you!" he bellowed, "and fifty Hail Marys! And it'll cost a thousand dollars to fix it!"

You can't run from a bishop. He has God on his side. He puffed over to us and stretched out his hand to heaven, and I followed his jeweled finger up, up, to the big round window. Something had gnawed a great hole in the top of it.

Mom pulled off the batter's hat and dropped it on the ground. "Did I do that?" she exclaimed.

"I'll show you what you did," hissed the bishop. He edged in to cut off our escape, and clapping his hands on our shoulders, he herded us inside. My eyes were so brimming with sunlight I couldn't see anything but darkness till we turned out of the side aisle into the sanctuary. It smelled so heavy and sweet, I looked around for flowers. I saw nothing but candles flickering at the feet of a saint in a brown robe, holding a baby in his arms. Over the high altar, I saw God the Father in the window. On the day I came here with Mrs. Fitzpatrick to pick up Philip, He was wearing a hat, all round and layered like a beehive. Now the maple leaves outside were brushing the broken space over His head.

I wondered if it was proper to pray for a miracle, and in that instant my tooth dropped out and I bit my tongue. At the taste of blood, I let out a shriek.

"Be still," cried the bishop. "This is a holy place."

"I lost my tooth," I whispered.

"Give it to me," said Mom. She held out her hand.

"I ate it. By accident."

And at the loss of that tooth I'd been banking on for months, I burst into tears. My tongue felt huge. I opened my mouth and showed Mom my bloody gums. Bishop O'Hara looked startled.

"Here," he said, drawing out his handkerchief and dangling it at me. "I've got some Kleenex in my office."

We followed him down a cold, dark corridor that ended in the most elegant office I've ever seen. On the ceiling a giant chandelier sparkled like a bush full of diamonds. The desk directly under it was so big that I could have tap-danced on it. A big gold box, a piece of marble with a pen sticking in it, and two typewriters sat on top of it. How can anybody use two typewriters? And pictures of people in halos, looking apologetic.

I lay down on a big leather sofa and pressed the bishop's handkerchief to my mouth.

"Cold water," he ordered Mom and handed her Kleenex. "Go fetch cold water from the drinking fountain in the hall."

Mom ducked out, and he slippered over to me and folded his arms over his cassock.

"Now, who really put that ball through the window?"

"My mom," I said.

He still didn't look convinced, so I explained that today was her final exam and Tristram was going to make us trash his marigolds if we lost. The bishop sighed deeply. I could see he was impressed.

"Is this her last lesson?"

I nodded.

THE HIGHEST HIT

"Good."

He didn't look so fierce to me now. Still, I was glad to see Mom bringing the cold water and the Kleenex. She handed him back his handkerchief and laid an icy-cold compress on my mouth. I didn't dare tell her it had stopped bleeding.

"I understand you've just finished your last baseball lesson, madam," said the bishop, addressing himself to a flower on the carpet.

"It better be," said Mom.

"Our Lord teaches us to forgive, not just seven times but seventy times seven."

Pause.

"Does that mean we don't have to pay a thousand dollars?" I asked.

"It means, don't ever play baseball around here again," said the bishop, and he wiped his handkerchief across his forehead. It left a thin streak of blood between his eyebrows. I sat up, completely cured.

"We won't, ever again," I promised.

Walking home, Mom and I didn't say much to each other until we saw a little boy sitting behind a big box selling lemonade. The sign said:

FIVE CENTS FOR A DIRTY CUP
TEN CENTS FOR A CLEAN ONE

"I need a lemonade," said Mom. She laid down two dimes. "Two clean ones, please."

The boy rummaged around for a clean cup but found none.

"Make it four dirty ones," said Mom.

I drank one cup and Mom drank three, one right after the other.

"I'll take one more," said Mom.

The boy watched admiringly as she finished it off.

"You mighty thirsty," observed the boy. "You come from far away?"

"My mom and I been playing baseball," I said. "She's gonna be in the Guinness Book of World Records."

"For drinking lemonade?" asked the boy. Mother was pouring herself a fifth.

"For hitting the highest ball," I answered.

Mom laid down another nickel, and he pocketed it.

"How high?" he asked, just as if Mom couldn't speak for herself. But I understood why she couldn't tell him. It's for us losers to praise the winners, not for the winners to praise themselves.

"She knocked off God's hat," I told him. "That's how high."

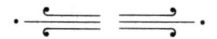

NANCY WILLARD (1936–) won the Newbery Medal in 1982 for *A Visit to William Blake's Inn: Poems for Innocent and Experienced Travelers,* the first book of poetry to be thus honored. Among her other distinguished books for young readers are *The Well-Mannered Balloon* (1976), *The Highest Hit* (1978), *The Nightgown of the Sullen Moon* (1983), and *Sailing to Cythera: And Other Anatole Stories* (1974) and *The Island of the Grass King: The Further Adventures of Anatole* (both winners of a Lewis Carroll Shelf Award).

ELIZABETH YATES

THE HASTE-ME-WELL QUILT

*A story of sickness and strength,
time travel and a patchwork quilt...*

SIMON LAY VERY STILL in his bed. Outside, birds were singing in the apple tree; cows were mooing by the pasture bars as they did when it was time to be milked.

Sometimes the wind flapped a little at the drawn shade, lifting it and letting in a flash of sunshine to frolic through the darkened room. But Simon only turned restlessly on the bed, kicking at the sheet and sending his books and toys onto the floor. He was tired of lying still, tired of being sick. He was cross at the world.

A set of crayons that his father had brought him that morning toppled off the bed. The blue one lay broken. Simon was glad it was broken and wished they all were. He did not want to use them. He hated crayons. He hated everyone. He—

Then the door opened slowly. It was Grandmother, with something over her arm. She went quietly across to the window, raising the shade so the sunlight could come into the room. The scent of lilacs came, too, and the song of birds.

Simon screwed up his eyes and said crossly, "Don't want any light, want darkness."

Grandmother laid the quilt she was carrying across the end of his bed; then she sat down on the bed and took one of Simon's hands in hers. She put her other hand on his forehead. Her touch was cool and gentle, like the water of a brook on a summer day. Simon opened his eyes and stared at her.

" 'Truly the light is sweet, and a pleasant thing it is for the eyes to behold the sun,' " Grandmother said slowly. "That's in the Bible, Simon. Grandfather read it to me this morning before he went out to plant the corn."

Simon opened his eyes wider. Grandmother had put something at the end of his bed. It was a patchwork quilt. Simon looked at it curiously. It was made not of odd-shaped patterns sewn together, but of tiny pictures of real things.

"Granny, what have you got?" he asked, forgetting how cross he was at the world, forgetting his hot, heavy head.

"This, Simon, is a quilt that we have always laid on the bed of sickness. Because of that it is called the Haste-Me-Well Quilt."

Deftly she shook it out of its folds and spread it over Simon, saying as she did so, "Grandfather needs you to help him on the farm. Your father wants to take a strong boy back to the city with him. It's time that you got well."

THE HASTE-ME-WELL QUILT

"Is it a magic quilt?" Simon asked, fingering it warily.

Grandmother nodded. "Perhaps, but a very special kind of magic."

Then something happened to Simon. He smiled. And because he had not smiled for a week but only thought how sorry he was for himself, his lips were a little stiff at the corners. But the smile lived on in his eyes, dark and deep, almost as dark as his thick black hair.

"Tell me about it, please," he said, snuggling down under the quilt and pulling Grandmother's hand up to his chin.

"Long ago, Simon," she began, "more than a hundred years ago, my grandmother—"

"*Your* grandmother!" he exclaimed—such a long way that seemed to reach back into the past.

"Yes," Grandmother nodded, "Lucy, her name was, made the quilt. She lived on a farm on the moors close to the Scottish border. She was not much older than you when she started it, and she finished it when she was seventeen—in time for her marriage. All of her friends were making quilts, but they made them out of bits and pieces of calico cut into squares or circles or triangles and sewed together into pretty patterns. Lucy was gay and strong, with quick fingers and a lively mind. She wanted to do something different, so she cut out her bits of calico into little pictures."

Grandmother bent over the quilt, and Simon propped his head up to follow her finger's journey across it.

"See, here is the farmhouse where she lived on the edge of the moors. Here are the chickens and the old tabby. Here is the postman, the muffin man with his bell, and the peddler who came with trinkets and ribbons and pots and pans. Here is her father, going off with his crook for the sheep. Here is a teakettle and the footstool at her feet, tables and fire tongs, watering cans and a bellows, horses and snails, a great castle, and a coach with dashing horses. Things she read about in books are here, like dragons and kangaroos and gladiators, as well as the latest fashion in bonnets and a mirror to try them on before"—Grandmother got more and more excited as her fingers flew across the quilt and she pointed out its wonders.

"It *is* a magic quilt," Simon agreed.

"Whatever young Lucy saw as interesting, useful, or amusing," Grandmother went on, "she snipped out of calico and sewed onto a white square, which was sewed to all the other white squares. Then, see, Simon, around the border she planted an old-fashioned garden!"

"It's like your garden, Granny, here at Easterly Farm!" Simon exclaimed.

"That's because it was *her* garden," Grandmother said quietly.

"It was?"

"Yes. When Lucy married, she and her husband came to America, here to this New England countryside. It was close to wilderness then, you must remember, but with their own hands they built this house; and while Silas cleared the fields and planted his crops and raised his stock, Lucy brought up her family—five boys and five girls, each one with a name from the Bible."

"And the quilt?"

"It must have meant everything to her in those days, for it was all her past—beautiful and orderly and gracious—and she brought it forward into a life of hardship and toil and privation. To her it was the tale of an age that was gone forever, costumes and customs, the little things used in a house and the larger things that though never seen were talked about; and she made it the background of a new life."

"How did it get its name, Granny? You haven't told me that."

Grandmother smiled. "The quilt used to lie on the guest bed, for all to admire it and for its occasional use. Then one day Peter was sick. He was the eldest of the five boys. He was wracked with chills and nothing they could do seemed to warm him. Lucy put all the blankets she had over him, and finally the quilt. Soon, oh, much sooner than anyone thought possible, the chills shivered themselves away and he went to sleep. Ever after that the quilt was put on the bed of a child who was sick."

"Was it ever on my father's bed?" Simon asked.

"Yes." Grandmother looked away. "Once when he fell from the barn during the haying and hurt his back, the doctor said that he could not do anything for him because he could not keep him still long enough." Grandmother smiled and turned back to look at Simon. "Grandfather and I didn't give up so easily. We put the quilt on his bed and for days and days afterward your father had wonderful adventures with it. He was always going to tell me about them, but he always forgot to."

Simon was looking drowsy, so Grandmother smoothed the folds of the quilt as it lay over him and stole softly from the room.

Simon moved his fingers lovingly over the quilt. He stroked the furry rabbit and called to the horse galloping across the field. He waved to the coach as it dashed along the road to London, and he bought a muffin from the muffin man. Then he opened the gate in the white fence that enclosed the farmhouse from the rolling moors and went up to the wide front door. Seeing it from a distance, he had not thought he could possibly go through the door, but the nearer he got to it the more of a size they were, and he found himself going into the house.

Inside, it was cool and quiet. His steps echoed a bit on the polished brick of the floor, but the sound did not disturb the tabby sleeping by the hearth. On the hob hung a fat kettle with a wisp of steam coming from its spout, saying as clearly as any words that whoever might be passing would be welcome to a dish of tea.

Simon went to the end of a passage and pushed open another door. A young girl was sitting by an open window. Grandmother had not told him what Lucy looked like, but Simon knew right away that this was Lucy. The quilt lay in a heap on the floor beside her; on a table nearby were scissors and thread, and bits and pieces of cloth. Simon crossed the room and stood beside Lucy. She looked up at him.

"I have a little boy in the quilt," she said. "There's no room for you."

"That's all right," Simon replied, "but mayn't I sit down and watch you?"

"If you wish," she smiled, "but it's all finished."

Simon sat down, tailor fashion before her, cupping his chin in his hands.

"Two hundred and seventy-four squares around a center panel, bordered by flowers," Lucy went on. "It's all done, but it's well it is for I'm going away next week."

"Where are you going?" Simon asked.

"To the New World." Lucy looked out of the window and Simon thought her voice throbbed, like a bird's on a low note. "I shall never see England again, never the rolling moors, nor the mountains of Scotland."

"*Never?*" Simon echoed. What a long time that was.

She shook her head slowly. "Ever since I was a little girl I have been cutting out and patching together the things that are my world. Now I can take my old world with me into the new. Once I wished I could draw pictures, go to London, and study to be an artist, but—"

"Why didn't you?" Simon demanded.

"If I had been a man I should have, but a girl doesn't do those things. Scissors, thread, thimble, calico—those are my artist's tools. Fingers are wonderful things, aren't they, little boy? You put a tool

THE HASTE-ME-WELL QUILT

in them—it doesn't matter what it is—a hoe, a churn, a needle, a spoon—and they do the rest."

"My father gave me crayons to draw with," Simon confided. "I want to be an artist someday."

"Crayons?" Lucy looked as if the word were strange to her. "They'll not make you an artist, but fingers will."

"Why?"

"Because they are friends to all you're feeling. I didn't know when I started this quilt that it would mean so much to me. Now, though I'm going far away, everything I love is going with me."

Simon stroked the quilt. "It will be nice to have it on your bed, won't it?"

She laughed. "Oh, it won't ever be on my bed. It's too good for that! It'll be in the spare room, for guests to use when they come to stay with us."

"And it will be on the children's beds whenever they are sick," Simon went on.

Lucy looked at him, amazed. "What a strange idea!"

"It will make them well."

"Do you really think so, little boy?" Lucy looked incredulous, then her eyes gazed far away as if she did not see Simon at all and she said slowly, "The quilt could never do that, but perhaps the thoughts I have sewed into it could." Her eyes came back from the faraway place and she looked closely at Simon. "What is your name, little boy? I would like to know in case we meet again."

"Simon."

She wrinkled her brows. "Yes, Simon. For a moment I thought you were one of my boys." She went on looking at him as if wondering why he seemed so familiar, then she shook her head.

"There's magic in the quilt," Simon commented, reaching out and touching it.

"Magic? What strange words you use."

301

"But there is," Simon insisted. "How did you put it in?"

She laughed gaily. "What you call magic is just being happy in what you are doing, loving it the way you love the morning or the new lambs every spring. There's strength in happiness."

The blind was flapping at the window. The scent of lilacs filled the air. The sun, dropping low over the hills, was coming into the room like an arrow of gold. Simon drew his hands over the quilt and propped himself up on his elbows. On the floor lay his crayons, one of them broken.

He slipped out of bed and gathered the crayons together into their box, then he pushed the pillows up straight and climbed back into bed. Leaning against the pillows, he curved his knees up so his drawing pad might rest against them. He was sad that the blue crayon was broken, for so much blue was needed to arch the sky over the rolling moors and give life to Lucy's eyes. But he would manage somehow.

Quickly he worked, his fingers strong and free, eager with happiness, hurrying to do something for Grandmother that he might have a present for her when she came back to his room.

The door pushed open a little, then wider as Grandmother saw Simon. On the table by his bed she laid a small tray.

"There's a glass of milk from the afternoon's milking, Simon," she said. "Grandfather sent it up to you, and I thought you'd like a molasses cookie from a batch I've just made."

Simon finished his picture quickly.

"See, Granny, I have a present for you!"

Grandmother smiled as she took the drawing. It was a happy picture; well-done, too. Simon's father would be pleased with it. A young girl and a patchwork quilt, and in the background a small stone farmhouse. Grandmother looked closer. It was the Haste-Me-Well Quilt and Lucy looking at the world with eyes of wonder.

"Thank you, Simon, thank you very much, but I did not tell you my grandmother's eyes were blue, did I?"

Simon shook his head. "Were they?"

"Yes, blue as morning light on the mountains, and her fingers were fine and strong."

Fingers were wonderful things, Simon thought. It didn't much matter what they held if they held it with joy. Simon looked dreamily across the room. He was trying to remember something to tell Grandmother, but whatever it was it was slipping from him like a rainbow before full sunshine.

"May I get up now, Granny, please?" he asked.

A surprised smile lighted Grandmother's face. She nodded and began to fold up the Haste-Me-Well Quilt.

ELIZABETH YATES *(1905–)* won the Newbery Medal in 1951 for *Amos Fortune, Free Man*. Her other honors include the Jane Addams Award in 1955 and the Sarah Josepha Hale Award in 1970. She brings American history alive in her many books, such as *Prudence Crandall, Woman of Courage* (1955), and *Mountain Born* (a Newbery Honor Book in 1944).

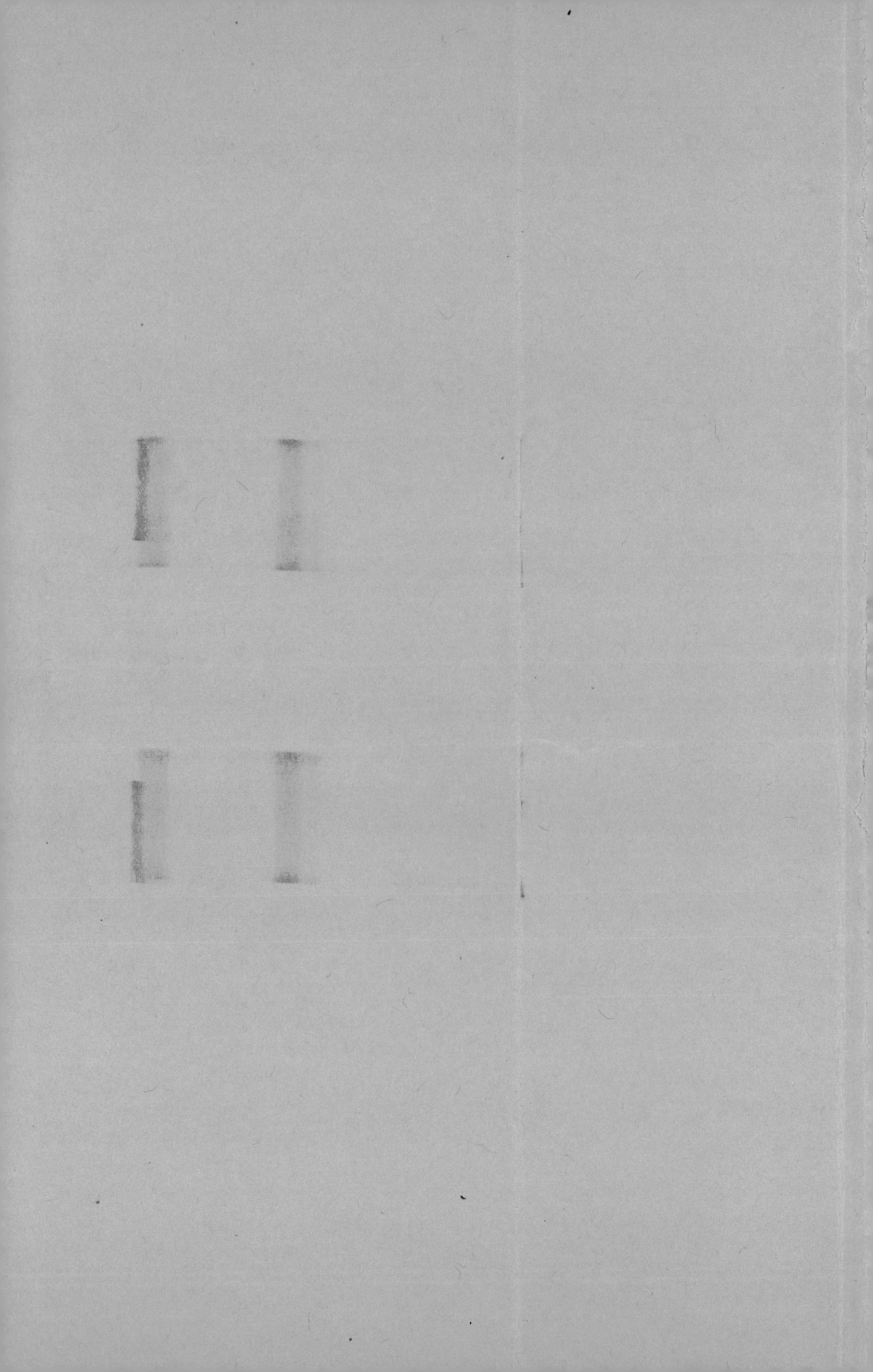